NUKE 101

PROFESSIONAL ... VISUAL EFFECTS

048x1556 bbox: 0 0 1 1 channels: none   x=1302 y= 816   0.00000 0.00000 0.00000 0.0000

fps 24

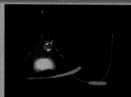

Ron Ganbar

NUKE 101
Professional Compositing and Visual Effects

Ron Ganbar

Peachpit Press
1249 Eighth Street
Berkeley, CA 94710
510/524-2178
Fax: 510/524-2221

Find us on the Web at www.peachpit.com
To report errors, please send a note to errata@peachpit.com
Peachpit Press is a division of Pearson Education

Senior Editor: Karyn Johnson
Development Editor: Corbin Collins
Production Editor: Cory Borman
Technical Editor: Mark Christiansen
Copyeditor: Kelly Kordes Anton
Proofreader: Scout Festa
Indexer: Valerie Haynes Perry
Interior Design and Composition: Kim Scott, Bumpy Design
Cover Design: Charlene Charles-Will
Cover Illustration: Alicia Buelow
Cover images: *Adrenalin Lemmings* (2008) by Crew 972, www.crew972.com

ISBN-13: 978-0-321-73347-4
ISBN-10: 0-321-73347-9

9 8 7 6 5 4 3 2 1

Printed and bound in the United States of America

"I don't always like writing, but I very much like having written."
—William Gibson

CONTENTS

INTRODUCTION

The Foundry's Nuke is fast becoming the industry leader in compositing software for film and TV. Virtually all the leading visual effects studios—ILM, Digital Domain, Weta Digital, MPC, Framestore, The Mill, and Sony Pictures Imageworks—now use Nuke as their main compositing tool. This is not surprising, as Nuke offers a flexible node-based approach to compositing, has a native multi-channel workflow, and boasts a powerful integrated 3D compositing environment that delivers on the artist's needs.

Nuke was first developed as the in-house compositing tool at Digital Domain, the visual effects studio behind the *Terminator* series, *The Fifth Element*, *Tron: Legacy*, *The Curious Case of Benjamin Button*, and other major films. The software has been developed by artists for artists to meet the immediate needs of actual top-level productions. Nuke is now developed by The Foundry (www.thefoundry.co.uk), which remains committed to making Nuke the best tool for compositing artists working in the trenches.

ABOUT THIS BOOK

Learning Nuke is a must for visual effects artists who want to master high-end compositing techniques and artistry. My goal with this book is to get you up-and-running with the program and give you the skills you need for doing your own compositing projects in Nuke.

Who this book is for

This book is for anyone interested in learning Nuke. Whether you're an artist experienced in using Adobe After Effects, Autodesk Flame, Apple Shake, or Eyeon Fusion, or you only have a basic understanding of compositing and image manipulation concepts, this book will guide you through the necessary theory and practice you need to use Nuke—from a basic level to Nuke's more advanced toolset.

How this book is organized

This book was written as a series of lessons, each focusing on a part of the interface, a tool, or a technique. Chapters 1 through 3 discuss Nuke basics, which are important for understanding where things are and how to create simple composites. Chapters 4 through 7 cover important tools and techniques. In Chapter 8 and onwards, advanced tools and techniques are explained.

What this book covers

This book teaches how to use Nuke from its very basic interface to its very advanced toolsets, including the 3D engine, Camera Projection, and Camera Tracking. Although the book teaches a fair amount of compositing theory, there is not enough space here to cover that topic in depth. Some of the theory discussed in this book may be new to you, but my intention is to cover just enough to understand how to use Nuke. If you want to dive further into the theory, two of my favorite books are Ron Brinkmann's *The Art and Science of Digital Compositing* and Steve Wright's *Digital Compositing for Film and Video*.

How to use this book

As you advance through the chapters in this book, the later lessons rely on knowledge you learned in the previous lessons. Chapter 2 relies on what you learned in Chapter 1, and so on. Because of this, I recommend completing the exercises in the chapters in order.

In the book you will find explanatory text and numbered steps. Ideally, you should complete each numbered step exactly as it is written—without doing anything else (such as adding your own steps). Following the steps exactly as written will give you a smooth experience. Not going through the steps as they are written might result in the next step not working properly, and could well lead to a frustrating experience. Each series of steps is also designed to introduce you to new concepts and techniques. As you perform the steps, pay attention to why you are clicking where you are clicking and doing what you are doing, as that will truly make your experience a worthwhile one.

You can use this book on your own through self-study or in a classroom.

- **Using the book for self-study:** If you're reading this book at your own pace, follow the instructions in the previous paragraph for your first read-through of the chapters. However, as you are not limited by any time frame, I recommend going through chapters a second time, trying to do as much of the work without reading the steps. Doing so can help you better understand the concepts and tools being taught. Also, the book leaves a lot of room for further experimentation. Feel free to use the tools you're learning to take your compositions further the second time you run through a chapter.

- **Using the book in a classroom setting:** You can use this book to teach Nuke in a classroom. As a course, the material is designed to run for roughly 40 hours, or five eight-hour days. I suggest the trainer run through a chapter with the students listening and writing down notes, explaining the steps as they are shown on-screen to the class while taking questions and expanding on the text where necessary. Once a chapter has been presented from start to finish, give students time to run through the same chapter on their own in the classroom in front of a computer, using the book to read the instructions and follow the steps. This second pass will reiterate everything the trainer has explained and, through actual experience, show the students how to use the software with the trainer still there to answer questions and help when things go wrong.

INSTALLING NUKE

While this book was originally written for Nuke version 6.2v1, The Foundry updates Nuke on a regular basis and the lessons can be followed using more recent updates. Small interface and behavior updates might slightly alter the Nuke interface from version to version, especially for so-called "point" updates (such as if Nuke version 6.3 were released). I recommend using this book with Nuke version 6.2v1 if you haven't already downloaded the most current version and you want the exact results as shown in the book.

You can download Nuke in a variety of versions from The Foundry's web site at www.thefoundry.co.uk as discussed in the next sections.

Different flavors of Nuke

Nuke comes in three different flavors with different features at different prices. There is only a single installation file for Nuke, but the license you purchase determines which type of Nuke you will be running. The Foundry offers a 15-day trial license, so you can try it before you purchase it (see "Getting a trial license" later in this section).

Here are the three flavors of Nuke.

1. **Nuke PLE (Personal Learning Edition):** This license (or lack of) is free—as in, you pay nothing. You can install Nuke on your computer and not purchase a license. With the PLE you can use Nuke as much as you want, although certain limitations apply. These include the placement of a watermark on the Viewer and on renders, and the disabling of WriteGeo, Primatte, Framecycler, and Monitor Output.

2. **Nuke:** This is regular Nuke—the flavor this book covers. Nuke requires a trial license or regular paid license, which should cost about $4,500.

3. **NukeX:** This license includes all the regular Nuke features with a few additional high-end tools. These tools include the CameraTracker, PointCloudGenerator, LensDistortion, DepthGenerator, Modeler, FurnaceCore plug-ins, and PRman-Render (allowing for Renderman integration). NukeX costs in the region of $7,000. Chapter 10 covers the Camera Tracker and shows how to use it under the NukeX license; however, the exercises in the chapter can also be done without a NukeX license.

Downloading Nuke

To download Nuke, follow these steps.

1. Go to www.thefoundry.co.uk/products/nuke/product-downloads/.

2. Select the latest copy of Nuke for your operating system (Mac, Windows, or Linux). You can also download older versions of Nuke if necessary.

3. If you're downloading the latest version, you need to register and then you are directed to the download page. (Downloading older versions from the archive does not require registration.)

4. Follow the instructions for installation on your specific operating system.

Getting a trial license

After successfully installing Nuke, when you double-click the Nuke icon it explains that because you don't have a license yet, you can use Nuke under the PLE license. If you would like to use a fully licensed Nuke or NukeX, you will have to buy Nuke, rent Nuke (both available on the Foundry's web site shown below), or get a free 15-day trial license.

As there is no functional difference between getting a Nuke trial license or a NukeX trial license, I recommend getting a NukeX trial license. To get your free 15-day trial NukeX license, do the following:

1. Go to www.thefoundry.co.uk/products/nuke/try/.

2. Log in or sign up to get to the Free Trial page.

3. In the Free Trial page, fill in the form.

The System ID, which is the first entry to fill, is the unique code of your computer—the free license will be locked to that computer. The link to the right of the entry field explains where to find this number on your computer.

4. After you complete the form and click Continue, follow the rest of the instructions on the Foundry's web site for how to install the license on your operating system.

Staying up to date

Because Nuke is updated often, please visit the web site at www.peachpit.com/nuke101 for periodic updates to the book. I will strive to publish notes about behavior in new versions of Nuke as they come out if they differ from what's written in the book.

Also, I will periodically publish additional information and more tutorials on the web site that will add further content to the book.

ADDITIONAL TECHNICAL REQUIREMENTS

Nuke is a very powerful piece of software, even though its system requirements are pretty low. If you bought your computer in the last couple of years, you are probably OK. The requirements are listed on The Foundry web site but there are three things you should really check:

- Workstation-class graphics card, such as NVIDIA Quadro series, ATI FireGL series, R3D Rocket, or newer. Driver support for OpenGL 2.0.

- Display with at least 1280x1024 pixel resolution and 24-bit color.

- Three-button mouse. This kind of mouse is really a must as Nuke uses the middle mouse button extensively. A scroll wheel, by the way, can serve as the middle mouse button.

To copy the exercise files to your computer, you will need a DVD drive as well.

For a full list of Nuke's system requirements, visit www.thefoundry.co.uk/products/nuke/system-requirements.

ABOUT THE BOOK'S DISC FILES

At the back of the book you will find a DVD-ROM disc containing the files you need to complete the exercises in this book (or if you bought the ebook version, you'll be presented with a link to the files). The files are a mix of a real production that I or my colleagues created in recent years and some shot elements intended for use with this specific book.

What's on the disc

Each chapter has its own directory. Copy these directories to your hard drive to use the files properly. Some chapters use files from other chapters, so you need to copy all the directories to your hard drive.

How to install the files

1. Insert the Nuke101 DVD into your DVD drive.

2. Create a directory on your hard drive and name it **NukeChapters**.

3. Drag the chapters directory from the DVD into the NukeChapters directory on your hard drive.

ACKNOWLEDGMENTS

I've been teaching compositing since 2001. When Nuke started becoming the tool of choice for a lot of the studios around me, I decided to write a course that focused on it. I started writing the course in the spring of 2009 with help from The Foundry, whose staff was very kind and forthcoming. I would specifically like to thank Vikki Hamilton, Ben Minall, Lucy Cooper, and Matt Plec.

I finished writing the original course around the autumn of 2009. I taught it several times at Soho Editors Training in London, which was kind enough to let me try out the new course at their training facility. The course was well received, so between sessions I updated, corrected, and expanded on the original course.

About a year after that I approached Peachpit Press with the idea of turning the course into a book. Karyn Johnson, the book's senior editor, took on the project and after a long digestion period I sat down and started adapting the course into a book. Karyn made sure I had the best support I could possibly have, and with the help of the wonderful team at Peachpit, including Corbin Collins and Kelly Kordes Anton, I managed to complete the book to the high standard Peachpit expects of their writers. Thanks also go out to the kind friends and colleagues who gave me materials to use for the book: Alex Orrelle, Alex Norris, Hector Berrebi, Dror Revach, Assaf Evron, Menashe Morobuse, and Michal Boico.

It was quite a ride. You can see it took me three paragraphs to cover it all. But throughout this long period, which sometimes felt like it would last forever, my wife, Maya, and my two sons had to bear with my long days and long nights of writing, gave me the quiet and solitude I needed, and believed (and prayed) that I would finish the book. And so I have.

In so many ways, this book is for them.

GETTING STARTED WITH NUKE

Nuke uses a *node-based* workflow to drive image manipulation. Starting from a source image or images, various types of processors, called *nodes*, are added in succession until the desired result is achieved. Each node performs a specific, often very simple, function, and its output is passed on to the next node's input using a connector called a *pipe*. Using this workflow creates a very easy-to-understand, easy-to-manipulate compositing setup. This series of nodes is usually called a *process tree* or a *flow*.

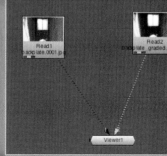

A Nuke project usually starts by bringing in images from your hard drive. More nodes are inserted after the image nodes and connected with pipes until a desired look is achieved. The process tree is rendered to disk for the final result and can also be saved in what's called a Nuke script to be opened later for changes.

In this lesson I explain the nuts and bolts of the Nuke interface so you will feel at ease clicking where you need to. It may seem boring, but it's a must. Knowing the components of the Nuke interface is the foundation of all the cool stuff you'll do later.

COMPONENTS OF THE GRAPHIC USER INTERFACE

Nuke's interface consists of a large window that can be split in various ways. By default the Nuke interface appears as in **FIGURE 1.1**.

The default layout is split into four key areas, called *panes*, populated by five *panels*. Yes, that's right, panes are populated by panels. Confusing terminology, I agree. The first pane, the strip at the very left, is populated by the Nodes Toolbar panel. The black pane at the top half of the screen is populated by the Viewer. Beneath that there's the pane populated by the Node Graph, which is also called the DAG

Nodes Toolbar   Viewer   Node Graph /Curve Editor   Properties Bin

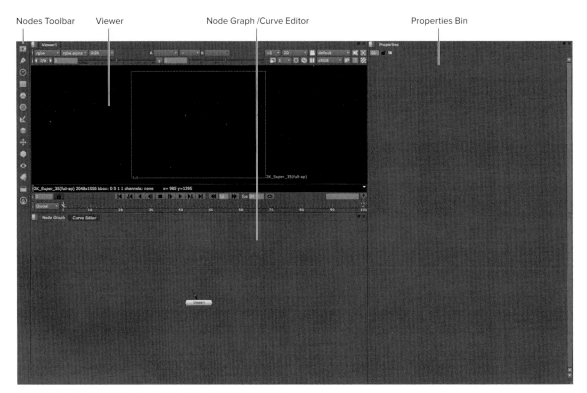

FIGURE 1.1 The default Nuke interface is split into four panes.

(Directed Acyclic Graph), and the Curve Editor panel. The large empty pane on the right is populated by the Properties Bin.

At the top left of every pane there's a tab with the name of that panel (except for the Nodes Toolbar). The pane containing the Node Graph panel also contains the Curve Editor panel. You can click the respective tabs to switch between the Node Graph and the Curve Editor.

The Content menu

The Nuke interface is completely customizable. You can split the interface into as many panes as you want and have as many tabs in each of them as you want, populated by whichever panels. Use the Content menus to do all this, which are the gray boxes in the top-left corner of each pane (**FIGURE 1.2**).

You should become familiar with the Content menu, which is located to the left of the tab name. This menu enables you to split the current pane either vertically or horizontally, creating another pane in the process. It also lets you detach the pane or tab from the rest of the interface, allowing it to float above the interface (there are several uses for this that I cover later on). You can also use the Content menu to populate the associated pane with any panel, be it a Curve Editor, Node Graph, Script Editor, and so on.

Hover your mouse pointer between the Node Graph and the Viewer, and the cursor will change to show that you can move the divide between the two panes to make the Viewer bigger or the Node Graph bigger. You can drag any separating line to change the size of the panes.

FIGURE 1.2 The Content menu is used to control the Nuke window layout.

Hover your mouse pointer in the Node Graph and press the spacebar on your keyboard to turn the whole window into the Node Graph. Click again to get the rest of the interface back. You can do this with any pane; simply hover your mouse pointer in that pane. This procedure is very useful if you want to look at only the Viewer.

A rundown of the various panels

The different Nuke panels are as follows:

- **Curve Editor** enables you to edit animation curves.

- **Dope Sheet** is a timeline representation of your clips and keyframes.

- **Nodes Toolbar** contains all the different nodes one can use to drive Nuke. These are split into several sections or toolboxes represented by little icons.

- **Node Graph** or DAG. The process of building the process tree happens here.

- **Properties Bin** contains sliders and knobs to control your various nodes.

■ **Progress Bar** is the window that tells you how long to wait for a process to finish, be it a render, a tracking process, or anything that takes a significant amount of time. This panel pops up whenever it's needed, but you can dock it in a pane, which some find convenient.

■ **Script Editor** is a text window where you can write Python scripts to automate various features of Nuke.

■ **New Viewer** opens a new viewer where you can view, compare, and analyze your images.

Using the Content menu, you can change the interface to fit the specific needs and preferences of different users.

The menu bar

The menu bar at the very top of the Nuke interface holds more functionality. Here's an explanation of the various menus (**FIGURE 1.3**).

FIGURE 1.3 The menu bar (on Mac OS X).

■ **File** contains commands for disk operations, including loading, saving, and importing projects—but not images.

■ **Edit** contains editing functions, preferences, and project settings.

■ **Layout** facilitates restoring and saving layouts.

■ **Viewer** helps in adding and connecting viewers.

■ **Render** is used to launch a render as well as various other related commands.

■ **Help** contains access to a list of hot keys, user documentation, training resources, tutorial files, and Nuke-related email lists.

Using the Content menu, you can customize the user interface. You can then use the Layout menu to save and retrieve the layout configuration.

Let's practice this in order to place the Progress Bar at the bottom right of the interface.

1. Launch Nuke.

2. Click the Content menu next to the Properties tab near the top right of the screen (top of the Properties panel).

3. From the Content menu choose Split Vertical (**FIGURE 1.4**).

FIGURE 1.4 Using the Content menu to split a pane into two panes.

You now have another pane, which holds no panel, at the bottom right of the interface. Let's populate it with the Progress Bar panel (**FIGURE 1.5**).

4. Click the Content menu in the newly created pane and choose Progress Bar (**FIGURE 1.6**).

FIGURE 1.5 The newly created pane holds no panel yet.

FIGURE 1.6 Creating a Progress Bar panel to populate the new pane.

The Progress Bar has been created and is populating the new pane. You don't need too much space for this panel, so you can move the horizontal separating line above it down to give more space to the Properties Bin.

5. Click the line separating the Properties Bin and the Progress Bar and drag it down.

I like having the Progress Bar docked as a panel in a pane at the bottom right of the interface. It means I always know where to look if I want to see a progress report, and it prevents the progress panel from jumping up and interfering when I don't need it. If you like this interface configuration, you can save it. You can use the Layout menu to do that.

6. From the Layout menu choose Save Layout 2 (**FIGURE 1.7**).

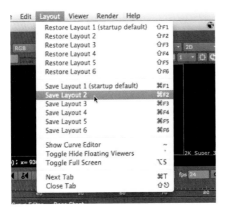

FIGURE 1.7 Saving the Layout using the menu option.

The layout has now been saved. Let's load the default layout and then reload this new one to make sure it has been saved.

7. From the Layout menu, choose Restore Layout 1.

You can now see the default window layout. Now let's see if you can reload the window layout you just created.

8. From the Layout menu, choose Restore Layout 2.

Presto! You now have full control over Nuke's window layout.

The contextual menu

FIGURE 1.8 An example of a contextual menu.

Using a two-button mouse, you can right-click an interface or image element to quickly access appropriate editing options. To display a context menu using a one-button mouse, Ctrl-click the interface or image element. (Generally, you right-click on Windows and Ctrl-click on Mac.) The contextual menus vary depending on what you click, so they are covered within discussions throughout this book (**FIGURE 1.8**).

Hot keys

Like most other programs Nuke uses *keyboard shortcuts* or *hot keys* to speed up your work. Instead of clicking somewhere in the interface, you can press a key or combination of keys on your keyboard. You are probably familiar with basic hot keys such as Ctrl/Cmd-S for saving.

Keyboard shortcuts in Nuke are location specific as well. Pressing R while hovering in the Node Graph will produce a different result than pressing R while hovering the mouse pointer in the Viewer.

NODES

Nodes are the building blocks of the process tree. Everything that happens to an image in Nuke happens by using nodes.

Let's explore the node's graphical representation (**FIGURE 1.9**).

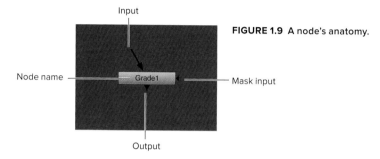

FIGURE 1.9 A node's anatomy.

Input

Node name

Grade1

Mask input

Output

NOTE Nuke is cross-platform, meaning it works on Windows, Linux, and Mac OS X. Windows and Linux machines use the modifier key called Control (Ctrl), but on the Mac this is called Command. I will use the short form for these, but will always mention both options. Ctrl/Cmd-S means press Control or Command and the S key simultaneously.

A node is usually represented by a rectangular shape with the name of the node in the middle. There's usually an input (or more than one) at the top of the node, and a single output at the bottom. On some nodes there is a mask input on the side of the node, the functionality of which is discussed in more detail in Chapter 3.

Creating a node

There are several ways to create nodes. Probably the best way is to choose a node from the Nodes Toolbar. The Nodes Toolbar is split into several *toolboxes*, as shown in **TABLE 1.1**.

TABLE 1.1

Icon	Name	Description
	Image	Image read and write nodes, built-in Nuke elements, and Viewer nodes.
	Draw	Roto shapes, paint tools, film grain, lens flares, sparkles, other vector-based image tools.
	Time	Retiming tools.
	Channel	Channel and layer set management.
	Color	Applying color correction effects.

continues

TABLE 1.1 The various toolboxes in the Nodes Toolbar (continued)

Icon	Name	Description
●	Filter	Applying convolve filters, such as blur, sharpen, edge detect, and erode.
✎	Keyer	Extracting procedural mattes.
▤	Merge	Layering tools.
✛	Transform	Translating, scaling, tracking and stabilizing, and distorting elements.
⬢	3D	3D compositing nodes and tools.
◉	Views	Nodes for working with views and stereoscopic or multi-view material.
◣	Metadata	Metadata-related nodes.
◉	Furnace Core	Furnace Core plug-ins are bundled in with NukeX.
▢	Other	Additional operators for project and viewer management.

As mentioned, there are other ways to create nodes. You can choose a node from the Node Graph's contextual menu, which mirrors the Nodes Toolbar (**FIGURE 1.10**).

The easiest way to create a node, if you remember its name and you're quick with your fingers, is to press the Tab key while hovering the mouse pointer over the Node Graph. This opens a dialog box in which you can type the name of the node. As you type, a "type-ahead" list will appear with matching node names, beginning with the letters you are typing. You can then use the mouse or the up and down arrows and the Enter key to create that node (**FIGURE 1.11**).

FIGURE 1.10 The contextual menu in the Node Graph.

FIGURE 1.11 Pressing the Tab key in the Node Graph allows you to create and name a new node.

The Read node

Unlike in many other applications, you import footage into Nuke in the same way you do everything else in Nuke—using a node.

Let's practice creating a node by importing a bit of footage into Nuke. This will also give you something to work with. Do either one of the following:

- Click the Image toolbox in the Nodes Toolbar and then click the Read node (**FIGURE 1.12**).

- Hover the mouse pointer over the Node Graph, or DAG, and press the R key.

The Read node is a bit special: When creating it, you first get the File Browser instead of just a node.

FIGURE 1.12 The Image toolbox gives access to image creation nodes.

The File Browser

The File Browser is used whenever reading or writing images to and from the disk drive. It is a representation of your file system much like the normal file browser found in Windows or Mac OS X.

Nuke doesn't use the basic operating system's file browser, as it requires extra features such as video previews and it needs to be consistent across all operating systems.

See the image below for an explanation of the browser's anatomy (**FIGURE 1.13**).

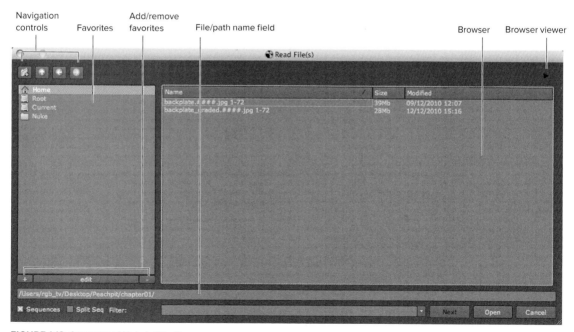

FIGURE 1.13 Anatomy of Nuke's File Browser.

NOTE Please read the Introduction of this book over carefully to learn how to copy the files from the book's disc onto your hard drive.

Let's walk through the File Browser together by using the files on this book's disc.

1. Browse to the Nuke101 folder that you copied onto your hard drive from this book's disc and click the chapter01 folder.

2. Click the little arrow at the top right-hand corner of the browser to bring up the browser's viewer.

3. Click once (don't double-click) the file named backplate.####.jpg 1-72 (**FIGURE 1.14**).

FIGURE 1.14 The File Browser's viewer can be used to preview images prior to importing them.

4. Scrub along the clip by clicking and dragging on the timeline at the bottom of the image.

   This viewer makes it easy to see what you are importing before importing it in case you are not sure what, for example, Untitled08 copy 3.tif is.

5. Click the Open button.

There is now a node in your Node Graph called Read1 (**FIGURE 1.15**)! Hurrah!

FIGURE 1.15 The new Read node is now in your DAG near your Viewer1 node.

Another thing that happened is that a Properties panel appeared in your Properties Bin. This Properties panel represents all the properties that relate to the newly created Read1 node (**FIGURE 1.16**).

You will learn about editing properties in Chapter 2.

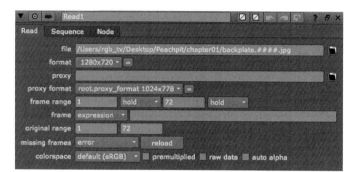

FIGURE 1.16 Using the Properties panels you can change the functionality of your nodes.

THE VIEWER

Another important part of the Nuke user interface is the Viewer. Without it, you will be lost as far as compositing goes. The Viewer is used to view your work as you go, receive feedback when editing nodes, compare different images, and manipulate properties on the image. You will explore each of these as you work through this book.

Notice that aside from the Read1 node you created there's also another node in your Node Graph, called Viewer1. Also notice that your Viewer panel is called Viewer1. Every Viewer node represents an open Viewer panel. To view an image in Nuke, you simply connect the Viewer node's input to the output of the node you want to view. It will then appear in the Viewer panel itself.

You can connect any node to a Viewer node in two ways.

- You can click the Viewer node's little input arrow and drag it from the input of the Viewer node to the node you want to view.

- You can do the reverse and drag the output of the node you want to view to the Viewer node.

Either method will connect the node to the Viewer node's first input, called input 1.

The connecting line that appears between the two nodes is called a *pipe*. It simply represents the connections between nodes in the Node Graph (**FIGURE 1.17**).

FIGURE 1.17 A process tree is a series of pipes.

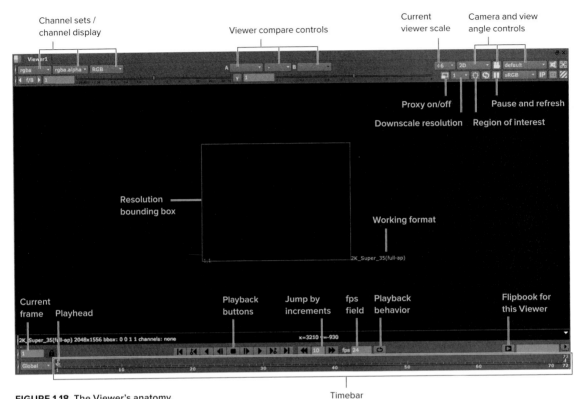

FIGURE 1.18 The Viewer's anatomy.

Another way to connect a node to the Viewer node's input 1 is by selecting the node you want to view and pressing the number 1 on the keyboard.

1. Select the Read node by clicking it once.

2. Keep hovering over the Node Graph and press 1 on the keyboard.

Viewer1 now shows the image you brought into Nuke—an image of a run-down staircase.

FIGURE 1.18 illustrates the Viewer's anatomy. The buttons are explained in more detail in further chapters.

Navigating the Viewer

While compositing, you often need to view different parts of an image, zoom in to closely inspect an aspect, and zoom out for an overall view. Because you do this so often, a few shortcuts are worth remembering and listed in **TABLE 1.2**.

TABLE 1.2 How to navigate the Viewer

Shortcut	Action	Comment
Alt/Opt-left-click	pan image around	
Alt/Opt-middle-click-drag	zoom image in and out	with a regular mouse
Scroll wheel up and down	zoom image in and out	for a scroll wheel mouse
Two fingers on track pad up and down	zoom image in and out	for Apple laptops
+ or -	zoom image in and out	left of backspace
F	centers frame and zooms	zooms to closest integer
H	fill image in Viewer	zooms to none integer
R	view the red channel	
G	view the green channel	
B	view the blue channel	
A	view the alpha channel	
Y	view the luminance of the image	
M	view a matte overlay	

NOTE All these hot keys will also let you navigate the DAG and Curve Editor.

Using the Viewer

Let's say you want to view the different color channels of the image you just brought in. Here's how you would go about it.

1. While hovering the mouse pointer over the Viewer, press the R key to view the red channel.

   The channel display box on the far left is now labeled R. You can also change which channel you are viewing by clicking in the channel display drop-down menu itself (**FIGURE 1.19**).

2. Press R again to display the three color channels again.

   You're now back to viewing all three color channels, and the channel display box changes back to RGB (**FIGURE 1.20**).

FIGURE 1.19 The channel display box shows R for the red channel.

FIGURE 1.20 The channel display box is back to showing RGB.

Now let's load another image and view it:

3. Hover your mouse pointer over the Node Graph and press R on the keyboard. The File Browser opens again.

    Notice how pressing R while hovering the mouse pointer in the Viewer and in the Node Graph produces different results.

4. Double-click the file named backplate_graded.####.jpg to bring it into Nuke.

    You now have another Read node in your interface. If one Read node is overlapping the other you can click and drag one of them to make space. Let's view the new Read node as well.

5. Select the new Read node by clicking it once and pressing 1 on the keyboard.

You now see the new image, which is a *graded* (color corrected) version of the previous image. Otherwise, the two images are the same.

Viewer inputs

Any Viewer in Nuke has up to 10 different inputs and it's very easy to connect nodes to these inputs in order to view them. Simply by selecting a node and pressing a number on the keyboard (like you pressed 1 before) you're connecting the node to that number input of the Viewer. This will result in several different parts of the process tree being connected to the same Viewer. You will then be able to change what you're looking at in the Viewer with ease.

Let's connect the first Read node to the first Viewer input and the second Read node to the second Viewer input.

1. Select the first Read node (Read1) and press 1 on the main part of the keyboard.

2. Select the second Read node (Read2) and press 2 on the the keyboard (**FIGURE 1.21**).

    To view the different inputs of a viewer, hover the mouse pointer over the Viewer itself and press the corresponding numbers on the keyboard.

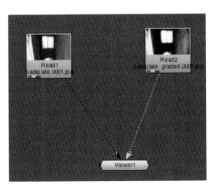

FIGURE 1.21 Two nodes connected to two different inputs of Viewer1.

3. Hover your mouse pointer over the Viewer and press 1 and 2 several times. See how the images change from one input to another.

Using this method you can keep monitoring different stages of your composite as you are working. This is also a good way to compare two images.

Playing a clip in the Viewer

Playing a clip is kind of mandatory in a compositing package. Let's see this piece of moving image playing in realtime.

This notion of realtime is very subjective in relation to the specific footage you are using. For film, realtime is 24fps (frames per second). For PAL video, it's 25fps. For some other purpose it might be 100fps. Some computers will simply never be able to play realtime footage of some resolutions and frame rates simply because they are too slow, no matter what tricks you try to apply to them.

This aside, you can strive to play clips in realtime. First, you can attempt to play footage in the Viewer itself. You will need to define what realtime is for your footage. This footage is 25fps. Let's set the Viewer to 25fps. You do this in the fps field above the Timebar. When playing, this field will show how fast playback really is instead of how fast it is supposed to be playing.

FIGURE 1.22 Viewer fps field.

1. Set the Viewer fps field to 25 (**FIGURE 1.22**).

   Now when you click Play, Nuke will load each frame from the disk, apply any calculations to it, and present it in the Viewer. It will also cache this image in its cache file. It will then move on to the next frame. Once Nuke caches all the frames, it will start to load those into the Viewer instead of going back to the originals. This will allow Nuke better speed in playback. Nuke will now attempt to play the given frame rate. The fps field will display the actual frame rate that is playing whether it's realtime or not.

2. Click the Play Forward button on the Viewer controls. Let it loop a couple of times to cache, and then see how fast it is actually playing.

3. Click Stop.

   Chances are it played pretty well, and close to if not exactly 25 fps. Let's give it something more difficult to attempt.

4. Change the value in the fps field to 100.

5. Click Play and again watch how fast Nuke is playing the footage.

Nuke probably isn't reaching 100fps, but it should be telling you what it is reaching. How thoughtful.

NOTE The cache file is a folder on your hard drive where Nuke can place temporary files. You can set that to be any folder and any size by changing the disk cache setting in Nuke's preferences.

TIP The hot keys for playing in the Viewer are easy to use and good to remember. They are exactly the same as in Final Cut Pro: L plays forward, K pauses, and J plays backwards. Pressing L and J one after the other enables you to easily rock 'n' roll your shot.

If you have the PLE (Personal Learning Edition) of Nuke, this is the only way to review your work aside from rendering and viewing the renders with a third-party application.

If you have a fully licensed version of Nuke, there is another option. Even if you only have the PLE at the moment, you should know about what's available, so read on.

FRAMECYCLER

The other option for rendering and viewing, which you are likely to use predominantly in your work, is Framecycler, an application bundled with Nuke. Framecycler functions as Nuke's built-in player.

NOTE Framecycler uses RAM to play back images. RAM is the fastest memory available to the computer, and you need it to use your computer for everything else, too. So remember to quit Framecycler when you're not using it to free up RAM.

Framecycler is a playback system developed by Iridas. It is the industry leader in uncompressed playback of frame-based and video file formats at high resolutions. You get it for free when you buy Nuke, but it's a version you can only open from within Nuke. Once it's open, though, Framecycler is fully functional.

You can do a lot of things with Framecycler besides viewing playback. It's a complete software program in its own right, but limited space prevents me from covering it in detail in this book. A manual for Framecycler is included in your installation. In this book, I cover how to use Framecycler for playback.

Let's look at how to load a *flipbook*, which is what Framecycler calls a sequence of frames loaded for viewing. I will also use flipbook as a verb, which is a standard way of saying you want to view something playing in realtime in Framecycler.

TIP You can also use the Flipbook This button in the Viewer itself, which will flipbook whatever you are currently viewing.

1. Click Read1 in the Node Graph, and then choose Flipbook Selected from the Render menu (or press Alt/Opt-F).

   A little panel appears called the Flipbook panel (**FIGURE 1.23**). This panel allows you to change what it is you want to flip and how. Most of the properties here will become apparent as you learn more about Nuke. The main thing this panel is asking is what range of frames you would like to render into a flipbook. This is the Frame range property.

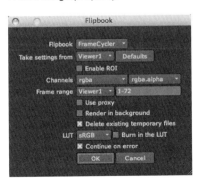

FIGURE 1.23 The Flipbook panel.

2. You want to view the whole range, so leave the Frame range field at its current value and press OK.

   You see a little splash screen showing the Iridas logo, and Framecycler fills the screen. The little bar at the bottom filling with green shows what's loaded into RAM.

Nuke defines frame ranges with a dash. To define a frame range of 1, 2, 3, 4, 5, for example, you would enter **1-5** in step 2. **TABLE 1.3** lists other possibilities.

TABLE 1.3 Frame range input

Frame Range	Expands To	Description
1-5	1, 2, 3, 4, 5	from 1 to 5
1-10x3	1, 4, 7, 10	from 1 to 10 in steps of 3
-5--1	-5, -4, -3, -2, -1	from -5 to -1
1-5 8-11 22	1, 2, 3, 4, 5, 8, 9, 10, 11, 22	multiple ranges separated by a space

Nuke uses this same system to define frame ranges for all aspects of its interface, such as rendering to disk. Unfortunately, Framecycler doesn't support some of these options.

TABLE 1.4 shows a list of Framecycler shortcuts.

TABLE 1.4 Framecycler shortcuts

Shortcut	Description
. (period) >	play forward
, (comma) <	play backwards
Spacebar	start/stop
- (minus on the numeric keypad)	zoom out
+ (plus on the numeric keypad)	zoom in
Middle mouse button	move around the frame
Scroll wheel up and down	step frame back/forward
Ctrl/Cmd + Scroll wheel	zoom in/out
Right Arrow	step frame forward
Left Arrow	step frame back
I or Home	go to in point
O or End	go to out point

continues

TABLE 1.4 Framecycler shortcuts (continued)

Shortcut	Description
Shift-I	set in point
Shift-O	set out point
F	toggle full/windowed frame
Shift-Home	center and set zoom to 100%
D	loads File Browser

I like to work with Framecycler filling the entire screen—simply because it makes viewing images an uncluttered experience.

3. Press F to maximize Framecycler.

4. Press spacebar to start playing the sequence.

NOTE At the end of each chapter, quit Nuke to start the next chapter with a fresh project.

5. Feel free to play around with Framecycler's controls. When finished, quit Framecycler to free up the RAM it was using.

6. Quit Nuke.

That's it for now. We will do actual compositing in the next lesson. Thanks for participating. Go outside and have cookies.

TOURING THE INTERFACE WITH A BASIC COMPOSITE

In this chapter you will create a simple composite: a color-corrected foreground over a background. In the process, you will learn the basic building blocks of the Nuke process tree and some additional things about the interface.

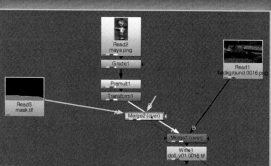

Digital compositing is about taking several often widely different sources and combining them into one seamless whole. As you will learn in this chapter, Nuke gives you the right toolset to do just that. A successful composite might involve many different tools that need to be combined in a specific order, such as those for keying, color correction, matte extraction, 2D or 3D tracking, and more. The final image will rely on your, the artist's, talent; however, having an easy-to-access toolset will help drive your vision instead of slowing it down.

WORKING WITH PROCESS TREES

A *process tree* is a very intuitive way to change the appearance of images. It is essentially a graphical representation of the process the image or images are going through. If you know what process you want your images to go through, the process tree will represent the process you are thinking of.

Nuke has several kinds of image manipulation tools. By placing them in a specific order one after another, you can create your desired effect. This process is similar in any compositing application, but in Nuke everything is open and at your control. Having each individual process exposed achieves a greater level of control, which enables you to keep tweaking your work to your or your client's needs quickly and with relative ease.

Usually, you start a composite with one or more images brought in from disk. You manipulate each image separately, connect them together to combine them, and finally render the desired result back to disk. This process builds a series of processors, or *nodes*, which together look like a tree, which is why it's called a process tree. Note that Nuke uses a second analogy to describe this process, that of the flow of water. A tree can also be called a *flow*. As the image passes from one node to another, it flows. This analogy is used in terms such as *downstream* (for nodes after the current node) and *upstream* (for nodes before the current node). Nuke uses these two analogies interchangeably.

A Nuke process tree is shown in **FIGURE 2.1**. In it, you can see a relatively basic tree with two images—the smiling doll on the top left and the orange image on the top right. The images are being passed through several nodes—a resolution changing node, a color correction node, a transformation node—until they merge together at the bottom of the tree with another node to form a composite. The lines connecting the nodes to each other are called *pipes*.

Trees usually flow in this way, from top to bottom, but that is not strictly the case in Nuke. Trees can flow in any direction, though the tendency is still to flow down.

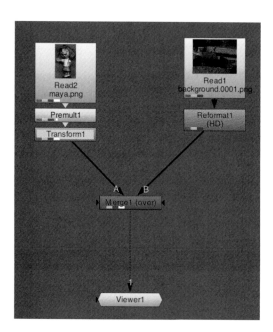

FIGURE 2.1 This is what a basic Nuke tree looks like.

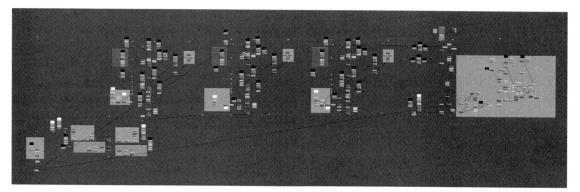

FIGURE 2.2 This is what a more complex Nuke tree looks like.

Another example of a Nuke process tree is shown in **FIGURE 2.2** and this is a much more complex tree. The black boxes are all images that are being processed and connected together with a large variety of nodes. The flow of this tree is down and to the left. At the very end of this tree is a yellow box, which is where this tree ends. Pretty daunting image. However, when you are building this flow of nodes, you know exactly what each part of the tree is doing.

CREATING A SIMPLE PROCESS TREE

Let's start building a composite in order to better understand the process tree. If you recall from Chapter 1, a tree is a collection of nodes (**FIGURE 2.3**) connected via pipes.

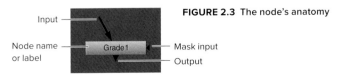

FIGURE 2.3 The node's anatomy

The tree flows from the output of one node to the input of the next node. Not all nodes have all these elements. A Read node, which you will use again in a moment, only has an output because it is the beginning of the tree and has no use for an input. Some nodes don't have a Mask input (explained in Chapter 3), and some nodes have more than one input.

You know from Chapter 1 how to read images from disk using a Read node, so let's do that again and learn a few more options along the way.

1. Launch Nuke.

2. While hovering the mouse pointer over the DAG (the Directed Acyclic Graph, also called the Node Graph), press the R key.

3. Navigate to the chapters directory, which you selected when you copied the files from the disc in the introduction. Navigate to the chapter02 directory.

In Chapter 1 you used a File Browser to bring in one sequence, then another File Browser to bring in another sequence. However, if you select more than one sequence, or image, more than one Read node will be created.

You can multiple-select files in the File Browser in several ways.

- Click and drag over several file names.

- Shift-click the first and last files to make a continuous selection.

- Ctrl/Cmd-click to select several files not immediately next to each other.

- Press Ctrl/Cmd-A to select all.

- You can also use Ctrl/Cmd-click to deselect files.

- Select one file name, then press the Next button at the bottom right, and then select another file and press the Next or Open button again.

4. Select the file called background.####.png and click the Next button, then select maya.png and click the Open button or press the Enter/Return key on your keyboard.

You now have two new Read nodes in the DAG (**FIGURE 2.4**). The first, Read1, should also be labeled background.0001.png. The second, Read2, should also be labeled maya.png. This second line of the label is generated automatically by Nuke and shows the current image being loaded by the Read node.

Let's view the images to see what you brought in.

5. Click Read2 (maya.png), hover the mouse pointer over the DAG, and press 1 on the keyboard.

    You're now viewing Read2 (maya.png), which is an image of a little doll. If you look at the bottom-right or top-right corner of the image in the Viewer (you might need to pan up or down using Alt/Option-click-drag or middle mouse button-drag) you will see two sets of numbers: 518, 829. These numbers represent the resolution of this image—518 pixels x 829 pixels (**FIGURE 2.5**). This odd resolution simply came about from placing this doll on my flatbed scanner, scanning, and then cropping the image. Nuke can work with any resolution image and mix different resolutions together.

FIGURE 2.4 After bringing in two files, your DAG should look like this.

NOTE If the file called maya.png isn't Read2, you did not complete the steps as presented. This is not necessarily a problem, but you'll have to remember that my Read2 is your Read1.

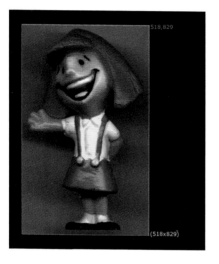

FIGURE 2.5 The resolution of the image is shown at the bottom-right corner in the Viewer.

Let's look at the other image.

6. Click Read1 (background.####.png) and press 1, like before.

    This image you are looking at is part of a file sequence. It's a rather dark image of a painter's toolbox. I shot this image in HD, and indeed if you look at the same corners of the image in the Viewer, you can see that the resolution for this sequence is 1920x1080. Since this is a defined format (more on this in Chapter 8), the bottom-right corner displays the name of the format rather than the resolution. The bottom-right corner shows HD.

Your goal in this chapter is to place the doll image inside the artist's toolbox—and for it to look believable. Let's start by placing the doll image over the background image.

MERGING IMAGES

The definition of compositing is combining two or more images into a seamless, single image. You definitely need to learn how to do that in Nuke. In layer-based systems, such as After Effects and Flame, you simply place one layer on top of another to achieve a composite. In Nuke you combine two images by using several different nodes—chief among which is the Merge node.

The simplest way to create and connect a node to an existing node is to select the existing node (after which the new node will be inserted) and then call the node you want to create, either by clicking it in the Nodes Toolbar or pressing the Tab key. The new node is then created, and its input is connected to the selected node's output. Let's do this.

TIP You can also use the hot key M to create a Merge node.

1. Select Read2 (maya.png) and choose Merge from the Merge toolbox.

    The Merge node has a slightly different anatomy than a standard node. It has two inputs rather than just the one (**FIGURE 2.6**).

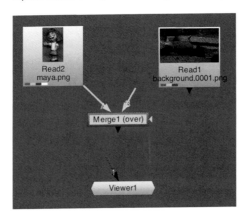

FIGURE 2.6 The Merge node you created has a free input.

NOTE To see all the different layering operations the Merge node is capable of, click the Operation property in the Merge node's Properties panel. To see the math of the operations, hover your mouse pointer over the Operation drop-down menu until a tooltip appears. Tooltips are available on practically every button in Nuke.

The Merge node can connect two or more images together using various layering operations such as Overlay, Screen, and Multiply. However, the default operation called Over simply places a foreground image with an alpha channel over a background image. The A input, already connected, is the foreground input. The unconnected B input is the background input. Let's connect the B input.

2. Click and drag Merge1's B input towards Read1 and release it over Read1 (**FIGURE 2.7**).

3. Select Merge1 and press 1 on the keyboard to view the result in the Viewer (**FIGURE 2.8**).

    The image, however, looks wrong—it is washed out in an odd light purple color.

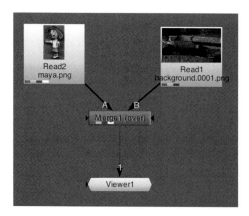

FIGURE 2.7 Both inputs are now connected, creating a composite.

FIGURE 2.8 All this light purple discoloration wasn't here before.

Maybe you don't have an alpha channel? Let's have a look.

4. Click Read2 and press 1 on the keyboard to view it in the Viewer.

5. While hovering your mouse pointer over the Viewer, press the A key to view the alpha channel (**FIGURE 2.9**).

   You can clearly see an alpha image here. It represents the area where the doll is. The black area represents parts of the doll image that should be discarded when compositing. So why aren't they being discarded?

6. Press the A key again to switch back to viewing the RGB channels.

   Notice that the black areas in the alpha channel are a light purple color, same as the discoloration in your composite. Maybe this is the source of your problems?

Normally, the Merge node assumes the foreground input is a *premultiplied image.* What's that you say? You've seen that term *premultiplied* before but never quite figured out what it means? Read on.

FIGURE 2.9 The doll's alpha channel.

Merging premultiplied images

The Merge node expects the foreground image to have both RGB channels and an alpha channel. The alpha is used to determine which pixels of the foreground image will be used for the composite. Another assumption is that the foreground RGB channels have been multiplied by the alpha channel. This results in an image where all black areas in the alpha channel are also black in the RGB channels. This multiplication is usually the result of 3D software renders or that of a composite partway through the tree. It is also the user's choice, in whatever software package, to multiply the RGB channels with the alpha channel, thus producing a premultiplied image, whether users are aware of this or not.

Nuke's Merge node expects the foreground image to be a premultiplied one, so it is important to know whether your image has been premultiplied or not. An image that hasn't been premultiplied is called either a *straight* image or an *unpremultiplied* image. How do you know whether an image is premultiplied? Generally speaking, you should ask the person who gave you the image with the incorporated alpha if he or she premultiplied the image (that person might very well be you). But here are a few rules of thumb:

- Most 3D software renders are premultiplied.

- Images that don't have incorporated alpha channels are straight.

- If black areas in the alpha channel are not black in the RGB channels, the image is straight.

- If you are creating the alpha channel (using a key, a shape creation node, or another method), you should check whether your operation created a premultiplied image or not. As you learn the alpha-channel creation tools, I will cover premultiplied again.

Another reason you need to know the premultiplication state of your image is color correction. Why? *Because you can't color correct premultiplied images.* You are probably not aware of this fact, as other software packages hide it from you. In Nuke, however, it is something that needs to be taken care of by the user—and that means you. Unpremultiplying is performed by dividing the premultiplied RGB channels with the alpha, thus reversing the multiplication. This produces a straight image that you can then color correct, then reapply the multiplication. You will learn how to do this later in the chapter.

Here are some dos and don'ts:

- The Merge node expects a premultiplied image as the foreground image for its Over (most basic and default) operation.

■ Never *color correct* premultiplied images. Chapter 4 is all about color correction.

■ Always *transform* (move around) and *filter* (blur and so forth) premultiplied images.

You control premultiplication with two nodes in the Merge toolbox: Premult and Unpremult.

The rule says that if an image's RGB channels aren't black where the alpha channel is black, then it isn't a premultiplied image. When you looked at Read2 you noticed exactly this. The black areas in the alpha channel were a light purple color in the RGB channels (**FIGURE 2.10**). This means this image is a ... what? A straight image!

Because the Merge node expects a premultiplied image as its foreground input, you need to premultiply the image first.

1. While Read2 is selected, press Tab and type **pre**. A drop-down menu displays with the Premult option. Use the down arrow key to navigate to it and press Enter/Return. Alternatively, you can choose the Premult node from the Merge toolbox (**FIGURE 2.11**).

FIGURE 2.10 This image shows both the alpha and RGB channels.

   There's now a Premult node called Premult1 connected to Read2. The area outside the doll's outline is now black (**FIGURE 2.12**). It is now a premultiplied image. You can proceed to place this image over the background.

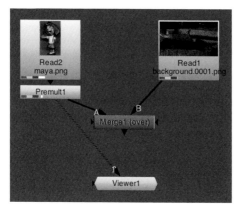

FIGURE 2.11 The Premult node sits in between Read2 and Merge1.

FIGURE 2.12 The area that was light purple is now black.

2. Click Merge1 and press 1 on your keyboard.

   All that purple nastiness has disappeared. You are now seeing a composite of the foreground image over the background (**FIGURE 2.13** next page).

FIGURE 2.13 Your first composite should look like this.

Is it really the Premult node that fixed this? Let's double-check by disabling it and enabling it.

3. Select Premult1 and press D on the keyboard to disable the node (**FIGURE 2.14**).

   A cross appears on Premult1, indicating that it is disabled. If you look at the image, you can see you are back to the wrong composite. This shows that indeed it is the Premult1 node that fixed things. Let's enable it again.

FIGURE 2.14 You have just disabled Premult1.

NOTE Disabling a node means that the flow of the pipe runs through the node without processing it. You can disable any node, and it's a very handy way of measuring what you did.

4. With Premult1 selected, press D on the keyboard again.

   What you now see is a classic Nuke tree: two streams flow into one. The foreground and background connect through the Merge node. Incidentally, to combine more images, you simply create another Merge node.

Before you go further, and there's much further to go, you should save your Nuke script. What's a script? You're about to find out.

Saving Nuke scripts

Nuke saves its project files, or *scripts*, as ASCII files. An *ASCII* file is a text file that you can open in a text editor. ASCII files stand in contrast to *binary* files, which don't make any sense when opened in a text editor and are only readable by specific applications. The ASCII file format of the Nuke script is great, and you explore this feature in Chapter 12. Nuke scripts have the .nk file extension.

All Nuke script-related functions are accessible through the File menu and respond to standard hot keys for opening and saving files.

1. Press Ctrl/Cmd-S to save the file, or choose File > Save.

2. In the browser that displays, navigate to the chapter02 directory (that you copied onto your hard drive from this book's disc). Name the script. Please use chapter02_v01. Nuke automatically adds the file extension.

3. Press Enter/Return.

   Nuke just saved your script. You can quit Nuke, go have a coffee, come back, open the script, and continue working.

By default Nuke autosaves your project every 30 seconds, or if you are not moving your mouse, it will save once after five seconds. But it doesn't autosave if you haven't saved your project yet. *You* have to save your project the first time. That's why it is important to save your project early on.

NOTE You can change the amount of time between autosaves in the Preferences pane.

Another great feature in Nuke is the Save New Version option in the File menu. You will save different, updated versions of your script often when compositing, and Nuke has a smart way of making this easy for you. If you add these characters to your script name: "_v##", where the # symbol is a number, using the Save New Version option in the File menu adds 1 to that number. So if you have a script called nuke_v01.nk and you click File > Save New Version, your script will be saved as nuke_v02.nk. Very handy. Let's practice this with your script, which you named chapter02_v01.nk earlier.

4. With nothing selected, press the Q key. This brings up the Current Info panel (**FIGURE 2.15**).

TIP If you are not sure what a hot key does or you don't remember the hot key for something, you can choose Key Assignment from the Help menu.

FIGURE 2.15 The Current Info panel is a quick way to see which script you are working on.

The Current Info panel shows that the name of your current script contains "_v01" in it. Let's save this as "_v02."

5. Click OK to close the Current Info panel.

6. Choose File > Save New Version.

7. Press the Q key again. Notice that your script is now called chapter02_v02.nk.

This same treatment of versions, using "_v01," is also available when working with image files. For example, you can render new versions of your images in the same way. You will try this at the end of this chapter.

INSERTING AND MANIPULATING NODES IN THE TREE

In the composite you are working on, the doll is obviously not in the right position to look like it's following basic laws of physics. You would probably like to move it and scale it down. To do that, you need to (what else?) add another node to the doll stream—a Transform node this time. The Transform node is a 2D axis that can reposition an image on the X and Y axes and rotate, scale, and skew (skew is sometimes called *shear*).

Because you only want to reposition the foreground image, you need to connect the Transform node somewhere in the foreground (the doll) stream. Remember from the explanation of premultiplication earlier in this chapter that you should always strive to transform premultiplied images. Now you're going to insert the Transform node after the image has been premultiplied. It is important, when compositing in the tree, to think about the placement of your nodes as in this example.

The Transform node resides in the Transform toolbox in the Nodes Toolbar. It also has a hot key assigned to it (T).

You have already inserted a node—the Premult node—but let's cover how to do this properly.

Inserting, creating, branching, and replacing nodes

When you create a node with an existing node selected in the DAG, the new node is inserted between the selected node and everything that comes after it. This is called *inserting* a node. If there is nothing selected, a node will be created at the center of the DAG, and will not be connected to anything. This is called *creating* a node.

1. Click Premult1 once and then press the T on the keyboard to insert a Transform node after it.

    A new node called Transform1 is inserted between Premult1 and Merge1 (**FIGURE 2.16**).

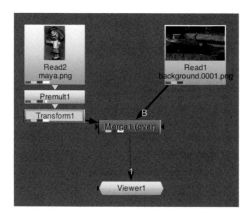

FIGURE 2.16 After adding the Transform node, your tree should look like this.

Sometimes what you want to do is to start a new branch from the output of an existing node. That lets you manipulate it in a different way, and then later, most likely, connect it back to the rest of the tree. This is called *branching*. To branch, you select the node you want to branch from and then hold Shift while creating the new node. You don't need a branch now, but let's practice it anyway.

2. Select Transform1, hold down Shift, and press T.

   A new node called Transform2 is now branching away from Transform1 (**FIGURE 2.17**). If you want to create the node by clicking it in a toolbox or using the Tab key, all you have to do is hold Shift and it will work in the same way.

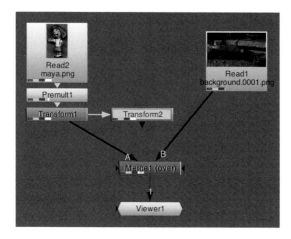

FIGURE 2.17 Branching to create a new stream.

But hold on, I was mistaken. I didn't want you to create another Transform node, I wanted you to create a Blur node. This happens a lot. You create a node by mistake and you need to replace it with another node. This is called *replacing*. To do this, select the node you want to replace and then hold Ctrl/Cmd while creating a new node. Let's try this.

3. Select Transform2 and while holding down Ctrl/Cmd, click Blur from the Filter toolbox in the Nodes toolbar.

Transform2 was replaced by a new node called Blur1 (**FIGURE 2.18**).

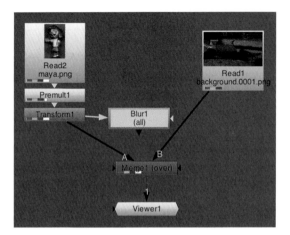

FIGURE 2.18 You have now replaced Transform2 with Blur1.

Here's a recap of the different ways to create nodes.

■ To insert a node, select a node in the DAG and create a new node. (Note that creating a node means to create an attached node. You do this by not having anything selected in the DAG before you create a node.)

■ To branch a node, hold Shift.

■ To replace a node, hold Ctrl/Cmd.

The next section covers a few more things you need to know about how to manipulate nodes in the DAG.

Connecting nodes

If you have an unconnected node that you want to connect, or if you have a node you want to reconnect in a different way, here's how:

■ To connect an unattached node, drag its input pipe to the center of the node to which you want to connect.

■ To move a pipe from one node to another, click the end you want to connect (input or output) and drag it to the node you want to connect it to (**FIGURE 2.19**).

■ To branch an existing output to an existing node, Shift-click the existing outgoing pipe and drag the newly created pipe to the existing node (**FIGURE 2.20**).

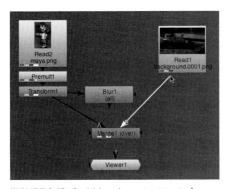
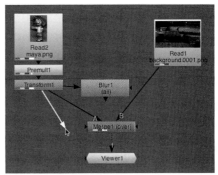

FIGURE 2.19 Grabbing the output part of the pipe.

FIGURE 2.20 Holding Shift and dragging the input end of the pipe.

Selecting nodes

You've been selecting nodes for a while now, but I never really explained this properly. Well done for succeeding without detailed instructions.

▨ To select one node, click once in the center of the node.

▨ To select multiple nodes, click and drag around them to draw a marquee, or Shift-click to select more than one node.

▨ To select all upstream nodes from a node, Ctrl/Cmd-click the bottom node and drag a little. Upstream nodes mean all the nodes that go up from the current node. In **FIGURE 2.21**, notice that Merge1 isn't selected as it's not upstream from Blur1.

▨ To deselect nodes, Shift-click a selected node.

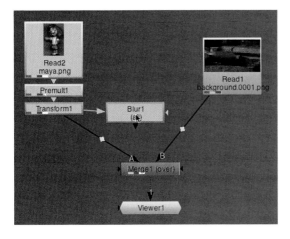

FIGURE 2.21 Holding Ctrl/Cmd and dragging to select all upstream nodes.

Arranging nodes

It is also good practice to keep a tree organized. The definition of "organized" is subjective, but the general idea is that looking at the tree makes sense, and following the flow from one node to the next is easy. Here are a few ways to keep an organized tree:

■ Nodes snap to position when they get close to other nodes both horizontally and vertically.

■ To arrange a few nodes together, select them, and then press L on the keyboard. Use this with caution—you can get unexpected results because Nuke uses simple mathematical rules instead of common sense. You might expect that the Read nodes would be on top, but sometimes they're on the side.

■ You can also create backdrops around part of your tree that remind you where you did certain things—a kind of group, if you will. Access these Backdrop nodes through the Other toolbox. You will learn this shortly.

Disabling and deleting nodes

In addition to adding nodes, you need to be able to remove them when you change your mind.

■ To disable a node, select it and press D on the keyboard. To enable it, repeat.

■ To delete a node, select it and press Backspace/ Delete on the keyboard.

Now that you know how to do all these things, let's delete the unneeded Blur1 node.

1. Click Blur1 to select it.

2. Press the Delete key to delete the node.

    Your tree should now have only the added Transform1 node and should look like **FIGURE 2.22**.

Now back to using the Transform node to place the doll in the correct place in the artist's toolbox.

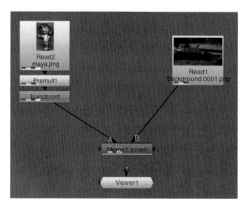

FIGURE 2.22 Your tree should look like this.

CHANGING PROPERTIES

Notice that the Viewer now displays a new set of controls. Some nodes, such as the Transform node, have on-screen controls, which mirror properties in the node's Properties panel but are more interactive and easier to use. On-screen controls display when a node's Properties panel is loaded in the Properties Bin. When a node is created, its Properties panel is automatically loaded into the Properties Bin. The controls that are now on-screen belong to the newly created Transform1 node. You can use these controls to change the position, scale, rotation, skew, and pivot of the image, as shown in **FIGURE 2.23**.

X scale   Rotate

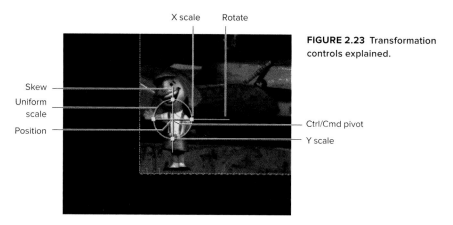

Skew
Uniform
scale
Position

Ctrl/Cmd pivot
Y scale

FIGURE 2.23 Transformation controls explained.

1. Go ahead and play around with Transform node controls to familiarize yourself with their functionality.

   When you are finished playing, reset the node's properties so you can start fresh. You do that in the node's Properties panel.

2. Right-click (Ctrl-click) an empty space in Transform1's Properties panel and then choose Set Knobs to Default from the contextual menu (**FIGURE 2.24**).

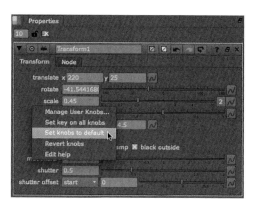

FIGURE 2.24 This is how you reset a node's properties.

TIP A good way to do the last fine bit of repositioning is to click the axis once to highlight it (a dot will appear in the center of the axis to represent this) and then use the numeric keypad to nudge the image into place. It's very intuitive, as the 4 on most keyboards' number keypads is left, 6 is right, 2 is down, 8 is up, and numbers 1, 3, 7, and 9 are diagonals. Hold down Shift to move in bigger increments, and hold down Ctrl/Cmd to move in smaller increments. You need a keyboard with a numeric keypad for this.

Now that you have reset the doll, you can proceed to position the doll at the front, bottom right of the painter's toolbox as shown in **FIGURE 2.25**.

FIGURE 2.25 This is where you want the doll image to end up.

3. Position the doll according to Figure 2.25 by using the on-screen controls, or simply type in the following values for the corresponding properties in Transform1's Properties panel:

- Translate.x = 1048
- Translate.y = −20
- Scale = 0.606.

Color correcting the image

NOTE Remember that you cannot color correct premultiplied images. Find the right place in the branch to insert the color correction node.

The color of the doll isn't exactly right. It's almost a match, but the doll is too cold in color and too bright in relation to the background. You can fix this using the Grade node in the Color toolbox.

The preceding note poses a question: How, or rather, where, are you going to color correct the doll image? One way to color correct it is to unpremult the image after the transformation, color correct it, and then premult it again. However, there is really no reason to do that. The great thing about the node/tree paradigm is that you have access to every part of the comp all the time. You can simply color correct the doll image before you premult it—right after the Read node.

1. Select Read2.

2. Press G on the keyboard to create a Grade node between Read2 and Premult1. Alternatively, you can pick a Grade node from the Color toolbox.

The Grade node gives you control over up to four channels using the following properties: Blackpoint, Whitepoint, Lift, Gain, Multiply, Offset, and Gamma. These properties are covered in Chapter 4.

You are now going to learn how to manipulate various types of properties in a Properties panel. Grade1's properties will come to your aid.

Using the Properties Bin

In order to properly use properties, I feel a quick explanation of the Properties Bin is in order. The Properties Bin holds nodes' *Properties panels* (**FIGURE 2.26**). The Properties panels hold a node's properties, controls, sliders, or whatever it is you called them until now. Nuke calls them *properties*, and the user interface elements used to change them are called *knobs*. So for example, you use a slider knob to change a color property. Or you can use a number-box knob to change a position property.

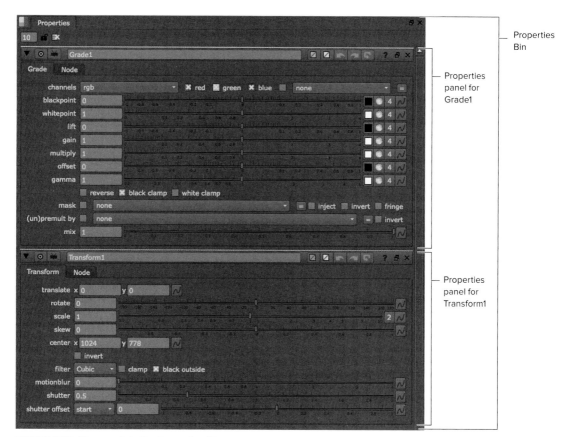

FIGURE 2.26 The panels in the Properties Bin.

You should have Grade1's and Transform1's Properties panels loaded into the Properties Bin. This happened when you first created the nodes. However, if you closed it by mistake, or want to learn how to close it, keep reading (**FIGURE 2.27**).

▪ To load the node's Properties panel in the Properties Bin, all you need to do is double-click the node. Newly created nodes' Properties panels load automatically.

NOTE If you hover your mouse pointer over the Empty Properties Bin button a tooltip appears that reads: Remove all panels from the control panel bin. Don't let that confuse you. The button is called Empty Properties Bin. The tooltips don't always use the same terminology as the rest of the interface, or the Nuke User Manual.

- To remove a node's Properties panel from the Properties Bin, click the close panel button. You do this for various reasons, chief of which is to get rid of on-screen controls that are in the way.

- Sometimes you want to clear the Properties Bin for specific functions, and to keep things organized. To do this, click the Empty Properties Bin button.

- You can open more than one Properties panel in the Properties Bin at a time. How many depends on the Max panels number box at the top left of the Proper-ties Bin.

- The Lock Properties Bin button locks the Properties Bin so that no new panels can open in it. If this icon is locked, double-clicking a node in the DAG displays that node's Properties panel as a floating window.

- Another way to display a floating Properties panel is to click the Float panel button.

- The Node Help button provides information about the functionality of the node.

- There is an interesting undo/redo functionality in Nuke. In addition to a gen-eral undo/redo function in the Edit menu, there is also an individual undo/redo function for every node's Properties panel, as shown in Figure 2.27. Using these buttons undoes only the last actions in the specific node being undone, while actions done in the interface and in other nodes are ignored.

Using these options, you can create a convenient way to edit properties in the Properties Bin.

FIGURE 2.27 Explana-tions of the Properties Bin and Properties panel's buttons.

Adjusting properties, knobs, and sliders

You will now use Grade1's properties to change the color of the doll image to better fit that of the background image. To do this, you need to understand how these prop-erties are controlled.

You manipulate properties using interface elements called *knobs*. These can be rep-resented as sliders, input fields, drop-down menus, and so on. Whatever they actually are, they are called knobs.

When changing a slider, for example, you are changing the knob (the property's value). A good thing about Nuke is that all values are consistent. All transformation and filtering values are in pixels, and all color values are in a range of 0 for black to 1 for white.

Look at the Gamma property under Grade1's Properties panel in the Properties Bin. A color slider is one of the most complex slider knobs you can find in Nuke, so it's a good slider to learn (**FIGURE 2.28**).

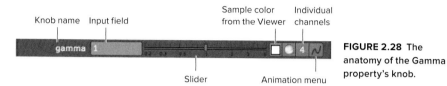

FIGURE 2.28 The anatomy of the Gamma property's knob.

Here are some ways to manipulate properties:

- Click in the Input field and type in a new number.

- Place the cursor in the Input field and use the up and down arrows to nudge digits up and down. The magnitude of change depends on the initial position of your cursor. For example, to adjust the initial value of 20.51 by 1s, insert your cursor to the left of the 0.

- Hold down Alt/Option and drag up and down with the left mouse button. In the same way as using the arrow keys, the magnitude depends on where in the Input field the cursor was when you clicked.

- Use the scroll wheel on your mouse if you have one.

- Use the slider (how original!).

The next two options refer only to color-related properties that have a Sample color button and a Color picker button.

- Use the Sample color from the Viewer button. By sampling colors from the Viewer, you can change the value of the color property. To do so, click the Sample color button to turn it on and then hold Ctrl/Cmd and drag the screen to pick a color. This will change the value of your property to mirror the value of the picked color. When you are finished picking colors, click the Sample color button to turn it off (to make sure you don't accidentally pick colors from the Viewer).

- Use the Color picker.

Using the Color Wheel and Color Sliders panel

The Color Wheel and Color Sliders panel is a great tool for working with color. It is invoked every time the Color Wheel icon is clicked, whether it be as part of a color correction node, changing the color in part of the interface, or anything else that needs a color selected (**FIGURE 2.29**).

FIGURE 2.29 Use the color wheel to choose a color.

You can pick color with the RGB, HSV, and TMI sliders. By default, only the HSV and RGB sliders are available, but the TMI button at the top of the color wheel will display the TMI sliders.

1. Click the Color picker button for Grade1's Gamma property.

2. Go ahead and play with the color wheel. When you're finished, close it.

Notice you no longer have a slider. Instead, you have four numeric fields (**FIGURE 2.30**).

FIGURE 2.30 Your single Gamma slider turned into four numeric fields.

Where's your slider gone? Every property in the Grade node can control all four channels, RGB and alpha, separately, but how can this happen with just one slider? As long as all four values remain the same, there is no need for four different fields, so there is just the one field with a slider. However, when the colors for the different channels are different, the slider is replaced by four numeric fields—one for each channel.

You can switch between the one slider and the four fields using the Individual channels button to the right of the Color Wheel icon. If you have four fields and click this button you are back to only having a single field. The values you had in the first field will be the value of the new single field. The other three values will be lost.

Using the Animation menu

The Animation button/menu on the right side of any property deals with animation-related options. Choose options from this menu to create a *keyframe*, load a *curve* onto the *curve editor*, and set the value of a property to its default state. The Animation menu controls all values grouped under this property. So, in the following example, the Animation menu for the Gamma property will control the values for R, G, B, and alpha. If you right-click (Ctrl-click) the field for each value, you get an Animation menu for just that value (**FIGURE 2.31**).

FIGURE 2.31 The Animation menu controls a property's value curve and animation-related functions.

Color correction is covered in depth in Chapter 4, so for now I just want you to input some numbers in the fields.

First, let's reset what you did.

1. Click the Animation menu at the far right of the Gamma property's knob and choose Set to Default.

2. Click the Individual channels button to the left of the Animation menu to display the four separate fields.

3. Enter the following numbers into the Gamma numeric fields:

    - R = 0.778
    - G = 0.84
    - B = 0.63
    - A = 1

Entering these numbers into the fields makes the doll image darker, and a little more orange. This makes the doll look better connected to the background, which is dark and has an orange tint to it.

RENDERING

You should be happy with the look of your composite now, but you have a ways to go. To be safe, however, let's render a version of the Nuke tree to disk now. *Rendering* means to process all your image-processing instructions into images that incorporate these changes.

Using the Write node

To render your tree, you need to use a Write node, which contains several functions. The Write node defines which part of the tree to render, where to render to, how to call your file or files, and what type of file you want to create. You're now going to add a Write node at the end of your tree. The end of your tree is where you can see the final composite. In this case, it's Merge1.

1. Click Merge1 at the bottom of the tree and press the W key. You can also choose Write from the Image toolbox in the Nodes Toolbar or use the Tab key to create a Write node by starting to type the word **write** (**FIGURE 2.32**).

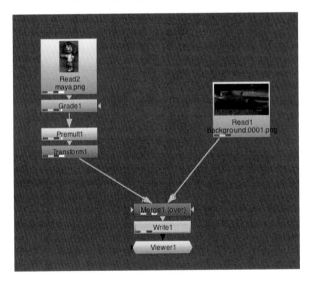

FIGURE 2.32 Inserting a Write node at the end of your tree.

You need to define the path you're going to write to, the name of the file, and the type of file you're going to write to disk. The plan is to create a folder in your Nuke101 folder called student_files and render a TIFF image sequence there called doll_v01.

2. In the Write1 Properties panel, look at the File property line. At the far right there's an icon of a folder (the top one, the bottom one belongs to something else called Proxy). Click it (**FIGURE 2.33**).

3. In the File Browser that opens, navigate to the NukeChapters/chapters folder.

FIGURE 2.33 It's small, so make sure this is what you are clicking.

File Folder button

4. Click the Create New Folder icon at the upper left of the browser.

5. Create a folder called **student_files** and click OK.

By navigating to this path, you have chosen the path to which you want to render. The first step is complete. In the field at the bottom, you need to add the name of the file you want to create at the end of the path. Make sure not to overwrite the path.

You are going to render a file sequence instead of a movie file such as a QuickTime file. File sequences are generally faster for Nuke to process as Nuke doesn't have to unpack the whole movie file to load in just one image.

But how will you call this file sequence? How are you going to define the number of digits to use for frame numbers? The next section explains these issues.

Naming file sequences

There are two ways to render moving images. One is by rendering a single file that holds all the frames, as is the case with QuickTime and AVI. The other, which is preferred for various reasons, is the *file sequence* method. In this method, you render a file per frame. The way you keep the files in order is by giving every file a number that corresponds to the number of the frame it represents. This creates a file called something like myrender.0001.jpg, representing the first frame of a sequence. Frame 22 would be myrender.0022.jpg. And so on.

When you tell Nuke to write a file sequence, you need to do four things:

- Give the file a name. Anything will do.

- Give the file a *frame padding structure*—as in: How many digits will be used to count the frames? There are two ways to tell Nuke how to format numbers. The first is by using the # symbol, one for each digit. So #### means four digits, and ###### means seven digits. The second method is %04d, where 04 means the number of digits to use—in this case, four. If you want two digits, you write %02d. I find the second method easier to decipher. Just by looking at %07d you can tell that you want seven digits. Using the other method, you actually have to count. Please note that you have to add frame padding yourself. Nuke won't do this for you. Nuke uses the # symbol by default when displaying file sequence names.

- Give your file an extension such as: png, tif, jpg, cin, dpx, iff, or exr (there are more to choose from).

- Separate these three parts of the file name with dots (periods).

The first bit can be anything you like, though I recommend not having any spaces in the name due to Python scripts, which have a tendency to not like spaces (you can use an underscore if you need a space). The second bit needs to be defined in one of the ways mentioned previously, either the %04d option, or the #### option. The last bit is the extension to the file type you want to render, such as: jpg, exr, sgi, tif, etc.

An example of a file name, then, is filename.%04d.png, or file_name.####.jpg.

To render a single file, such as a QuickTime file, simply give the file a name and the extension .mov. No frame padding is necessary.

1. In the field at the bottom, at the end of your path, add the name of your file sequence. Use: doll_v01.####.tif. Don't forget the dots and the *v01* (**FIGURE 2.34**).

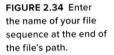

2. Click Save.

   You now have the path and file name under the File property. You might have noticed that the Write1 Properties panel changed a little. It now accommodates a property called Compression, which is, at the moment, set to a value called *deflate*.

Let's change the compression settings.

3. Choose LZW from the Compression drop-down menu (**FIGURE 2.35**).

   LZW is a good, lossless compressor that's part of the TIFF architecture. Lossless means that, although the file size will be smaller, no quality is lost in the process. In contrast, JPG uses lossy compression.

You are now ready to render using the Render button on Write1's Properties panel (**FIGURE 2.36**). You can also use the Render All and Render Selected commands in the Render menu in the menu bar.

FIGURE 2.35 Changing the Compression property to LZW.

FIGURE 2.36 The Render button is the quickest way to start a render.

Call me superstitious, but even with the autosave functionality I still like to save on occasion, and just before a render is one of those occasions.

4. Save your Nuke script by pressing Ctrl/Cmd-S.

5. Click the Render button.

6. In the Render panel that displays, click OK.

    The Render panel lets you define a range to render. The default setting is usually fine.

    The render starts. A Progress Bar panel displays what frame is being rendered and how many are left to go (**FIGURE 2.37**).

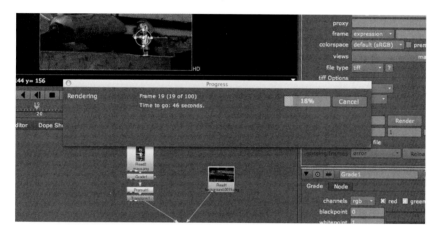

FIGURE 2.37 The Progress Bar shows the progress of each frame as it's being rendered.

You now need to wait until the render is finished. Once it is, you probably want to look at the result of your render. Let's do that.

If you are running the PLE version of Nuke, please use the following steps. (Even if you are not running the PLE, read this section as you can use this method too—otherwise you should pick up from step 11.)

Every Write node can double as a Read node. If the Read File check box is selected the Write node will load the file that's written in its File property (**FIGURE 2.38**).

FIGURE 2.38 This little check box turns the Write node into a Read node.

TIP Using the Content menu, you can place the Progress Bar panel in a specific place in the interface. I prefer the bottom right as you did in Chapter 1. This way the Progress Bar doesn't pop up in the middle of the screen, which I find annoying because it hides the image.

7. In Write1's Properties panel, click the Read File check box to turn it on.

    Your Write node should now look like the one in **FIGURE 2.39** (next page). It now has a *thumbnail* like a Read node does.

TIP All nodes can have thumbnails. You can turn them on and off by selecting a node and using the Alt/Option-P hot key.

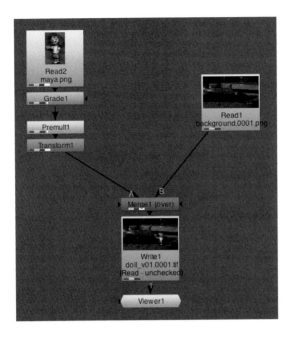

FIGURE 2.39 The Write node now has a thumbnail.

8. Make sure you are viewing Write1 in the Viewer and then click the Play button to play forward. When you're finished, remember to click the Stop button.

9. Also, when you're finished, uncheck Read File.

For those who have a licensed copy of Nuke, perform the next couple of steps.

10. Select Write1 and press Alt/Option-F on your keyboard to load Write1 into Frame-cycler. In the Flipbook panel that opens, click OK.

   This should happen very fast. When loading a Write node into Framecycler, Nuke doesn't render a flipbook, but rather looks at the File property for a file name and path and loads that instead.

11. Press Play and watch your work. When you are finished, quit Framecycler.

So, not too shabby. You still have a little work to do. If you look carefully, you might notice that the doll's feet are actually on top of the front edge of the artist's toolbox instead of behind it, so the doll does not yet appear to be inside the toolbox. Another problem is that around halfway through the shot the background darkens, something that you should mirror in the doll. Let's take care of the doll's feet first.

DELVING DEEPER INTO THE MERGE NODE

To cut the doll's feet so the doll appears to be behind the front edge of the artist's toolbox, you need another matte. You will learn to create mattes in Chapter 6. Until then, you will read the matte as an image from the disk.

1. While hovering over the DAG, press R on the keyboard to create another Read node.

2. In the File Browser that opens, navigate to the chapter02 folder and double-click mask.tif to import that file.

3. Select Read3 and press 1 on the keyboard to view this image in the Viewer.

    What you see in the Viewer should be the same as **FIGURE 2.40**. You now have a red shape at the bottom of the image. Mattes are usually white, not red. How will you use this? Do you need to key it perhaps? Let's take a better look at this image.

FIGURE 2.40 The matte image looks like this.

4. While hovering the mouse pointer over the DAG, press the R key to view the red channel (**FIGURE 2.41**).

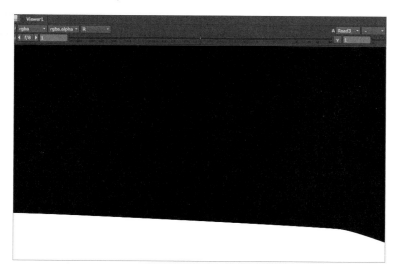

FIGURE 2.41 Viewing just the red channel.

This is what I usually expect a matte to look like: white on black. Let's see what the other channels look like.

5. While hovering the mouse pointer over the DAG, press the B key to view the blue channel, then the G key to view the green channel, then the A key to view the alpha channel, and finally the A key again to view the RGB channels.

Did you notice that all the other channels are black? This image was saved like this to conserve space. There is only information in one channel, the red channel, rather than having the same information in all four channels, which adds nothing but a bigger file. Just remember that your matte is in the red channel.

The Merge node's default layering operation is Over, which places one image over another. But Merge holds many more layering operations. You will look at a few throughout this book.

Now you will use another Merge node to cut a hole in the doll's branch before it gets composited over the background. Because you want to cut this hole after the doll has been repositioned—but before the composite takes place—place the new Merge node between Transform1 and Merge1.

6. Select Read3 and press M on the keyboard to create another Merge node (**FIGURE 2.42**).

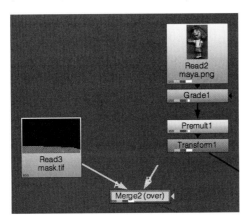

FIGURE 2.42 The newly created Merge2 node's A input is connected to Read3.

Merge2 has been created with its A input connected to Read3. You need to connect Merge2's B input to Transform1 and Merge2's output to Merge1's A input. You can do this in one step.

7. Drag Merge2 on top of the pipe in between Transform1 and Merge1, and when the pipe turns white, as in **FIGURE 2.43**, release the mouse button.

Look at Merge2's Properties panel (**FIGURE 2.44**). It shows that the Operation property is still Over. You need to change that to something that uses the A input to punch a hole in the B input.

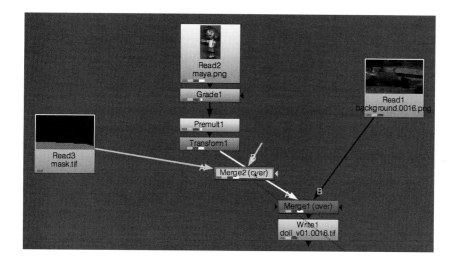

FIGURE 2.43 Using this method, you can insert a node to an existing pipe.

FIGURE 2.44 The Operation drop-down menu.

The Stencil operation does exactly that. It creates a hole in the B input where the alpha channel of the A input is white. Let's change the operation to Stencil.

8. Change Merge2's Operation property from Over to Stencil.

9. Select Merge1 and press 1 on the keyboard to view it.

Look at the image in the Viewer (**FIGURE 2.45**). It appears unchanged. The doll's feet are still visible in front of the artist's toolbox. This is because the Stencil operation uses the A input's alpha channel, but your matte is in the red channel. To solve this, move the red channel into the alpha channel using a node called Shuffle.

FIGURE 2.45 The doll's feet are still in front.

Using the Shuffle node

The Shuffle node is one of the most useful nodes in Nuke. A lot of times you need to move channels around from one location to another—taking the alpha channel and placing a copy of it in the three color channels, for example. Think of it as if you were moving a piece of paper from one location in a stack to another location (**FIGURE 2.46**).

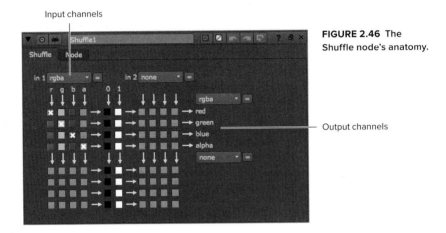

FIGURE 2.46 The Shuffle node's anatomy.

The Shuffle node looks like a matrix built from a source at the top to the destination on the right. To understand the flow of the Shuffle node, follow the arrows from the In property at the top till you reach the Out property on the right.

You need to move the red channel of the mask image so you'll have a copy of it in the alpha channel. Using the check boxes, you can tell the Shuffle node to output red into the alpha.

1. Select Read3, and in the Channel toolbox click Shuffle.

   A new node called Shuffle1 has been inserted between Read3 and Merge2 (**FIGURE 2.47**). Shuffle1's Properties panel was automatically loaded into the Properties Bin.

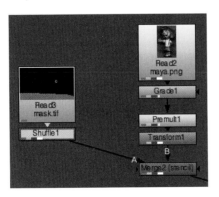

FIGURE 2.47 Shuffle1 is now inserted after Read3.

2. In Shuffle1's Properties panel, check all the red boxes on the very left column, as shown in **FIGURE 2.48**. This places the R channel in the R, G, B, and alpha channels.

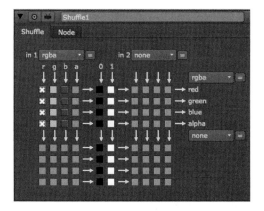

FIGURE 2.48 Setting up the Shuffle node to copy the red channel into all the four channels.

Now that you copied the red channel into the alpha channel, Merge2 works and the doll's feet now appear to be behind the wooden box (**FIGURE 2.49**).

FIGURE 2.49 That's more like it. The doll's feet are now behind the front of the toolbox.

Viewing a composite without rendering

Let's look at your composite so far. To do that, you need to render your tree as a flipbook into Framecycler.

> **NOTE** If you're using the PLE version of Nuke, you will not be able to preview your work using Framecycler, as it's a blocked feature under the PLE license. If that's the case, simply click Play in the Viewer and wait for it to cache. This might not result in perfect playback.

1. Select Merge1 and press Alt/Option-F to render a flipbook of the selected node and load it into Framecycler.

2. In the Flipbook panel that displays, leave the frame range at 1-100 and press OK.

   A Progress Bar displays to show you the frame count as they are rendered. This is slightly different than the way you used Framecycler in Chapter 1 and previously in this chapter, as you are now actually processing a tree and not just loading Read or Write nodes into Framecycler.

   What's happening now is the tree is being rendered into a temp directory, and those temp frames will get loaded into Framecycler. When you close Framecycler, those frames will be deleted.

3. When Framecycler loads, press the Spacebar to play the clip.

   Notice the dark flash that occurred during the playback. It starts at frame 42. You will need to make the doll mimic this light fluctuation. So far all the values you set for various properties were constant values—not changing from frame to frame. Now you need to change those values over time. For that purpose you have keyframes.

4. If Framecycler is still open, close it.

CREATING ANIMATION WITH KEYFRAMES

Keyframes specify that you want animation. To do this, the property needs to change its value over time. So if you want your image to have a Blur value of 20 to begin with and then, at frame 10, to have a value of 10, you need to specify these two pieces of information: a value for frame 1 and a value for frame 10, and the application will interpolate the in-between values.

In Nuke, practically every property can be keyframed. You are going to create another Grade node and use that to change the brightness of the doll branch to match the changes to the lighting in the background.

1. In the Viewer, go to frame 42 by clicking the Timebar (**FIGURE 2.50**).

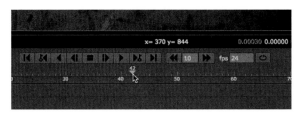

FIGURE 2.50 Move to frame 42 using the Timebar.

2. Select Grade1 and press G on the keyboard to create another Grade node.

    Your tree should now have a new Grade node in it called Grade2 (**FIGURE 2.51**).

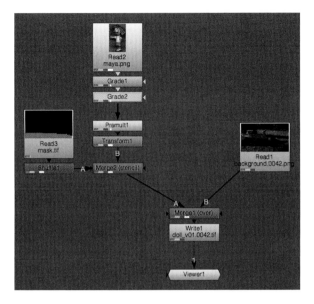

FIGURE 2.51 Grade2 is inserted after Grade1.

NOTE You could have used the existing Grade node instead of adding another one, but using another Grade node gives you greater freedom. Each node has a purpose. The first matches the color of the foreground to the background, and the second Grade node will take care of the brightness change. You can always delete or disable one without affecting the other, for example, which is quite handy.

TIP If, unlike my tree, your tree is really messy, it will be hard for you to understand the flow of information and therefore read your tree. Sure, this is a simple tree. But if it were bigger, and you saved it and went back to it over the weekend, things might start to no longer make sense. Keeping an organized tree is always a good idea.

Frame 42, which you are on at the moment, is the last frame of bright lighting you have before the background starts to darken. This will be the location of your first keyframe, to lock the brightness of the doll to the current brightness level.

3. In Grade2's Properties panel, click the Gain property's Animation menu and choose Set Key (**FIGURE 2.52**).

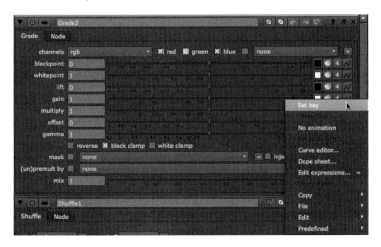

FIGURE 2.52 Set Key holds the current value at the current frame in place.

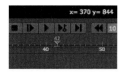

FIGURE 2.53 The blue field indicates this frame has a keyframe.

FIGURE 2.54 The blue boxes on the Timebar indicate keyframes.

This creates a keyframe for the four values (R, G, B, and Alpha) associated with the Gain property. Notice that the field turns a blueish color—this is to show that a keyframe is present on this frame for this property (**FIGURE 2.53**).

The Timebar also displays a blueish-colored little box to indicate on which frame you have keyframes (**FIGURE 2.54**). The markings on the Timebar are shown for all open property panels that have keyframes. To see the keyframes on the Timebar for a specific node, make sure only that node's Properties panel is open in the Properties Bin.

4. Advance one frame by hovering over the Viewer and pressing the right arrow on your keyboard.

Notice that the color of the property's Gain field is now showing a subtler blue color (**FIGURE 2.55**). This indicates that there is animation for the property, but there is no keyframe at this point in time.

FIGURE 2.55 A light blue field indicates that this property has animation, but no keyframe at the current frame.

5. Play with the Gain slider until you reach a result that matches the doll's brightness to that of the background. I stopped at 0.025.

A keyframe is now automatically added. Once the first keyframe is set, every change in value to the property will result in a keyframe on the frame you are currently on. Notice the color of the numeric box changed from the light blue color to a bright blue color, indicating a keyframe has been created for this frame.

TIP Remember that one way of manipulating values is to click in the field and then use the arrow keys to change every decimal point number by placing the mouse cursor to the left of it. This makes fine adjustments easy!

6. Advance another frame forward to frame 44 and adjust the gain again. I stopped at 0.0425.

7. Repeat the process for frames 45 and 46 as well. I had 0.41 and then 1.0.

We have now created several keyframes for the Gain property, resulting in animation. The animation can be drawn as a curve in a graph called an *Animation curve*. The X axis will represent time and the Y axis value.

Let's set the Animation curve for this property in the Curve Editor.

8. Choose Curve Editor from the Gain property's Animation menu (**FIGURE 2.56**).

You can see the curve for the animation you just created (**FIGURE 2.57**). The Curve Editor is explained in more detail in Chapter 6.

9. Click the Node Graph tab to go back to the DAG.

Look at Grade2. What's that on the top right? Notice it has a little red circle with the letter A in it (**FIGURE 2.58**). I wonder what that's for? It's an *indicator*, which is explained in the next section.

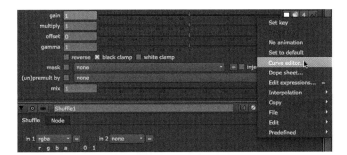

FIGURE 2.56 Using the Animation menu to load a curve into the Curve Editor.

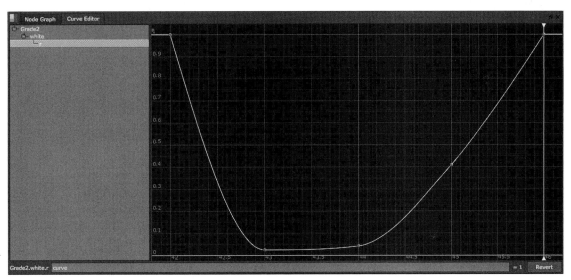

FIGURE 2.57 This is what an Animation curve looks like.

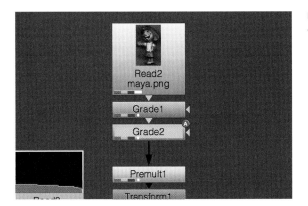

FIGURE 2.58 Node indicators can be very useful at times.

Indicators on nodes

Several indicators may display on nodes in the Node Graph, depending on what you are doing. **TABLE 2.1** describes what each indicator means.

TABLE 2.1 Node indicators

Indicator	Context	Definition
		The wide rectangles indicate the channels the node processes. The thin rectangles indicate the channels that are passed through the node untouched.
M		The node's effect is limited by a mask from the node's primary input.
X		The node has been disabled by pressing D or clicking the Disable button.
/		The node has been disabled using an expression.
C		The node has been cloned. The indicator displays on both the parent and the child node.
A		One or more of the node properties are animated over time.
E		One or more of the node properties are being driven by an expression.
V		You are working with a multiview project and have split off one or more views in the node's controls.
		You are working with a multiview project and have split off one or more views in the node's controls; dots also display on the node to indicate which views have been split off. For example, if you are using red for the left view and split off that view, a red dot displays on the node.
X		The full effect of the node is not in use, because you have adjusted the mix slider in the node's controls.

Having little "tells" like these indicators on the nodes themselves really helps in reading a tree. The A indicator, for example, can help you figure out which of your two Grade nodes is the one you added animation to.

You should now be happier with your comp (**FIGURE 2.59**). The doll appears to be standing inside the artist's toolbox, and the light change is matched. Let's save and render a new version of the composite.

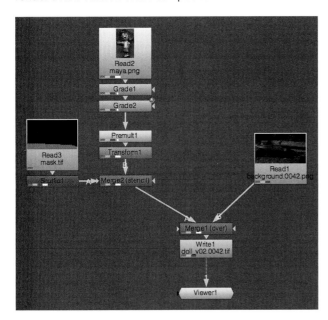

FIGURE 2.59 The final tree should look like this.

Rendering a new version and comparing

Since you updated the Nuke project, and the shot now looks so much better, it is a good idea to create another version of your render. Sure, you can always overwrite what you rendered before, but it would be a shame not to have something to compare to.

Nuke's versioning system, which you used at the beginning of this lesson to save a new version of the script, also works with Read and Write nodes.

Remember from earlier in this chapter how you set up your Write node to have a "_v01" in the file name? Well, that's what's going to change. Using a hot key, change this to one version up, meaning "_v02."

1. Select Write1 and press Alt/Option-Arrow Up key to change the file name to v02.

    The whole file name should now be doll_v02.####.png. Going up a version (and going down) is as easy as that.

2. To render a new version, press F5 on your keyboard (hot key for Render All) and then click OK.

Comparing images

It would be great to compare the two versions. Any Viewer in Nuke has up to 10 different inputs, and it's very easy to connect nodes to these inputs to view them as you did in Chapter 1. You can also split the screen in the Viewer as long as the images are connected to two of the Viewer's inputs.

When the render is finished, compare the previous render to this one in the Viewer. Let me walk you through this.

1. While hovering your mouse pointer over the DAG, press R on the keyboard to display a Read File browser.

2. Navigate to the student_files directory and double-click doll_v01.####.tif to load it in.

You now have Read4 with the previous render; Write1 can become the new render by turning it into a Read node like so:

3. In Write1 click the Read File check box.

To compare the two versions, you will now load each one to a different buffer of the Viewer, then use the Viewer's composite controls to compare them.

4. Click Read4 and press 1 on the keyboard.

5. Click Write1 and press 2 on the keyboard (**FIGURE 2.60**).

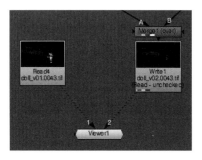

FIGURE 2.60 Using two Viewer inputs.

6. Go to frame 43 in the Timebar.

7. From the Composite button/menu at the center of the Viewer, choose Wipe (**FIGURE 2.61**).

With the Composite controls set in this way, there's a new axis on the Viewer—the image to the left of this axis is Write1 and the image to the right of this axis is Read4.

You can move the axis using the controls shown in **FIGURE 2.62**.

8. Reposition the axis at the center of the doll (**FIGURE 2.63**).

You can clearly see that the half doll on the left has been darkened, while the half doll on the right is still bright.

FIGURE 2.61 Turning on the Wipe option in the Viewer Composite controls.

Split position   Split fade   Split rotate

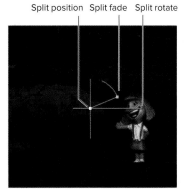

FIGURE 2.62 The Viewer Composite controls axis.

FIGURE 2.63 Repositioning the axis at the center of the doll.

You can even compare the two halves while playing.

9. Click the Play button in the Viewer.

   Look at them roll! The two streams are playing side by side, and you can see that only the stream on the left shows the doll darkening when needed. Also only the doll on the left has its feet appearing behind the artist's toolbox. Well done! See how much you advanced? It's only Chapter 2.

10. Use the hot key Ctrl/Cmd-S to save your script for future reference.

11. Quit Nuke.

This ends the practical introduction. You should now start to feel more comfortable working with the interface to get results. In the next chapter you work with a much bigger tree. Get ready to be dropped into the pan.

COMPOSITING CGI WITH BIGGER NODE TREES

These days, Computer Generated Imagery, or CGI, primarily refers to images that are rendered out of 3D software such as Maya, XSI, and Houdini.

Rendering in 3D software can be a very long process. Calculating all the physics required to produce a convincing image is very processor intensive. A single frame can take anything from a minute to eight hours or more to render. Because of this, 3D artists go to great lengths to give the compositor as much material as possible so that the compositor can modify the 3D render without having to go back to the 3D package and re-render.

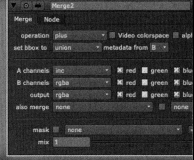

A compositor finds it very hard to change the animation or shape of a 3D model. But color and quality are a compositor's strong suit, and those are the main things a compositor deals with when having to composite a 3D render. To facilitate the ease of changing color and quality in compositing, 3D renders are usually rendered in *passes*. Each pass represents a part of what makes up the final image. The amount of light that falls on the object, for example, is rendered separately (represented as a color image where bright pixels are strong light and dark pixels low light) from its color. Reflections, shadows, and specular highlights are all examples of how an image might be split into different passes. The compositor's role then is to take all these elements in and rebuild what the 3D program usually does—creating the *beauty pass*, the composite of all these passes together.

Once the layers are composited, it is very easy for the compositor to change the look of the beauty pass, as there is easy access for anything that makes up the look of the render. For example, because the light is separate from the color, it's easy to color correct it so it is brighter—meaning more light—or to change the reflection so it is a little blurry, making the object look like its material is a little worn, for example. Rendering just a single final image from the 3D software, on the other hand, means that changing the look (such as adding blur) will be more difficult.

WORKING WITH CHANNELS

Down deep, digital images are really an array of numbers representing brightness levels. There is a brightness value for each location in the X and Y resolution of the image. A single location in X and Y is called a *pixel*. An array of a single value for each pixel is called a *channel*. A color image generally consists of the four standard channels: red, green, blue, and alpha. Nuke allows you to create or import additional channels as masks, lighting passes, and other types of image data. A Nuke script can include up to 1023 uniquely named channels per compositing script.

All channels in a script must exist as part of a *channel set* (also called a *layer*). You're probably familiar with the default channel set—RGBA—which includes the channels with pixel values for red, green, blue, and also the alpha channel for transparency.

All channels in a composite must belong to a channel set. Channel names always include the channel set name as a prefix, like this: setName.channelName. So the red channel is actually called rgba.red.

NOTE OpenEXR has the .exr extension and is simply called EXR for short.

Most image file types can hold only one channel set—RGBA. The PNG file format holds only RGBA. The JPEG file format holds only RGB. However, TIFF and PSD can hold more channels. All the layers you create in Photoshop are actually other channel sets. One of the better multilayer file formats out there is called OpenEXR. It can support up to 1023 channels, is a 32-bit float format (meaning it doesn't clip colors above white and below black), and can be saved in a variety of compression types. 3D applications are using this file format more and more. Luckily, Nuke handles everything that comes in with OpenEXR very well.

Bringing in a 3D render

To start the project, you will bring in a 3D render from your hard drive (files copied from this book's disc).

1. Using a Read node, bring in chapter03/lemming/lemming.####.exr.

2. Connect Read1 to Viewer1 by selecting Read1 and pressing 1 on the keyboard.

3. Press the Play button in the Viewer to look at the clip you brought in. Let it cache by allowing it to play once; it will then play at normal speed.

4. Click Stop and use the Timebar to go to the last frame: 143 (**FIGURE 3.1**).

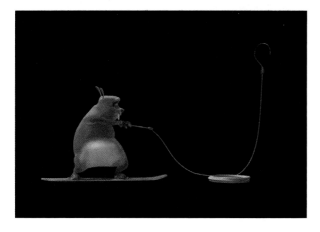

FIGURE 3.1 A 3D render of an Adrenalin Lemming.

NOTE This shot in Figure 3.1 is part of a short film by Crew 972 called Adrenalin Lemmings. Adrenalin Lemmings are just like ordinary lemmings, except they like extreme sports. You can (and should!) view the whole thing here: www. crew972.com.

5. By pressing Ctrl/Cmd-S, save your script (Nuke project files are called scripts, remember) in your student_files folder. Name it chapter03_v01.

Viewing channel sets with the Viewer

The 3D render displayed in the Viewer, which you brought in from the disk, is an EXR file that holds the beauty pass (a combination of all the other passes, if you will) in the RGBA channel set along with all the channel sets that make up the image. To view these other channels, use the Viewer's Channel buttons (**FIGURE 3.2**).

FIGURE 3.2 Use these three Channel buttons to display different channels in the Viewer.

FIGURE 3.3 The list of all the channel sets available in the stream being viewed.

NOTE As a side note, the Other Layers submenu at the bottom shows channels that are available in the project, but not through the currently viewed node. For example, if we had another Read node with a channel set called Charlie, it would show up in the Other Layers submenu.

The three buttons at the top left of the Viewer are the Channel buttons. The button on the left shows the selected channel set; by default the RGBA set is chosen. The button in the middle shows which channel to display when viewing the alpha channel; by default it is rgba.alpha. The button on the right shows which channel from the set you have currently chosen is being viewed; by default, it is RGB.

If you want to view the second channel of a channel set called Reflection Pass, for example, you need to change the leftmost button to show the Reflection Pass channel set, and then set the third button to green channel (G is the second letter in RGBA—hence, second channel).

1. Click the Channel Set Viewer button (the one on the left) and view all the channel sets you can now choose from (**FIGURE 3.3**).

    This list shows the channels available for viewing for the current stream loaded into the Viewer. In this case, Read1 has lots of extra channel sets besides RGBA, so they are available for viewing.

2. Switch to the Col channel set (short for *Color*) by choosing it from the Viewer drop-down menu.

    This pass, simply called the Color pass, represents the unlit texture as it's wrapped around the 3D object. It is essentially the color of the object before it's been lit (**FIGURE 3.4**).

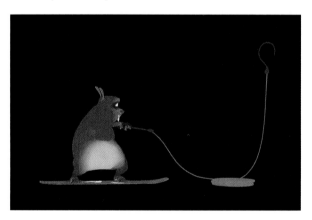

FIGURE 3.4 The Col channel set represents the unlit texture.

There are many ways to render separate passes out of 3D software. Not all of them include a Color pass, or any other pass you will use here. It is up to the people doing the 3D rendering and compositing to come up with a way that makes sense to the production, whatever it may be. Having a Color pass made sense for this production because we needed to be able to change the color of the lemming before it was lit.

3. Go over the different passes in the Viewer to familiarize yourself with them. See **TABLE 3.1** to understand what each pass is supposed to be.

4. When you are finished, go back to viewing the RGBA set.

TABLE 3.1 shows a list of the different render passes incorporated in this EXR file sequence.

TABLE 3.1 Lemming render passes

Channel Set Name	Common Name	Description
rgba	Beauty pass	All the passes layered together as they come out of 3D.
ao	Ambient occlusion	Contact and deep shadows.
col	Color	The unshaded texture of the surfaces.
eyes	Eyes	This is a pass specific for this shot. The eyes needed rendering separately.
hair	Hairs	Same as the eyes.
id	ID	A four-channel matte layer, each channel representing a different matte.
inc	Incidence	Incidence means the angle of the object to the camera. In this case, this pass was used to create fur texture for the areas not facing the camera.
ind	Indirect light	This is bounce light generated in Mental Ray's Final Gather.
lgt	Light	The light falling on the object with no shadows.
shdDrop	Drop shadow	A black-and-white matte representing the shadow from the object onto other objects.
shdSelf	Self shadow	The shadow contribution the object casts onto itself.
spc	Specular	The areas where the light source hits a shiny surface. In this specific case, reflections have been incorporated into this pass as well.

WORKING WITH CONTACT SHEETS

A good tool in Nuke is the ContactSheet node, which organizes inputs into an array of rows and columns. Using the ContactSheet node results in a handy display of all the inputs and is very handy for looking at everything together. For example, you can connect all the shots you are color correcting to a ContactSheet node and compare all of them in one sweep.

There's another version of the ContactSheet node called LayerContactSheet. It works exactly the same way, but instead of several inputs, it is designed to show you the different channel sets of a single input in an array.

You can use the LayerContactSheet node to look at all the passes you have.

1. Select Read1 and attach a LayerContactSheet node from the Merge toolbox.

2. Check Show Layer Names at the bottom of LayerContactSheet1's Properties panel (**FIGURE 3.5**).

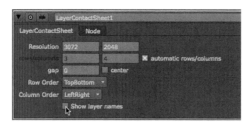

FIGURE 3.5 Clicking this check box will display the channel set names in the Viewer.

You can immediately see all the different channel sets laid out, with their names. This makes life very easy. The LayerContactSheet node is a very good display tool, and you can keep it in the Node Graph and refer to it when you need to (**FIGURE 3.6**).

FIGURE 3.6 The output of LayerContactSheet1 in the Viewer.

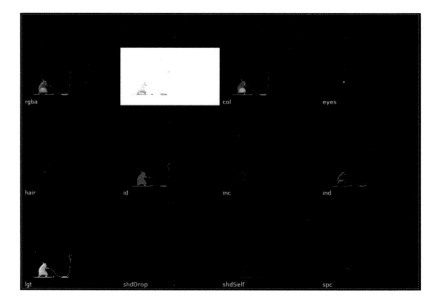

3. Delete LayerContactSheet1.

USING THE BOUNDING BOX TO SPEED UP PROCESSING

The *bounding box* is an element that Nuke uses to define the area of the image for processing. It is always there. Chapters 1 and 2 have bounding boxes all over them— you just may not have noticed them. To understand the bounding box, let's first look at the image properly.

1. Make sure Read1 (the lemming image) is loaded in Viewer1 by selecting it and pressing 1 on the keyboard.

2. Look at Read1's alpha channel by pressing A while hovering the mouse pointer over the Viewer. Now go back to viewing the color channels by pressing A again.

Normally, as in most other compositing software, Nuke processes the whole image. If you add a Blur to this image, every pixel is calculated. But that would be wasteful, because blurring all that blackness in the lemming image won't change that part of the image at all. There's a way to tell Nuke which part of the image to process and which to disregard without changing the resolution. You do this with a bounding box. The bounding box is the rectangular area that defines the area of the image that should be processed. Pixels outside the bounding box should not be processed and should remain black.

3. From the Transform toolbox, attach a Crop node after Read1.

4. Grab the top-right corner of the Crop controls and drag it down and to the left to frame the Lemming.

5. Close all Properties panels by clicking the Empty Properties Bin button, to hide the controls (**FIGURE 3.7**).

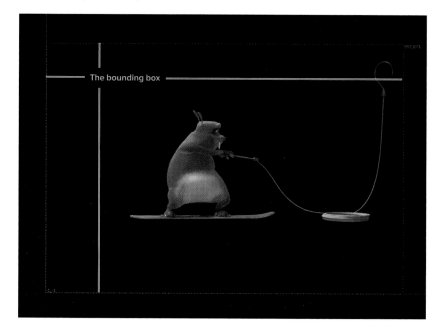

FIGURE 3.7 The bounding box.

The dotted line that formed where you placed the top-right corner is the bounding box. The numbers at the top right in Figure 3.7 are the top right location of the bounding box, in pixels on the X and Y axes. The resolution of the image itself didn't change, but pixels outside the bounding box will not be considered for processing.

Going frame by frame and animating the crop by changing the on-screen controls and adding a keyframe on every frame takes a long time and isn't very precise, so there's a tool to automate the process: the CurveTool node.

6. Insert a CurveTool between Read1 and Crop1 by clicking Read1 and then clicking CurveTool in the Image toolbox (**FIGURE 3.8**).

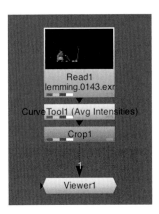

FIGURE 3.8 Inserting a CurveTool node after Read1.

7. View the output of CurveTool1 by selecting it and pressing 1 on the keyboard.

8. In CurveTool1's Properties panel, choose Avs Intensities from the Curve Type drop-down menu.

9. Click Go! In the panel that opens, click OK.

    The Auto Crop function is now looking for pixels that are black. Black pixels surrounded by non-black pixels will remain inside the new bounding box. However, black pixels that don't have any non-black pixels between them and the edge of the frame will be considered unimportant, because they are adding nothing to the image, so the new bounding box will not include them.

10. When the process finishes (it may take some time), click the AutoCropData tab.

Here you can see the four values (X, Y, Right, and Top) that are now changing from frame to frame according to the location of non-black pixels. Keyframes were created on every frame, as you can tell by the bright blue color of the fields (**FIGURE 3.9**).

FIGURE 3.9 The AutoCropData tab once the processing is complete.

LINKING PROPERTIES WITH EXPRESSIONS

The CurveTool does not apply any operations; it only accumulates data. To use the accumulated data, you need to use another node—in this case, a Crop node. You have one already, you just need to tell the Crop node to use the properties from the CurveTool's AutoCropData tab. You will create a link between CurveTool1's property called "autocropdata" and Crop1's property called "box" using an expression.

Expressions are programmatic commands used to change a property's value. Expressions can be simple math functions (such as 2+4), more complex math functions (sin[frame/2]), or a set of available functions that may be included as part of an expression such as *width* for the width of an image, or *frame* which is the current frame number. A few of these functions are explained throughout the book.

You can type an expression by hand (in fact, you will do this in Chapter 5) or you can make one by clicking and dragging, as you will now do:

1. Double-click Crop1 and then double-click CurveTool1 to display both their Properties panels, one on top of the other.

2. Ctrl/Cmd-click-drag down from CurveTool1's AutoCropData Animation menu to Curve1's Box Animation menu and release the mouse button (**FIGURE 3.10**).

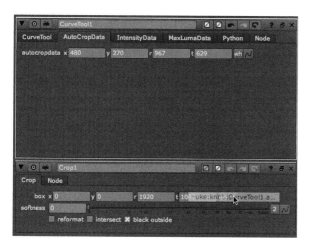

FIGURE 3.10 Dragging from one Animation menu to another while holding Ctrl/Cmd creates a linking expression.

Curve1's four Box fields turn light blue, which means you have successfully linked Crop1's property to CurveTool1's property (**FIGURE 3.11**).

FIGURE 3.11 The light blue color of the fields shows there is animation.

Let's learn a little bit more from this and see what this expression looks like.

3. From Crop1's Box property's Animation menu, choose Edit Expression to display the Expression panel (**FIGURE 3.12**).

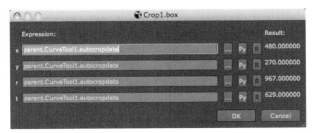

FIGURE 3.12 Crop1's Box property's Expression panel.

The Expression panel shows the four expressions for the four subproperties of the Box property (X, Y, R, and T).

The expression for each of the four subproperties is parent.CurveTool1.autocropdata. There are three parts to this expression, separated by dots.

▪ The first, *parent*, tells the current property to *parent* to another property, meaning copy values from another property.

▪ The second part tells which node, in this case CurveTool1, should look for a property.

▪ The third part tells which property to copy from.

You can see this is a very simple command, one that you can easily enter yourself. Simply use the node name, then the property name you need to copy values from.

Let's see the result of this expression in the Viewer—but first close the open Expression panel.

4. Click Cancel to close the open Expression panel.

5. Clear the Properties Bin by using the button at the top left of the Properties Bin.

6. View Crop1's output by selecting it and pressing 1 on the keyboard (**FIGURE 3.13**).

You can see in **FIGURE 3.13** that the bounding box has changed dramatically. If you move back and forth a couple of frames, you will see that the bounding box changes to engulf only the areas where something is happening. Having a bounding box that only engulfs the lemming, thereby reducing the size of the image that is being processed, dramatically speeds up processing.

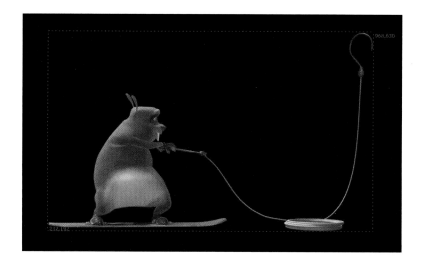

FIGURE 3.13 The bounding box is now a lot tighter.

SLAPPING THINGS TOGETHER: FOREGROUND OVER BACKGROUND

To achieve the desired results, the lemming needs to be composited over a background. Let's bring it in.

1. Using a Read node, read another sequence from disk: chapter03/bg/bg.####.png.

2. Load Read2 into the Viewer and click the Play button to view it. When done, stop and go to frame 143 in the Timebar.

    This is your background (**FIGURE 3.14**). The cheeky lemming is going to connect itself to the back of the car for a little surfing action.

FIGURE 3.14 The background image.

When working with 3D renders, a good first step is to start with what's technically called a *slap comp*. Slap comps are exactly what they sound like—a quick comp slapped together to see if things are working correctly. Slap comps tell you whether the animation is working with the background, whether the light direction is correct, and so on.

3. Select Crop1 and press M on the keyboard to create a Merge node.

4. Connect Merge1's B input to Read2, and view Merge1 in the Viewer.

NOTE Proxy mode, by default, shrinks all images to half resolution, reducing render and playback times considerably. Proxies are discussed more in Chapter 8.

5. While hovering the mouse pointer over the Viewer, click Ctrl/Cmd-P to switch to proxy mode.

6. Load Merge1 into Framecycler or use the Viewer to view it (**FIGURE 3.15**).

You can see that the result is already not bad. The good thing is that the lemming is tracked in place. The lemming is missing one frame, but don't worry about that as you are just using this as an exercise. What you should worry about, however, is the lemming looking as if it doesn't belong in the scene. Its color is all wrong for the background and it simply doesn't feel as if the lemming is there, shot on location, which is what compositing magic is all about.

FIGURE 3.15 The slap comp in all its glory.

7. Quit Framecycler or click the Stop button in the Viewer.

8. You no longer need the slap comp, so select Merge1 and delete it.

BUILDING THE BEAUTY PASS

Next you're going to take all the passes and start building the beauty pass as it was built in the 3D renderer. When you're finished doing that, you'll have full access to all the building blocks of the image, which means you'll be able to easily change some things, such as the color and brightness of passes, to make the comp look better.

The passes will be built like this: First you combine the Lgt and Col passes using a Merge node's multiply operation. Then you Merge with a plus operation in this order: the Inc, Ind, and Spc passes. You then subtract the shadow pass with a Merge node's operation. This is the way this image was created in the 3D software that created it, so this is how you recombine them in Nuke.

There are two ways to work with channel sets in Nuke. The first is by working down the pipe, and the second is by splitting the tree. First, you will look at how to work down the pipe and then move on to working with a split tree.

Working down the pipe

To start layering passes, first combine the Lgt and Col passes with a multiply operation. Let's connect a Merge node.

1. Select Crop1 and insert a Merge node after it by pressing the M key.

    Merge1 has two inputs. The B input is not connected. You want to combine two different channel sets that live inside the Read1 branch, so you simply connect the B input to the same output that the A input is connected to—the output of Crop1.

2. Move Merge1 below Crop1 and connect Merge1's B input to Crop1 (**FIGURE 3.16**).

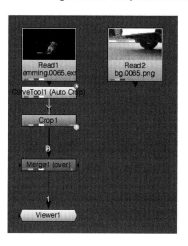

FIGURE 3.16 Both the A and the B inputs are connected to Crop1.

So how are you going to tell Merge1 to use different channel sets for this operation? So far you have been combining the RGBA of images, which is the default state of the Merge node. However, you can change that using the pull-down menus for each input (**FIGURE 3.17**).

FIGURE 3.17 The pull-down menus control which channel sets are combined.

Let's go ahead and use these pull-down menus to combine the Lgt and Col passes.

3. Make sure Merge1's Properties panel is loaded in the Properties Bin, and view Merge1.

4. From the A Channels pull-down menu, choose the Col channel set.

5. From the B Channels pull-down menu, choose the Lgt channel set.

6. Since you need to multiply the two, change the Operation property using the pull-down menu at the top, to Multiply (**FIGURE 3.18**).

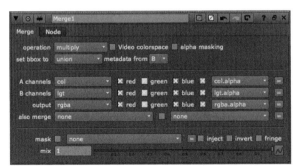

FIGURE 3.18 Merge1's Properties panel should look like this now.

You have now created a *diffuse* pass. A diffuse pass is the combination of the light and color of an object (**FIGURE 3.19**). Let's now add the Inc pass.

7. Insert another Merge node after Merge1.

8. Connect Merge2's B input to Merge1 as well (**FIGURE 3.20**).

FIGURE 3.19 Merge1's output should look like this in the Viewer.

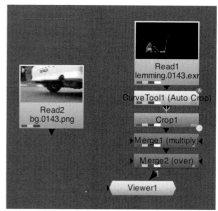

FIGURE 3.20 Inserting and connecting Merge2 should end up looking like this.

The output pull-down menu for Merge1 was set to RGBA (the default). You can change that if you want the output to be placed elsewhere. The result of the multi-plication of the Lgt and Col passes is now the RGBA. You want to add the Inc pass to that.

9. From the A Channels pull-down menu, choose the Inc channel set.

10. Since you want to add this pass to the previous passes, choose Plus from the Operation pull-down menu (**FIGURE 3.21**).

FIGURE 3.21 Merge2's Properties panel should look like this.

To see what you did, use the mix slider to mix the A input in and out (**FIGURE 3.22**).

FIGURE 3.22 Using the mix slider, you can make the A input transparent.

11. Play with the mix slider to see the Inc pass fade in and out and see what it does to the image. When you're finished, set the mix slider to 1.

You should now have something that looks similar to **FIGURE 3.23**.

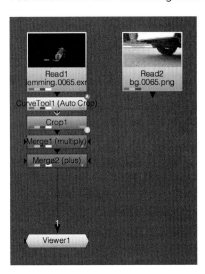

FIGURE 3.23 The tree so far, going down the pipe.

You can continue doing this until you combine all the passes. However, I find working in this way restricts the advantage of the tree, which is mainly easy access to every part of it. I prefer to have the Merge node just combine two streams and have the streams available outside the Merge node. Shuffling the channel sets inside the Merge node restricts that. Having everything out in the open, the way you will build this in the next section, is a lot more visual and open, and that gives you easier access and better control.

12. If you want, save this script with File > Save As, and give it a new name.

13. Click and drag to create a marquee to select Merge1 and Merge2, and then press the Delete key to delete them.

Splitting the tree

This time around, you will make branches for each pass as you go. This gives you instant access to every pass in your tree, which is very handy, but it also creates a very big tree. To not lose your bearings, you need to be very careful how you build the tree and where you place nodes.

One of the interface elements you're going to use a lot is the *Dot*. The Dot is a circular icon that enables you to change the course of a pipe, making for a more organized tree.

1. Select Crop1 and press . (period) on your keyboard.

2. Select the newly created Dot, and then insert a Shuffle node from the Channel toolbox.

3. Make sure you are viewing Shuffle1 in the Viewer, and then change the In 1 property to Lgt.

4. From the In 2 property's drop-down menu pick RGBA instead of None.

5. Check the In 2 alpha to alpha check box to direct the alpha from input 2 to the alpha output (**FIGURE 3.24**).

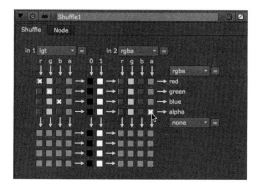

FIGURE 3.24 Using Shuffle you can mix channels from multiple channel sets.

What you did here was take the R, G, B from the Lgt channel set and the alpha from the original RGBA channel set, and output these four channels into a new RGBA. You did this so that your Lgt pass, which doesn't come with an alpha channel, will have the correct alpha channel.

Because you will do this a lot, it is a nice reminder if you name your Shuffle1 node according to the name of the input channel set. You can simply change the name of the node, but that is less advised. Instead, you have a label for each node, accessed via the Node tab in each node's Properties panel.

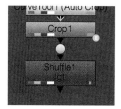

FIGURE 3.25 Whatever you type in the label box displays on the node in the DAG.

6. Switch to the Node tab in Shuffle1's Properties panel.

Whatever you type in the Label field will display on the node in the DAG.

7. In the Label field enter **lgt**.

    You can see that lgt displays under Shuffle1 (**FIGURE 3.25**).

You can simply type this for every pass. However, you can also use a little scripting to automate this process.

8. In the Label property's field replace lgt with [**knob in**].

Breaking down what you typed, the brackets mean you are writing a TCL script. The word *knob* means you are looking for a knob (knob = property). The word *in* is the name of the knob (the pulldown knob, in this case).

NOTE Text fields in Nuke generally use the scripting language TCL. Nuke used to be strictly TCL, but added Python as well. However, TCL remains useful for Properties panel manipulation. Check out www.tcl.tk as a good source for learning TCL scripting. Chapter 12 covers scripting in more detail.

FIGURE 3.26 The label should display this text.

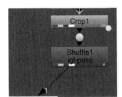

FIGURE 3.27 Shuffle1 in the DAG will display the new label with the TCL script resolved.

The result of this script shows the value of the property called "in." Therefore, you will see that the node in the DAG still displays as lgt.

9. To make this a little more readable, add a space and the word *pass* after the script, so it reads like this: **[knob in] pass** (**FIGURE 3.26**).

The word *pass* is just a word—because it's outside the TCL brackets it will simply display as the word (it's not part of the script). The node in the DAG now shows the label lgt pass (**FIGURE 3.27**).

Now, just by looking at the Node Graph, you can see that this is your Lgt pass branch. You will have a similar setup for your other passes.

Because the passes came in from the 3D software as premultiplied, and by multiplying and adding passes together you are actually doing color correction operations, you need to *unpremultiply* each of the passes before doing almost anything else with them. That's why you made sure you have an alpha channel for the pass by shuffling the rgba.alpha channel to the new rgba.alpha channel. The node Unpremult negates any premultiplication.

10. Insert an Unpremult node from the Merge toolbox after Shuffle1.

Use the Lgt pass as your background for all the other passes. It will serve as the trunk of your tree. The rest of the passes will come in from the right and connect themselves to the trunk of the tree. To do the next pass, you'll first create another Dot, to keep the DAG organized.

11. While nothing is selected, create a Dot by pressing the . (period) key.

12. Connect the newly created Dot's input to the previous Dot.

13. Drag the Dot to the right to create some space (**FIGURE 3.28**).

FIGURE 3.28 Keeping a node organized with Dots.

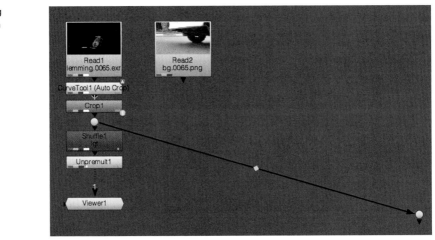

14. Hold down Ctrl/Cmd and drag the yellow Dot in the middle of the pipe between the two Dots to create a third Dot. Drag it to the right and up so it forms a right angle between the two Dots (**FIGURE 3.29**).

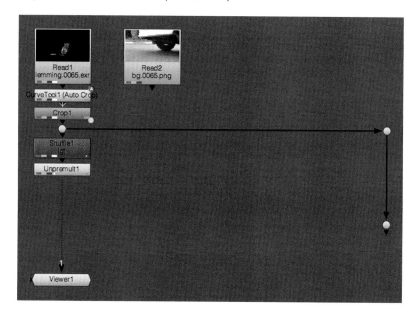

FIGURE 3.29 It's easy to snap elements to right angles in the DAG.

Now you will create the content for this new branch by copying everything, changing a few properties, and rearranging a few nodes.

15. Select both Shuffle1 and Unpremult1 and press Ctrl/Cmd-C to copy them.

16. Select the bottom right Dot and press Ctrl/Cmd-V.

17. Arrange Shuffle2 and Unpremult2 so that Shuffle2 is to the left of the Dot and Unpremult2 is to the left of Shuffle2 (**FIGURE 3.30**).

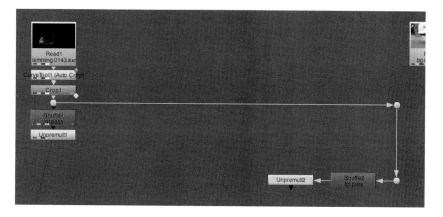

FIGURE 3.30 After arranging the nodes, the tree should look like this.

18. Double-click Shuffle2 to display its Properties panel and choose Col from the drop-down menu (**FIGURE 3.31**).

Notice how the label changed to reflect this in the DAG, thanks to our TCL script (**FIGURE 3.32**).

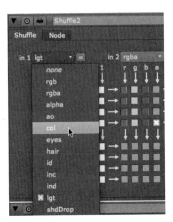

FIGURE 3.32 The TCL script made the label change automatically.

FIGURE 3.31 Picking another pass by choosing Col from the drop-down menu in the Shuffle node.

19. Select Unpremult2 and press M on the keyboard.

20. Connect Merge1's B input to Unpremult1.

21. Make sure Merge1's Properties panel is open and change the Operation property's drop-down menu from Over to Multiply.

22. Move Merge1 so it's directly underneath Unpremult1 and in a straight line from Unpremult2 (**FIGURE 3.33**).

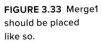

FIGURE 3.33 Merge1 should be placed like so.

The light multiplied by the unshaded texture essentially creates what's commonly called the diffuse pass (**FIGURE 3.34**).

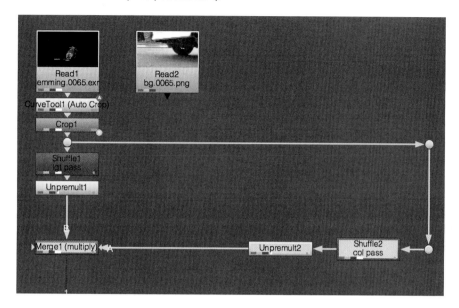

FIGURE 3.34 The Col pass added. The highlighted line will be duplicated for each additional pass.

Now for the next pass—the Inc pass (short for *Incidence* pass).

23. Select the horizontal line of nodes that starts with the Dot and ends with Merge1; press Ctrl/Cmd-C to copy it (it's highlighted in Figure 3.34).

24. Select the Dot at the bottom right of the tree and press Ctrl/Cmd-Shift-V to paste.

25. Drag the newly pasted nodes down a little and connect Merge2's B input to Merge1.

26. Double-click Shuffle3. Click Shuffle3's In property's drop-down menu and choose Inc.

27. Double-click Merge2. From the Operation property's drop-down menu choose Plus (plus, meaning: to add).

You have just added the Inc pass to the composite. You'll need to color correct it, but first you'll finish adding the rest of the passes (**FIGURE 3.35**).

NOTE You held Shift to branch a copy of the above group of nodes rather than insert.

FIGURE 3.35 With a few changes, each of these lines will represent a pass.

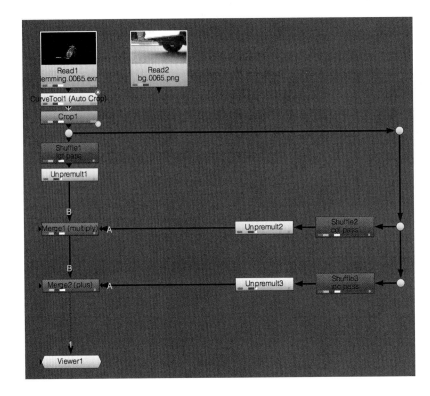

You'll repeat this process three more times to connect the Indirect (Ind), Specular (Spc), and ShdSelf (Self Shadow) passes. You will copy the same line and branch, and then paste it back into the last bottom right Dot, connecting the Merge node and changing the Shuffle node, and sometimes the Merge node's Operation property.

28. Repeat the process. Select the last line starting from the bottom right Dot and ending in the bottommost Merge node, copy, and then branch-paste to the bottom right Dot. Connect the new Merge's B input to the previous Merge node.

29. This time, change the Shuffle node's In property to Ind. Don't change the Merge node's Operation property.

30. Repeat the process, this time for the Spc pass.

31. Go through the process a third time. Choose ShdSelf for the Shuffle node's In property, and change the Merge operation to Minus.

32. Make sure you are viewing the output of the last Merge node, which should be called Merge5 (**FIGURE 3.36**).

Shadow is a *subtractive* pass. It is light that needs to be taken away, so it needs to be subtracted from the rest of the tree. Using the Minus operation sounds like the right thing to do—however, judging by the resulting image, something isn't right. It's all black.

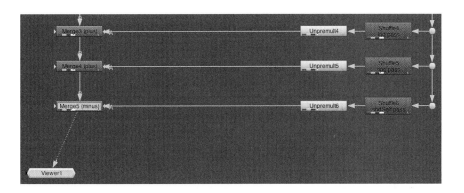

FIGURE 3.36 The bottom Merge node's Operation property is set to Minus.

The way the Merge node works is A then B. For the Over operation, normally this means A over B. For the Plus operation, this doesn't matter as 1+3 is the same as 3+1. For the Minus operation this means A minus B, which will work on some occasions, but in this case you need to subtract the shadow from the composite, not the other way around. You need B minus A. One way to do this is to switch inputs (the hot key Shift-X will take care of that and is worth remembering), but there's an alternative. The operation From does exactly what Minus does, only the other way around. It subtracts A from B.

33. Change the same Merge operation from Minus to From.

Using these passes, you completed the basic building of the lemming's beauty pass. Your tree should look like **FIGURE 3.37**.

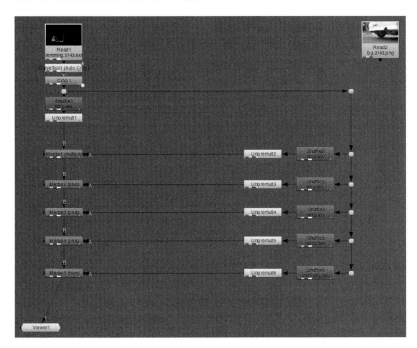

FIGURE 3.37 The tree at the end of the beauty pass build.

USING THE SHUFFLECOPY NODE

Now that you have finished building the lemming's beauty pass, you need to premultiply your composite to get rid of those nasty pixelated edges (**FIGURE 3.38**) and return to a premultiplied image that can be composited with other elements. To do this, you need to make sure you have the right alpha channel.

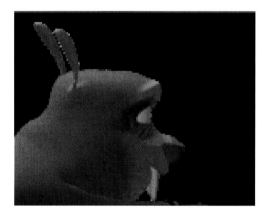

FIGURE 3.38 Time to get rid of those nasty edges.

If you look carefully, you might notice that as you added and multiplied various images together, you were also doing the same to the alpha channel. This means the alpha channel you now have in the pipe is a massively degraded one. You need to revert to the original unchanged one. The original alpha exists elsewhere in the tree—on the right side of the tree, where all the Dot nodes are, where you source all your branches.

To copy the channel from one branch to another, you use a node that's very similar to the Shuffle node you've been using. This one is called ShuffleCopy, and it allows you to shuffle channels around from two inputs instead of just one. You need to copy the ID pass's alpha channel from the branch on the right to the RGBA's alpha channel to your trunk on the left.

1. Select Merge5 (the one with the ShdSelf pass in the A input) and insert a Shuffle-Copy node after it from the Channels toolbox.

2. Connect ShuffleCopy1's 1 input to the last Dot on the right, then Ctrl/Cmd-click the yellow Dot on the pipe to create another Dot and create a right angle for the diagonal pipe (**FIGURE 3.39**).

FIGURE 3.39 The ShuffleCopy branch should look like this.

3. Change ShuffleCopy1's In 1 property to ID to copy the correct alpha for your lemming from the ID pass.

   By default, the ShuffleCopy node is set to copy the alpha channel from the selected channel set in input 1 and the RGB from the selected channel set in input 2, which is what you're after.

Since you started this exercise by unpremultiplying all the passes, it's time to premultiply again now that you have a correct alpha channel.

4. Select ShuffleCopy1 and connect a Premult node after it.

5. View Premult1 in the Viewer. Make sure to display the last frame.

You have now rebuilt the beauty pass with the correct alpha. You also ensured that you have easy access to all the various passes for easy manipulation (**FIGURE 3.40**).

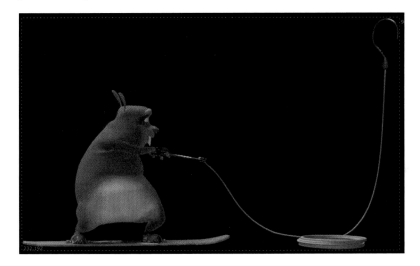

FIGURE 3.40
The beauty pass, premultiplied.

MANIPULATING PASSES

Now, by playing with the various branches, you can change the colors of elements that make up the lemming image—such as the amount of light falling on the object, how bright or sharp the specular highlights are, and so forth.

Let's start by changing the color of the Incidence pass. You want it to be a slightly brighter version of the fur color instead of the gray color it is now.

1. Click Unpremult3—this should be the one downstream from the Inc pass Shuffle node—and press the G key to insert a Grade node.

Because you're after a brighter version of the fur color, it would be a good idea to start by picking the color from the Viewer and then making it a little brighter.

2. Click the Sample Color From The Viewer button next to the gain slider (**FIGURE 3.41**).

FIGURE 3.41 Honestly, they should have thought of a shorter name for this little button.

NOTE Three modifier keys change the way sampling colors from the Viewer works. The Ctrl/Cmd key activates sampling. The Shift key enables creating a box rather than a point selection. The resulting color is the average of the colors in the box. The Alt/Option key picks the input image rather than the output image—meaning, picking colors before the Grade node changes them.

3. Hold Ctrl/Cmd-Shift in the Viewer and drag a box around the bright orange area of the lemming's fur—near his shoulder.

4. Click the Sample Color From The Viewer button again to turn it off.

5. To make the color brighter, click the Color Picker button for the Gain property to display the Color Wheel and Color Sliders panel (**FIGURE 3.42**).

FIGURE 3.42 The Color Picker button, in case you forgot what it is.

6. Drag the V slider up to a value of about 1.0, and then close the Color Wheel and Color Sliders panel (**FIGURE 3.43**).

7. Ctrl/Cmd-click the Viewer to remove the red sampling box.

   This made the rim part of the fur look more like part of the fur. Doing this to the fur using only the beauty pass would have been immensely difficult (**FIGURE 3.44**).

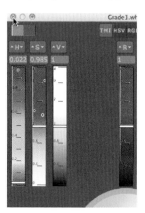

FIGURE 3.43 Close the Color Wheel and Color Sliders panel with the top left X button.

FIGURE 3.44 Your changes should create an image similar to this.

Next, add a little softening to the Specular pass. You're going to use a blur so you need to do this before the Unpremult operation. Remember: Always apply filters to premultiplied images.

8. Move Unpremult5 to the left to clear up some room between it and the Spc pass Shuffle node (should be Shuffle5).

9. Insert a Blur node after Shuffle5 by pressing B on the keyboard.

10. Change Blur1's Size property to 2.

To make the Specular pass a little less apparent, use Merge4's Mix property to mix it back a little.

11. Make sure Merge4's (the Merge that's adding the Specular pass) Properties panel is open by double-clicking it.

12. Bring down the Mix property to a value of around 0.6.

    The specular pass is softer now and sits better with the other passes. The specular part of your tree should look **FIGURE 3.45**.

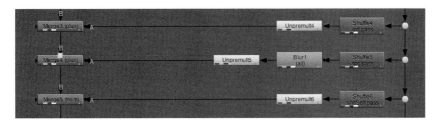

FIGURE 3.45 The Specular pass branch.

ADDING OTHER CGI IMAGES

There are two other elements to add to the lemming: the hair and eyes. These passes were rendered separately for several reasons that are not important here. These elements don't have passes—they only have a beauty pass. The hair will simply be added to the rest of the tree. However, the eyes need to be cut so they fit the eye sockets, so you will use the ID pass for that before adding them to the rest of the tree.

1. With nothing selected, create another Dot by pressing . (period) on your keyboard.

2. Connect the new Dot's input to the bottom right Dot, the one that ShuffleCopy1 is connected to.

3. Place the new Dot underneath that Dot to create a new branch to start with.

4. Copy Shuffle6 (ShdSelf pass) and paste it after the new Dot.

5. Change Shuffle7's In 1 property's pull-down menu to Hair.

6. Make sure all four channels are shuffled from the left—Hair input. This means you need to check on the alpha channel box on the left, In1, side (**FIGURE 3.46**).

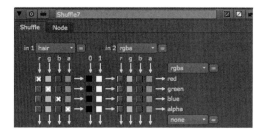

FIGURE 3.46 Changing the Shuffle node so that the alpha is copied as well.

7. Select Shuffle7 and press M on your keyboard to attach a Merge node to it.

8. Connect Merge6's B input to the output of Premult1 and place Merge6 under Premult1, and then view it in the Viewer (**FIGURE 3.47**).

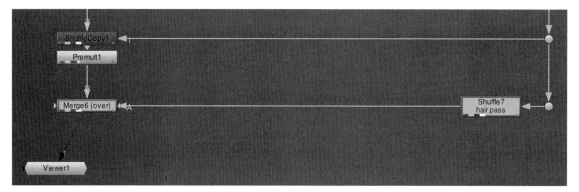

FIGURE 3.47 The hair elements should be added like this to the tree.

9. Go to frame 70 and view Merge6.

The hair element has been added. However, there is a little problem. The hair and the head are perfectly cut so they fit each other. This means the hair has been cut in such a way that the part that should be behind the head is not there anymore. When doing a normal Over operation in the Merge, this actually results in a little error due to the math involved. In these cases, an Over operation isn't enough. Let's see what this means.

10. Switch to the alpha channel by hovering the mouse pointer in the Viewer and pressing the A key.

Notice the thin black line where the hair and the head come together. You can fix this with a different Over operation designed especially for these kinds of situations (**FIGURE 3.48**).

11. In Merge6's Properties panel, change the Operation from Over to Disjoint-over.

Look at the place where the head and hair come together. You can see the line has disappeared and the matte looks correct now (**FIGURE 3.49**).

FIGURE 3.48 This thin gray line in the matte shouldn't be there.

FIGURE 3.49 The Disjoint-over operation saves the day.

12. Switch back to view the RGB channels by hovering the mouse pointer in the Viewer and pressing the A key.

Now for the eyes. Let's start by shuffling them into the RGBA channel set.

13. Copy Shuffle7 and the Dot to the right of it by selecting them and pressing Ctrl/Cmd-C.

14. Select the Dot to the right of Shuffle7 and press Ctrl/Cmd-Shift-V to *branch-paste* another copy. (To branch-paste, hold the Shift key to produce a branch rather than an insert operation.)

15. Change Shuffle8's In 1 property's pull-down menu to Eyes, and view Shuffle8 in the Viewer (**FIGURE 3.50**).

These are the lemming's eyes. The whole orb. It's not very often that one gets to see the whole of a lemming's eyes. That's because normally they are held inside eye sockets, which is exactly what you need to do now. Let's find the matte for that.

There is one more thing to do first, though. If you look carefully, you can see that the eyes are unpremultiplied. This is apparent due to the jagged edge you can see in Figure 3.50, which doesn't appear in the alpha channel. You need to make them premultiplied before you can put them over the rest of the tree.

16. Insert a Premult node after Shuffle8 (**FIGURE 3.51**).

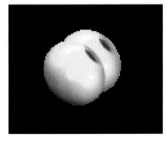

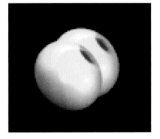

FIGURE 3.50 The lemming's eyes—the whole thing.

FIGURE 3.51 The edge of the eyes is no longer as jagged.

With that fixed, you can move on to finding your eye socket matte.

17. Make sure you are viewing Premult2.

The eye socket is still in this stream. The only thing you did to this stream, as far as channel manipulation goes, is move the eye channels to the RGBA. Everything else remains untouched.

18. In the Viewer, change the Channel Set pull-down menu from RGBA to ID.

You can see here that the eye socket matte is the green part of the ID pass. This doesn't mean you need to key this out. The green part means the green channel. Let's have a look at it.

19. In the Viewer, press the G key to display the green channel.

You can clearly see that the green channel is a black-and-white image, just like an alpha channel. Holding different mattes in different channels is a smart and economical way of doing things (**FIGURE 3.52**).

FIGURE 3.52 Setting up the Viewer to display only the ID channel set's green channel shows a matte for the eye sockets.

So, all you have to do is place the eyes inside the ID channel set's green channel. You will do this down the pipe, as explained earlier in this chapter, by connecting a Merge node's A and B input to the same node and changing the channel set to merge inside the Merge Properties panel.

20. Switch back to viewing the RGBA channel set and press G again to view the RGB channels.

21. Insert a Merge node after Premult2.

22. Connect Merge7's B input to Premult2.

23. Change Merge7's Operation property from Over to Mask.

The mask operation will mask input B inside of the alpha channel of input A. This means you have to tell Merge7 which channel to pick for channel A's alpha channel.

24. Change A Channel's last property from rgba.alpha to id.green using the pull-down menu.

FIGURE 3.53 shows Merge7's setup. The point to take to heart here is that you don't have to use a Shuffle node every time you want to use a channel that's not in the RGBA channel set. You can simply access it from the stream—down the pipe, in other words. Most of the time it's not as convenient. But in this case it was.

FIGURE 3.53 Using a Merge node to pull information from other channel sets.

Let's continue compositing the eyes.

25. Insert another Merge node after Merge7 and connect its B input to Merge6.

The lemming can see again (**FIGURE 3.54**). Good for him! You have been working in isolation so far and haven't seen how the lemming looks over the background. Guess what's next?

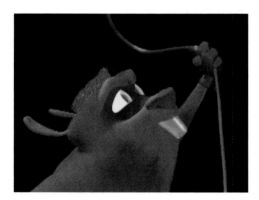

FIGURE 3.54 The eyes are now added to the lemming.

PLACING CGI OVER LIVE BACKGROUND

Now you're going to composite the lemming tree over the background. Only after you do that will you be able to really gauge your composite and use your complex CGI tree to its full potential. You will then be able to make the lemming feel more like it's in the scene.

Treat this whole tree as a single element—the foreground.

1. Click Merge8 (the very last Merge) and insert another Merge node after it.

2. Bring Read2 (the background) down to the area at the bottom of the tree and connect Merge9's B input to it.

3. Make sure you are viewing Merge9 to see the whole tree's output.

The lemming doesn't look like he's standing on the ground (**FIGURE 3.55**). One of the main reasons he appears to be floating is that the composite is missing the contact shadow elements. The drop shadow and the ambient occlusion need to be added.

FIGURE 3.55 The lemming over the background.

At the beginning of this chapter, you cropped the image according to the auto crop calculation of CurveTool1. This calculation was performed on the RGBA channel set and so it didn't include the shadow element, which sits outside the lemming area (it's dropping on the floor, so that's a given). If you call up the shadow or ambient occlusion elements from the bottom point in the stream, you'll be getting a cropped version of those elements. Therefore you have to go back up to a place before the crop, and pick those passes from there.

4. At the top of the tree, with nothing selected, create a Dot and connect its input to Read1. Drag it to the right until it passes the rest of the tree.

5. Select the new Dot and insert another Dot, connected to it. Drag the new Dot down until it passes the rest of the tree without passing Read2 (**FIGURE 3.56**).

6. Select the new Dot and insert a Merge node after it by pressing M.

7. Connect Merge10's B input to the final output of your comp (Merge9) and view Merge10 in the Viewer.

FIGURE 3.56 Using Dots to keep the tree organized.

Use this Merge node to combine the *Ambient Occlusion* pass (here simply called AO) with the whole comp (the pass affects both the lemming and the floor). Because the AO pass is wholly white, except for the dark parts representing the shadows, you'll use the Multiply operation in the Merge node.

8. In Merge10's Properties panel, change the A Channel property's drop-down menu from RGBA to AO.

9. Change Merge10's operation from Over to Multiply (**FIGURE 3.57**).

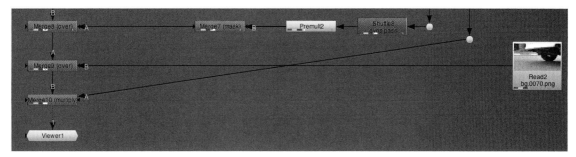

FIGURE 3.57 This is where Merge10 should be.

Here again you saved a Shuffle operation and did the shuffling inside the Merge.

You will combine the drop shadow pass in a slightly different way in the next section.

USING THE MASK INPUT

Another great way to use channels in Nuke is the Mask input. The Mask input is that extra input some nodes—including all the Merge, Color, and Filter nodes—have on the right-hand side. You can see the Mask input in **FIGURE 3.58**.

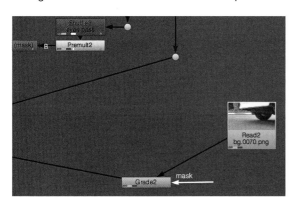

FIGURE 3.58 This is the Mask input. It says so when you click and drag it.

The Mask input limits the area where the node operates. It receives a single channel, and makes the node operate only where that channel is white. Gray areas in the mask image are going to make the node operate in that percentage—a 50% gray means 50% effect, and black means no effect. This makes it really easy to make a node affect only a specific area.

Note that the Mask input has nothing to do with alpha channels and merging streams together. Its only purpose is to limit the area a node operates in.

You'll use the Mask input with a Grade node, darkening the background where the drop shadow should be.

1. Press G on your keyboard to insert a Grade node after Read2.

2. Drag Grade2's Mask input to the Dot that supplied you with the uncropped CGI renders (**FIGURE 3.59**).

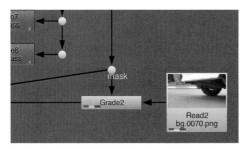

FIGURE 3.59 Make sure you connected the Mask input in the correct way.

Because you want to use the Shadow pass, call that up in Grade2's Mask Channel drop-down menu.

3. In Grade2's Properties panel, change the Mask property's drop-down menu, at the bottom, to shdDrop.alpha—calling up the ShdDrop channel set's alpha channel (**FIGURE 3.60**).

FIGURE 3.60 Changing the Mask property's drop-down menu to pick the correct single channel from the stream.

4. Now use the Gain property's slider or field to bring the color of the shadow down to 0.25, which should look about right (**FIGURE 3.61**).

FIGURE 3.61 Grade2 only has an effect where the drop shadow should be.

You can see here that the background is only getting darker in the area where the shadow should be dropping. You can turn off the Mask input to see its effect.

5. Uncheck the check box next to the Mask property's drop-down menu to turn off the mask channel.

   This is the difference between having the mask channel and not having it. This ability to limit the area an effect or a node works in is one of the really strong points in Nuke.

6. Check the check box next to the Mask property's drop-down menu to turn on the mask channel.

This almost concludes this chapter. But one last thing.

You can now look at this composite and see the result of all the work you did. You have a lemming over a background. Those with more experienced eyes may notice that there is a lot more work to do to get this lemming to look as if he was shot with the same camera and in the same location as the background image—but that's more of a compositing lesson than a Nuke lesson.

What's important now, though, is that you have access to every building block of what makes up the way the lemming looks. Having the separate passes easily accessible means your work will be easier from here on out.

For now, though, leave this composite here. Hopefully, it helped teach you the fundamental building blocks of channel use and how to manipulate a bigger tree (**FIGURE 3.62**).

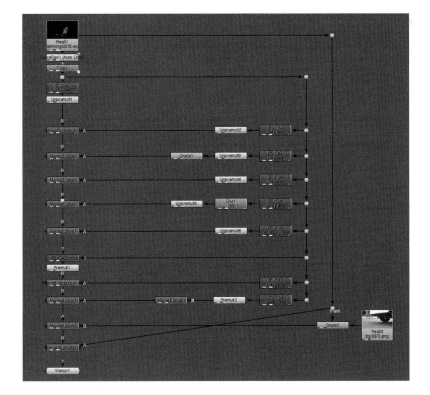

FIGURE 3.62 Your final tree should look like this.

COLOR CORRECTION

Wow. This is a bit naive. Calling a lesson "Color Correction." It should be a whole course on its own. But this book is about more than that, and limited space reduces color correction to a chapter. So let me start by explaining what color correction means.

Color correction is one of the most fundamental things you can do to an image. It refers to any change to the perceived color of an image. Making an image lighter, more saturated, changing the contrast, making it bluer—all of this is color correction. There are a lot of uses for color correction. The most obvious one is to make an image look different as a result of a stylistic decision. But you can also color correct to combine two images so they feel like part of the same scene. This is performed often in compositing when the foreground and the background should have colors that work well together. There are plenty

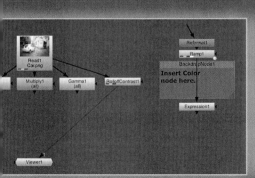

more uses for changing the color of an image. An image might be a mask or an alpha channel that needs to have a different color in some way—to lose softness and give it more contrast, for example.

Whatever reason you have for color correcting an image, the color correction will work according to the way Nuke handles color. Nuke is a very advanced system that uses cutting-edge technology and theory to work with color. It is important to understand Nuke's approach to color to understand color correcting within Nuke.

UNDERSTANDING NUKE'S APPROACH TO COLOR

Nuke is a 32-bit float linear color compositing application. A bit of a fancy description there, with potentially new words. I explain this bit by bit:

- *32-bit*: That's the amount of bits used to hold colors. Most compositing and image-manipulation programs are 8-bit, allowing for 256 variations of color per channel (resulting in what's referred to as "million of colors" when combining the three color channels). This is normally fine for displaying color, but is not good enough for some calculations of operations, and may result in unwanted results such as *banding*—inaccurate display of gradients where changes in color happen abruptly instead of smoothly. 32-bit allows for a whopping 4,294,967,296 variations of color per channel. That's a staggering amount that results in *much* more accurate display of images and calculations of operations. 8- or 16-bit images brought into Nuke will be bumped up to 32-bit, although that doesn't add any detail, it just enables better calculations from that point onwards.

- *Float:* Normally the color of an image is represented between black and white. In 8-bit images, for example, the 256 color variations are split evenly between black and white—so the value 1 is black, the value 256 is white, and the value 128 is a middle gray. But what about colors that are brighter than white? Surely the whiteness in the middle of a lit light bulb is brighter than a white piece of paper? For that reason, there are colors that are brighter than white called super-whites. There are also colors that are darker than black called sub-blacks (but there isn't a real-world analogy that can be used here short of black holes). Using 8 bits to describe an image simply doesn't allow enough room to describe colors beyond black and white. These colors get *clipped* and are simply represented as black or white. However, in 32-bit color, there is plenty of room and these colors become representable. As mentioned before, 8-bit color is normally enough to display images on-screen. Furthermore, the computer monitor can still display only white—and nothing brighter. However it is still very important to have access to those colors beyond white, especially when color correcting. Darkening an image that has both a piece of white paper and a light bulb in it will leave the light bulb white, while darkening the paper to a gray color results in an image that mimics real-world behavior and looks good and believable. Doing the same with a non-floating image will result in the white paper and the light bulb looking the same gray color—which will be unconvincing.

- *Linear:* Linear can mean lots of things. In terms of color, I mean *linear color space.* A computer monitor doesn't show an image as the image appears in reality, because the monitor is not a *linear* display device. It has a mathematical curve called *gamma* that it uses to display images. Different monitors can have different curves, but most often they have a gamma curve called *sRGB.* Because the monitor is not showing the image as it appears in reality, images need to be "corrected" for this. This is usually done automatically because most image capture devices are applying an sRGB curve too, in the opposite direction. Displaying a middle gray pixel on a monitor only shows you middle gray as it's being affected by the gamma curve. Because your scanner, camera, and image processing applications all know this, they color correct by applying the *reverse* gamma curve on this gray pixel that negates the monitor's effect. This process represents basic *color management.* However, if your image's middle gray value isn't middle gray because a gamma curve has been applied to it, it will react differently to color correction and might produce odd results. Most applications work in this way, and most people dealing with color have become accustomed to this. This is primarily because computer graphics is a relatively new industry that relies on computers that, until recently, were very slow. The correct way to manipulate imagery—in whatever way—is *before* the gamma curve has been applied to an image. The correct way is to take a linear image, color correct it, composite it, transform it, and then apply a reverse gamma curve to the image to view it correctly (as the monitor is applying gamma correction as well and negating the correction you just applied). Luckily, this is how Nuke works by default.

Still confused? Here's a recap: Nuke creates very accurate representations of color and can store colors that are brighter than white and darker than black. It also calculates all the compositing operations in linear color space, resulting in more realistic and more mathematically correct results.

Nuke has many color correction nodes, but they are all built out of basic mathematical building blocks, which are the same in every software application. The next section looks at those building blocks.

NOTE Nuke color values are displayed and are calculated in what's called "normalized values." This means that instead of defining black at a value of 0 and white at a value of 255, black is still 0, but white is 1. It's a very easy thing to remember that makes understanding the math easier.

COLOR MANIPULATION BUILDING BLOCKS

Color correction is a somewhat intuitive process. Often compositors just try something until they get it right. Understanding the math behind color correction can help you pick the right tool for the job when attempting to reach a specific result—which is better than trial and error. **TABLE 4.1** explains most of these building blocks.

TABLE 4.1 Basic Color Correction Functions

Math function	Node	Explanation	Names in Nuke	Other known names
Add	Add, Grade, ColorCorrect	Adds a constant value to a channel.	Add, Offset	
Multiply	Multiply, Grade, ColorCorrect	Multiplies the channel by a constant value.	Gain, Multiply	Brightness, Contrast, Exposure, Input/Output White
Gamma	Gamma, Grade, ColorCorrect	Applies a gamma curve to a channel.	Gamma	
Contrast	RolloffContrast, ColorCorrect	Applies a contrast curve to a channel. This is also a form of multiplication.	Contrast, RolloffContrast	
Lift	Grade	This function is similar to Multiply and Contrast. It's a contrast curve with a center at white. More below.	Lift	Pedestal, Input/Output Black
Lookup	ColorLookup	Applies a user-defined curve to a channel.	ColorLookup	Curves
Saturation	Adjusts the color intensity by reducing the differences between the RGB channels.	Saturation		

Dynamic range

When dealing with color correction, I usually talk about dynamic range and its parts. *Dynamic range* means all the colors that exist in your image, from the darkest to the brightest color. The dynamic range changes from image to image, but usually you are working with an image that has black and white and everything in between. The parts of the dynamic range, as mentioned, are split according to their brightness value as follows:

- The shadows or lowlights, meaning the darkest colors in the image
- The midtones, meaning the colors in the image that are neither dark nor bright
- The highlights, meaning the brightest colors

In Nuke, and in other applications that support colors beyond white and black (float), there are two more potential parts to the dynamic range: the super-whites, or colors that are brighter than white, and the sub-blacks, colors that are darker than black.

Let's look at these building blocks in several scenarios to really understand what they do and why you might choose one over another.

1. Launch Nuke.

2. Bring in a clip called Car.png by pressing R and navigating to the chapter04 directory.

3. Click Read1, then press 1 on the keyboard to view it.

   It's an image of a car. Did that catch you by surprise?

4. With Read1 selected, go to the Color toolbox and click Add in the Math folder.

   You have now inserted a basic color-correcting node after the car image. Let's use it to change the color of the image and see its effect.

5. In Add1's Properties panel, click the Color Picker button to display the Color Wheel and Color Sliders panel. Play with the R, G, and B colors to see the changes (**FIGURE 4.1**).

FIGURE 4.1 Using the Color Wheel and Color Sliders panel.

You can see everything changes when playing with an Add node—the highlights, midtones, and even blacks (**FIGURE 4.2**). An Add operation adds color to everything uniformly—the whole dynamic range. Every part of the image gets brighter or darker.

FIGURE 4.2 The whole image is becoming brighter.

6. When you're finished, close the Color Wheel and Color Sliders panel.

7. Select Read1 again and branch out by holding the Shift key and clicking a Multiply node from the Math folder in the Color toolbox.

8. While Multiply1 is selected, press 1 on the keyboard to view it.

9. In Multiply1's Properties panel, click the Color Picker button to display the Color Wheel and Color Sliders panel and experiment with the colors (**FIGURE 4.3**).

FIGURE 4.3 The changes affect the highlights more than the rest of the image.

You can see very different results here. The highlights get a strong boost very quickly while the blacks are virtually untouched.

10. Repeat the above process for the Gamma node. Remember to branch from Read1 (**FIGURE 4.4**).

You can see that gamma mainly deals with midtones. The bright areas remain untouched and so do the dark areas.

FIGURE 4.4 The midtones change the most when changing gamma.

You should now have three different, basic, math-based color correctors in your Node Graph that produce three very different results as shown in **FIGURE 4.5**.

FIGURE 4.5 The results from changing Add, Multiply, and Gamma.

Your DAG should look a little like **FIGURE 4.6**.

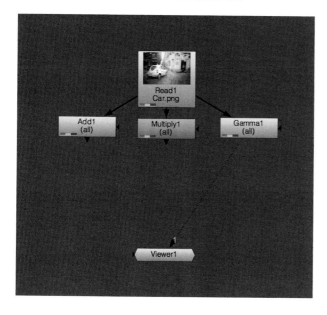

FIGURE 4.6 Branching three color correctors from a node.

Let's try some more color correction nodes.

11. Select Read1 and then Shift-click RolloffContrast in the Color toolbox to create another branch.

    I find it really annoying that they chose to call the Contrast node RolloffContrast, especially since it makes opening it via the Tab key so much harder because typing "contrast" won't display this node.

12. While viewing RolloffContrast1, open its Properties panel and play with the Contrast value (**FIGURE 4.7**).

FIGURE 4.7 A high Contrast value produces a high-contrast image.

    You can see how, when increasing the contrast above 1, the lowlights get pushed down and the highlights are pushed up.

13. Keep the Contrast property above 1 and bring the Center value down to 0.

    The Center property changed what is considered to be the highlight or lowlight. Colors above the Center value will be considered bright and pushed up, and colors below the Center value will be considered dark and pushed down.

You can see the result of the RolloffContrast operation now is very similar to that of the Multiply node. In fact, they are virtually the same. When setting the center value at 0, you lock that value in place. The value 0 is locked in place when multiplying as well.

14. Bring the Center value up to 1.

You haven't gone through an operation called Lift yet, but the RolloffContrast operation is virtually the same as that operation. With Lift, the value 1 is locked in place and the farther the values are away from 1, the bigger the effect. You will go through Lift when you learn about the Grade node later in this chapter.

To wrap up this part of the color introduction, here's an overall explanation:

- When dealing with color, there's usually a need to control the lowlights, midtones, and highlights separately.

- The Add operation adds the same amount of color to every part of the dynamic range.

- The Multiply operation multiplies the dynamic range by a value. This means that a perfect black doesn't change, lowlights are barely touched, midtones are affected by some degree, and highlights are affected the most. It is good to mention that a Multiply operation is virtually the same as changing the exposure in a camera or increasing light. It is the most commonly used color operation.

- The Gamma control is a specific curve designed to manipulate the part of the dynamic range between 0 and 1 (black and white, remember?), without touching 0 or 1.

- Contrast is actually very similar to Multiply, but has a center control. If you place the center point at 0 you get a Multiply node.

USING AN I/O GRAPH TO VISUALIZE COLOR OPERATIONS

And *I/O graph* (input versus output graph) is a great way to understand color operations. The X axis represents the color coming in, and the Y axis represents the color going out. A perfectly diagonal line therefore represents no color correction. The graph shows what the color operation is doing and the changes to the dynamic range.

To view an I/O graph like this, you can bring in a pre-made script I made.

1. Choose File > Import Script to load another script from the disk and merge it with the script you have been building.

2. In the File Browser that opens, navigate to chapter04 and click IO_graph.nk to import it into your current script.

   Notice that when you imported the script (which is only four nodes) all of its nodes were selected. This is very convenient as you can immediately move the newly imported tree to a suitable place in your Node Graph.

3. Make sure the imported tree is not sitting on top of your existing tree. Move it aside to somewhere suitable as in **FIGURE 4.8**.

FIGURE 4.8 You now have two trees in your DAG.

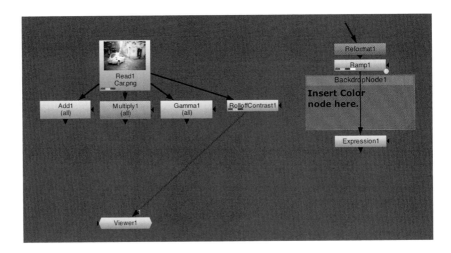

4. Make sure you are viewing the output of Expression1.

A quick explanation of the script you imported, node by node:

- The first node is a Reformat node, which defines the resolution of your image. In this case, 256x256. Notice that its input isn't connected to anything. This is a good way to set a resolution for your tree.

- The second node is a Ramp. This can be created from the Draw toolbox. This node generates ramps—in this case, a black to white horizontal ramp from edge to edge.

- The third node is a Backdrop node, used to highlight areas in the tree. You can find it in the toolbox called Other. It indicates where to add your color correction nodes in the next step.

- The fourth and last node is an Expression node. This is a very powerful node. It can be found in the Color > Math toolbox. It lets the user write an expression with which to draw an image. You can do a lot of things with this node, from simple color operations (such as adding or multiplying, though this is wasteful) to complex warps or redrawing of different kinds of images all together. In this case, you use this node to draw values of a horizontal black to white ramp (you have the ramp from above) on-screen as white pixels in the corresponding height in the image. A value of 0.5 in the ramp will generate a white pixel halfway up the Y resolution in the output of the Expression node. The left-most pixel is black in the ramp, and shows as a white pixel at the bottom of your screen. The middle pixel is a value of 0.5 and so shows as a white pixel in the middle of the screen. The right-most pixel is a value of 1 and so draws a white pixel at the top of the screen. All these white pixels together form a diagonal line (**FIGURE 4.9**). Changing the color of the ramp will change the line. This happens on each of the three color channels individually.

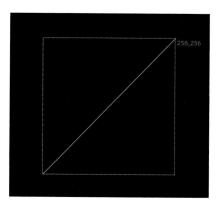

FIGURE 4.9 The I/O graph at its default state.

Let's start using this I/O Graph tree. You will insert a Color node in between Ramp1 and Expression1 and look at the resulting I/O graph.

5. Insert an Add node from the Color > Math toolbox after Ramp1 as shown in **FIGURE 4.10**.

6. Bring the value of Add2's value property to around 0.1.

    You can see, as in **FIGURE 4.11**, that the Add operation changes the whole dynamic range of your graph, and therefore, for any image.

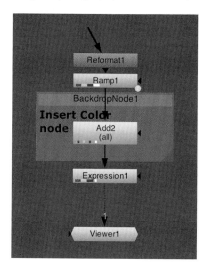

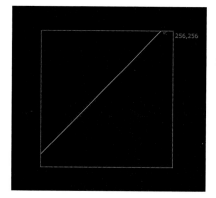

FIGURE 4.11 The whole graph is raised or lowered in unison.

FIGURE 4.10 Add2 has been inserted after Ramp1 and will change your I/O graph.

Let's replace your Add node with a Multiply node. You've never done this before, so pay attention.

7. With Add2 selected, Ctrl/Cmd-click the Multiply node in the Color > Math toolbox to replace the selected node with the newly created one.

8. Increase and decrease Multiply2's value.

9. You can also click the color wheel and change the RGB channels individually (**FIGURE 4.12**).

The Multiply operation has more effect on the highlights than the lowlights. You can see when you are moving the slider that the 0 point stays put, and the further away you go from 0 the effect becomes stronger.

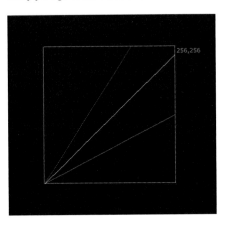

FIGURE 4.12 The graph changes more the further away it is from 0.

Let's try Gamma. Maybe you don't know what a Gamma curve looks like. Well, here's your chance.

10. Replace Multiply2 with a Gamma node from the Color or Math toolbox by holding down Ctrl/Cmd and clicking Gamma from the Color > Math toolbox.

11. Load Gamma2's Color Wheel and Color Sliders panel and play with the sliders for R, G, and B.

You should now get a similar result to **FIGURE 4.13**.

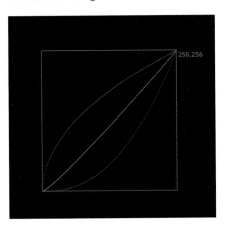

FIGURE 4.13 Notice that only the middle part of the graph moves.

The Gamma operation changes the midtones without changing the blacks or whites. You can tell that the point at the furthest left and at the furthest right are not moving.

Contrast is next.

12. Replace Gamma2 with a RolloffContrast node in the Color toolbox.

13. Bring RolloffContrast2's contrast value to 1.5.

The contrast operation pushes the two parts of the dynamic range away from one another (**FIGURE 4.14**).

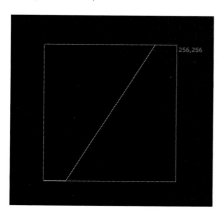

FIGURE 4.14 A basic contrast curve.

14. Play around with RolloffContrast2's Center property. When you are finished, set the value to 0.

Here you can see what actually happens when you play with the Center slider. It moves the point that defines where the lowlights and highlights are. When leaving the center at 1, you can see that the curve is identical to a Multiply curve (**FIGURE 4.15**).

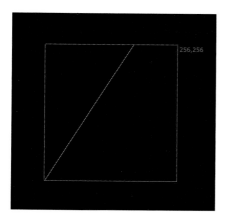

FIGURE 4.15 A Center value of 0 makes Contrast behave like Multiply.

15. Move the Center slider up to 1 (**FIGURE 4.16**).

    This is a Lift operation, which is covered later in this chapter. Your white point is locked, while everything else changes—the opposite of Multiply.

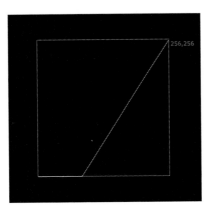

FIGURE 4.16 Moving the slider up to 1 is actually a Lift operation.

RolloffContrast has one other property you can see in the I/O graph. This property, called Soft Clip, is the property that gives this node its name. This property smooths out the edges of the curve so that colors don't all of a sudden turn to black or white and result in a harsh transition.

16. Move the center slider to 0.5 and start to increase the Soft Clip slider. I stopped at 0.55.

    FIGURE 4.17 shows what happens when you increase the soft clip. This creates a much more appealing result, which is unique to this node.

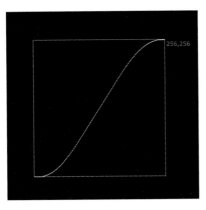

FIGURE 4.17 This smooth edge to the curve is what gives RolloffContrast its name.

If you have a fair amount of experience, you must have noticed that the I/O graph looks a lot like a tool you may have used in the past—something applications such as Adobe After Effects call Curves. In Nuke, this is called ColorLookup, and it is discussed in the next section.

CREATING CURVES WITH COLORLOOKUP

The ColorLookup node mentioned at the beginning of this lesson is actually an I/O graph you can control directly. This makes it the operation with the most amount of control. However, it's actually the hardest to control and keyframe due to its more complicated user interface. After all, it's easier to set a slider and keyframe it than move points on a graph.

Let's try this node on both the image and the I/O graph itself.

1. Replace RolloffContrast2 with a ColorLookup node in the Color toolbox (**FIGURE 4.18**).

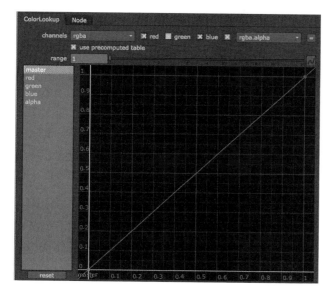

FIGURE 4.18
The ColorLookup interface.

The interface for this node has the narrow curves list on the left, and the curve area on the right. Choosing a curve at left displays that curve at right, which enables you to manipulate it. There are five curves. The first controls all the channels, and the next four control the R, G, B, and alpha separately. You can have more than one curve display in the graph window on the right by Shift-clicking or Ctrl/Cmd-clicking them in the list.

2. Click the Master curve in the list at left.

In the graph (Figure 4.18), you can now see a curve (a linear one at the moment). It has two points that define it, one at the bottom left and one at the top right. Moving them will change the color. For example, moving the top one will create a Multiply operation.

The ColorLookup's strength lies in making curves that you can't create using regular math functions. For that you need to create more points.

3. To create more points on the curve, Ctrl/Cmd-Alt/Option-click the curve in the graph window. It doesn't matter where on the curve you click.

You've just created another point. You can move it around and play with its handles. If you look at the I/O graph on the Viewer, you can see that it mimics what you did in the ColorLookup node. They are exactly the same (**FIGURE 4.19**).

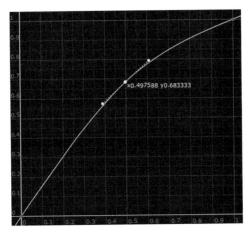

FIGURE 4.19 Changing the curve is just like working with an I/O graph.

Now let's use ColorLookup on the car image.

4. Select Read1 and Shift-click the ColorLookup node in the Color toolbox to branch another output.

5. Click ColorLookup2 and press the 1 key to view it in the Viewer.

6. Play around with ColorLookup2's curves. You can play with the separate RGB curves as well.

I ended up with **FIGURE 4.20**—pretty drastic. But that's the level of control you have with ColorLookup. The Reset button at bottom left allows me to reset this mess.

FIGURE 4.20 Extreme color correction courtesy of ColorLookup.

COLOR MATCHING WITH THE GRADE NODE

The Grade node is specifically built to make some color correction operations easier. One of these operations is matching colors from one image to another.

When matching colors, the normal operation is to match black and white points between the foreground and background (only changing the foreground), and then match the level of the midtones gray, and finally match the midtone hue and saturation.

Using the Grade node

The Grade node is made out of a few of the building blocks mentioned earlier. **TABLE 4.2** shows a list of its seven properties.

TABLE 4.2 Grade Node Properties

Property	Definition
Blackpoint	This is the reverse operation to Lift. It works in the same way, but higher numbers will result in stronger blacks instead of lighter blacks. Basically, the color chosen here will turn to black.
Whitepoint	This is the reverse operation to Multiply. It works in the same way, but higher numbers will result in lower highlights instead of stronger highlights. Basically, the color chosen here will turn to white.
Lift	A Lift operation.
Gain	A Multiply operation.
Multiply	Another Multiply operation.
Offset	An Add operation.
Gamma	A Gamma operation.

By using Blackpoint and Whitepoint to set a perfect black and a perfect white, you can stretch the image to a full dynamic range. When you have a full dynamic range you then can easily set the blackpoint and whitepoint to match those of the background using Lift and Gain. You then have Multiply, Offset, and Gamma to match midtones and for final tweaking.

Let's practice color matching, starting with a fresh script.

1. If you want, you can save your script. When you are finished, press Ctrl/Cmd-W to close the script and leave Nuke open with an empty script.

2. From your chapter04 folder bring in two images: CarAlpha.png and IcyRoad.png.

3. Make sure that CarAlpha.png is called Read1 and IcyRoad.png is Read2. You can change the name of a node in the top-most property.

NOTE If Nuke quits altogether, just start Nuke again.

You will quickly composite these images together and then take your time in color matching the foreground image to the background.

4. Select Read1 and press the M key to insert a Merge node after it.

5. Connect Merge1's B input to Read2 and view Merge1 in the Viewer (**FIGURE 4.21**).

FIGURE 4.21 The car is over the dashboard— this is wrong.

The composite is almost ready. You just need to punch a hole in the foreground car so it appears to be behind the snow that's piling on the windshield. For that, you'll bring another image in (you will learn how to creates mattes yourself in Chapter 6).

6. From your chapter04 folder bring in Windshield.png and display it in the Viewer.

Here you can see this is a matte of the snow. It is a four-channel image with the same image in the R, G, B, and alpha. You need to use this image to punch a hole in your foreground branch. To do that you will need another Merge node.

7. Select Read3 and insert a Merge node after it.

8. Drag Merge2 on the pipe between Read1 and Merge1 until the pipe highlights. When it does, release the mouse button to insert Merge2 on that pipe (**FIGURE 4.22**).

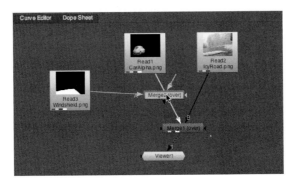

FIGURE 4.22 Inserting a node on an existing pipe.

9. View Merge1 (**FIGURE 4.23**).

FIGURE 4.23 All that white on the dashboard shouldn't to be there.

You can see here that this is not the desired result (**FIGURE 4.23**). You still need to change the Merge2 operation to something that will cut the B image with the A image. This operation is called Stencil. Stencil is the reverse operation from Mask, which you used in Chapter 3. Mask held image B inside the alpha channel of image A, and Stencil will hold image B outside image A.

10. In Merge2's Properties panel, choose Stencil from the Operation drop-down menu.

FIGURE 4.24 The car is now correctly located behind the dashboard.

Looking at your comp now, you can see that it works—short of a color difference between the foreground and background (**FIGURE 4.24**). Let's use a Grade node to fix this shift.

11. Select Read1 and press the G key to insert a Grade node after it.

As you know from Chapter 2, you are not allowed to color correct premultiplied images. It is often hard to tell if an image is premultiplied or not, but in this case it is. You can also look at the RGB versus the alpha channels and see that the areas that are black in the alpha are also black in the RGB.

Since you can't color correct premultiplied images you have to unpremult them. You can do this in one of two ways: using an Unpremult node before the color correction (in this case, Grade1) and then a Premult node after it, or using the (Un)premult By Switch in your Color nodes. Let's practice both.

12. Bring Grade1's Offset property up to around 0.4.

You can see that the whole image, except the dashboard area, turned brighter, even though you are only correcting the car image (**FIGURE 4.25**). This is due to the lack of proper premultiplication. Let's do the two-node method first.

FIGURE 4.25 The whole image turned brighter.

13. Click Read1 and from the Merge toolbox add an Unpremult node.

14. Click Grade1 and from the Merge toolbox add a Premult node and look at the Viewer (**FIGURE 4.26**).

FIGURE 4.26 The proper premultiplication fixed the problem.

The problem has been fixed. This is one way to use proper premultiplication. Let's look at another.

15. Select Unpremult1 and Premult1 and press the Delete key.

16. In Grade1's Properties panel, choose rgba.alpha from the (Un)premult By menu; this automatically selects the associated check box (**FIGURE 4.27**).

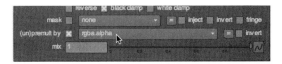

FIGURE 4.27 Using the (Un)premult By property does the same thing as the Unpremult and Premult nodes workflow.

The resulting image looks exactly as before (Figure 4.26). This technique does exactly the same thing as the first method, just without using other nodes. I usually prefer the first method as it shows clearly in the DAG that the premultiplication issues are handled. However, if you look at Grade1 in the DAG now, you will see that, although a smaller indication, Grade1 is showing that it is dividing the RGB channels with the alpha channel. The label now says "rgb/alpha" (**FIGURE 4.28**).

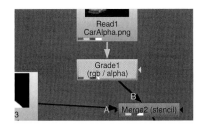

FIGURE 4.28 The node's label changes to show the Unpremult and Premult operations are happening inside the node.

Let's use the second method you have set up already. You will now be color correcting an unpremultiplied image, but outputting a premultiplied image. After a little rearranging, the tree should look like that in **FIGURE 4.29**.

17. Bring the Offset property back to 0.

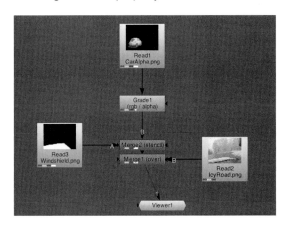

FIGURE 4.29 Your tree should look like this at this point.

Using CurveTool to match black and white points

Thinking back to the introduction of this section, how are you going to find the darkest and lightest points in these two images to match them together? One way, which is valid and happens often, is using your eyes to gauge which are the darkest and brightest pixels. However, the computer is so much better at these kinds of things, and doesn't have to contend with light reflections on the screen, etc.

The Node to use for this is the CurveTool node, which you used in Chapter 3 to find the edges of the lemming element. You can also use this node to find other color-related stuff about your image. Let's bring a CurveTool node in to gauge the darkest and brightest point in the foreground and use that data to stretch the foreground image to a full dynamic range.

1. Select Read1 and branch out by Shift-clicking a CurveTool node in the Image toolbox.

This time you are going to use the Max Luma Pixel Curve Type. This finds the brightest and darkest pixels in the image.

2. In CurveTool1's Properties panel, switch the Curve Type drop-down menu to Max Luma Pixel.

3. Click the Go! button.

4. In the dialog box that opens, click OK as you only want to process one frame.

5. Switch to the MaxLumaData tab and view CurveTool1 in the Viewer (**FIGURE 4.30**).

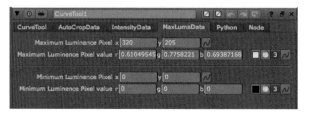

FIGURE 4.30 The MaxLumaData tab's two sections.

The purpose of this operation is to find the darkest and lightest pixels in the image. When switching to this tab you see two sections, the one showing the lightest pixel (Maximum) and the darkest pixel (Minimum). For each, the X and Y location and RGB values display.

NOTE A Constant node creates a solid color with a chosen resolution.

Looking closely you can see that the value of the minimum pixel is 0 in every property. This is because this image is a premultiplied image, and as far as CurveTool is concerned, all that black in the image is as much a part of the image as any other part of it. You need to find a way to disregard that black area. Let's do the following.

6. From the Image toolbox, create a Constant node.

7. Change Constant1's Color value to 0.5.

8. Select Read1 and branch a Merge node from it by pressing Shift-M.

9. Connect Merge3's B input to Constant1, and then view Merge3 in the Viewer (**FIGURE 4.31**).

FIGURE 4.31 The car is on a gray background.

What you did here was replace, momentarily, the black background with a middle gray background. This way you are getting rid of the black and replacing it with a color that is not the darkest nor the lightest in the image. This new image is the image you want to gauge using the CurveTool. You'll need to move the pipe coming in to CurveTool1 (**FIGURE 4.32**).

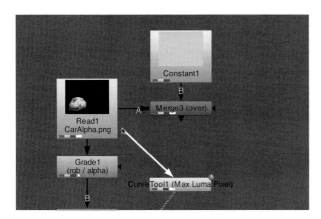

FIGURE 4.32 Moving the pipe from Read1's output to Merge3's output.

10. Click the top half of the pipe going into CurveTool1, which will enable you to move it to the output of Merge3.

11. Double-click CurveTool1 to display its Properties panel in the Properties Bin. Switch to the CurveTool tab (the first one), click Go! again, and click OK.

12. Switch to the MaxLumaData tab again and have a look (**FIGURE 4.33**).

FIGURE 4.33 The updated CurveTool1's MaxLumaData tab.

You can see now that the minimum values are far from being all 0. You are now getting a true result showing the lightest and darkest pixels. Let's make use of them.

13. Close all Properties panels in the Properties Bin to clear some room.

14. Double-click CurveTool1, and then double-click Grade1.

15. View Merge1 in the Viewer.

16. Click the 4 icon next to Grade1's Blackpoint, Whitepoint, Lift, and Gain to enable the four fields.

17. Ctrl/Cmd-drag from CurveTool1's Minimum Luminance Pixel value's Animation menu to Grade1's Blackpoint Animation menu and release the mouse button to create an expression link between them.

18. Do the same from Maximum Luminance Pixel value to Whitepoint (**FIGURE 4.34**).

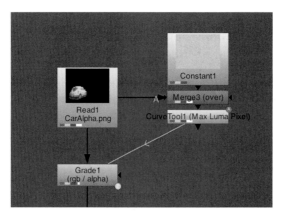

FIGURE 4.34 The green arrow shows the expression link between the two nodes.

The foreground image's dynamic range now spans from a perfect black to a perfect white. This enables you to push those colors to new black and white points to match these points to the background image. You'll need to use another CurveTool to find those points in the background image.

19. Click Read2 and by Shift-clicking, branch out another CurveTool from it.

This time there is no alpha and no black background to worry about. You can simply proceed to finding the black and white points.

20. In CurveTool2's Properties panel, choose Max Luma Pixel from the Curve Type drop-down menu.

21. Click Go! When asked, click OK.

22. When the processing is finished (you should see a quick flash of the Progress Bar) switch to the MaxLumaData tab.

You now have two sets of data to match to: new black points and white points. Let's link them to your Grade node.

23. Close all Properties panels in the Properties Bin to clear some room.

24. Double-click CurveTool2, then double-click Grade1.

25. Ctrl/Cmd-drag from CurveTool2's Minimum Luminance Pixel value's Animation menu to Grade1's Lift Animation menu to create an expression link between them.

26. Do the same from the Maximum Luminance Pixel value to Gain (**FIGURE 4.35**).

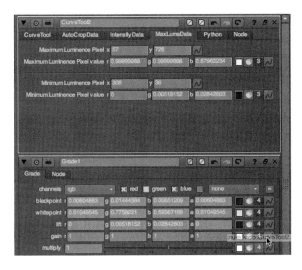

FIGURE 4.35 Dragging while holding Ctrl/Cmd creates a linking expression.

You have now matched the foreground's shadows and highlights to those of the background (**FIGURE 4.36**).

FIGURE 4.36 Shadows and highlights now match.

As you can see from the image, the shadows and highlights are matched, but the image is far from looking matched. The midtones, in this case, make a lot of difference.

Matching midtones by eye

You now need to match the midtones. This is a much more difficult task. You'll start by matching its luma level by eye. Because it is hard to tell what the midtones are, though, you are going to view the luminance of the image in the Viewer.

1. Hover your mouse pointer in the Viewer and press the Y key to view the luminance.

To change the midtones now, you will use the Gamma property. You can see that the whitish snow on the right is a darker gray than the whitish car. Let's bring down the whitish car to that level.

2. Start dragging the Gamma slider down. I stopped at around 0.6.

Notice that the midtones don't match well with a higher Gamma value. Now, however, the lower midtones aren't matching well. I need to use the Multiply property to produce a good match.

3. Bring the Gamma slider up to 0.85 and bring the Multiply slider down a bit to 0.9 (**FIGURE 4.37**).

4. Hover your mouse pointer in the Viewer and press the Y key to view the RGB channels (**FIGURE 4.38**).

FIGURE 4.37 The midtones match better now.

FIGURE 4.38 There is still work to be done on the color of the midtones.

OK, so the midtones' brightness is now better, but you need to change the color of the car's midtones. At the moment, the car is too warm for this winter's day. Matching color is a lot more difficult as you always have three options: red, green, and blue. Matching gray is a lot easier as you only need to decide whether to brighten or darken it. However, as each color image is made out of three gray channels, you can do that to match color too. Here's how.

5. Hover your mouse pointer in the Viewer and press the R key to view the red channel (**FIGURE 4.39**).

FIGURE 4.39 Viewing the red channel.

Now you are looking only at levels of gray. If you now change the red sliders, you will better match the color while still looking only at gray.

6. Display the Color Wheel and Color Sliders panel for the Gamma property by clicking the Color Wheel button.

You will also want to change the Multiply and Offset values to achieve a perfect result. This is because, even though you matched the black point and white point, the distance of the car from the camera means the black point will be higher and the white point lower. At the end of the day, it will only look right when it does, math aside.

Let's display those extra color wheels.

7. Ctrl/Cmd-click the Color Wheel button for the Multiply and Offset properties. Your screen should look like **FIGURE 4.40**.

FIGURE 4.40 Opening three color wheels to easily control three properties.

8. Since you are looking at the red channel in the Viewer, you should change the red sliders for Gamma, Multiply, and Offset until you are happy with the result. Little changes go a long way. I left mine at Gamma: 0.8, Multiply: 0.82, and Offset: 0.02.

9. Display the green channel in the Viewer, and then move the green sliders to change the level of green in your image. Mine is Gamma: 0.85, Multiply: 0.95, and Offset: 0.025.

10. Do the same for the blue channel. Mine is Gamma: 0.96, Multiply: 0.95, and Offset: 0.03.

11. Switch back to viewing the RGB channels (**FIGURE 4.41**).

FIGURE 4.41 Not a bad result at the end of it all.

This is as far as I will take this comp. Of course, you can use your already somewhat-developed skills to make this a better comp, but I'll leave that to you.

Save your script if you wish, and we will move on.

ACHIEVING A "LOOK" WITH THE COLORCORRECT NODE

Giving an image a "look" is a very different practice than matching color. While matching color has a very specific purpose and methodology, giving an image a look refers to an artistic practice that gives an image a different feel to how it was shot. For example, you might want it to look brighter, warmer, or colder, depending on the feeling you want to create.

Using the ColorCorrect node

The ColorCorrect node is a very good tool to use for this as it has a lot of control over the different parts of the image—even more control than the Grade node. But as with everything else, it is still made out of the basic mathematical building blocks covered in the beginning of this chapter.

Let's bring in an image and give it a look.

1. Press Ctrl/Cmd-W to close the color matching script and start a new one.

2. Press the R key and bring in, from the chapter04 folder, the Car.png image again.

3. While the newly imported Read1 node is selected, press the C key to create a ColorCorrect node. You can also find the ColorCorrect node in the Color toolbox.

4. View ColorCorrect1 in the Viewer (**FIGURE 4.42**).

NOTE If Nuke quits altogether, just start Nuke again.

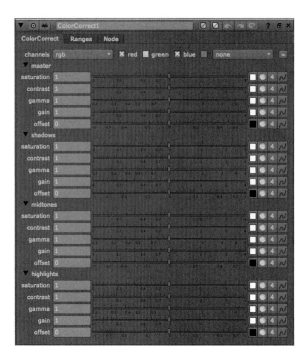

FIGURE 4.42 The ColorCorrect node's Properties panel.

As you can see in ColorCorrect1's Properties panel, the ColorCorrect node includes controls for Saturation, Contrast, Gamma, Gain (Multiply), and Offset (Add). This is performed over either the whole dynamic range—called Master—or parts of the dynamic range called Shadows, Midtones, and Highlights. This makes creating a look somewhat easier.

This idea of midtones, highlights, and shadows changes from image to image. An image of a dark room will have no whites, but in that darkness one can still define that the brighter areas will be that image's highlights, the slightly lighter blacks will be midtones, and the darkest colors shadows. This can also be defined in the ColorCorrect node's Ranges tab.

5. Click the Ranges tab in ColorCorrect1's Properties panel.

   In this tab (similar to ColorLookup, isn't it?) you have three graphs, all selected. One represents the shadows, another the midtones, and a third the highlights (**FIGURE 4.43**).

6. Check the Test check box at the top of the graph.

   This shows a representation in the Viewer of what parts of the image are shadow, midtone, and highlight. Highlights are represented by white, midtones as gray, and shadows as black. Green and magenta areas represent a mix of two ranges (**FIGURE 4.44**).

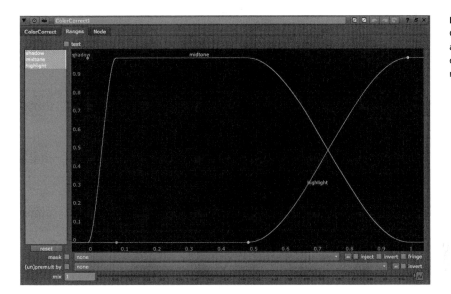

FIGURE 4.43 Color-Correct's Ranges is a lookup curve that defines the brightness ranges.

FIGURE 4.44 The test shows the parts of the dynamic range in the Viewer.

7. Click the Test button at the top of the graph again to turn it off.

    The ranges are fine for this image, so we won't change anything and we will continue working.

8. Switch back to the ColorCorrect tab.

You will now give this image a dreamy, car-commercial look—all soft pseudo blues and bright highlights. If you don't define the "look" you are after in the beginning, you can lose yourself very quickly.

Before changing the color of this image, I'll show you my preferred interface setup for color correcting.

9. In ColorCorrect1's Properties panel, click the Float controls button (looks like two boxes). This will float the Properties panel instead of docking it in the Properties Bin (**FIGURE 4.45**).

FIGURE 4.45 Click this button to float the Properties panel.

10. Hover your mouse pointer in the Viewer and press the Spacebar to maximize the Viewer to the size of the whole interface (**FIGURE 4.46**).

FIGURE 4.46 This is a good way to set the interface for color correction.

Since the Properties panel is floating, it is still there. This way, you can look at the image at its maximum size without wasting space on things like the DAG yet still be able to manipulate the ColorCorrect node.

What I am aiming for is something like that in **FIGURE 4.47**. You can try to reach that yourself, or you can follow my steps point by point.

11. I'll start by desaturating the whole image a little, so in the Master set of properties I set the Saturation property to 0.5.

12. Now for the shadows. I would like to color the shadows a little bluer than normal. Click the Color Wheel button for shadows.gamma.

FIGURE 4.47 This is the image look I am referring to.

13. From the Hue slider, choose a blue hue. I selected 0.6. Now display Saturation for the shadows.gamma color. I set it to 0.31. Finally, adjust the brightness, or Value, slider in the Color Wheel and Color Sliders panel. I have 1.22 (**FIGURE 4.48**).

FIGURE 4.48 Setting the shadow's Gamma properties using the Color Wheel and Color Sliders panel.

This results in RGB values of 0.8418, 0.993, and 1.22, respectively. It gives the image a nice-looking blue shadow tint. Notice that there are actually no hue and saturation sliders in the real Properties. The hue and saturation sliders in the Color Wheel and Color Sliders panel are only there so it will be easier to set the RGB sliders.

14. Close this Color Wheel and Color Sliders panel.

15. You have a lot more work in the midtones. First, set the Saturation to 0, so that the midtones are tinted black and white.

16. To create a flatter palette to work on, set the Contrast for midtones at 0.9.

17. To darken the midtones, set the Gamma to 0.69.

18. Use the Gain property to tint the midtones by clicking the Color Wheel button for midtones.gain.

NOTE If you need to make the Color Wheel and Color Sliders panel bigger, drag the bottom-right corner of the panel.

19. In the Color Wheel and Color Sliders panel that opens, click the TMI button at the top to enable the TMI sliders (**FIGURE 4.49**).

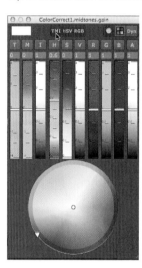

FIGURE 4.49 Turning on the TMI sliders.

20. Now, for a cooler-looking shot, drag the T (temperature) slider up towards the blues. I stopped at 0.72.

21. To correct the hue of the blue, use the M (magenta) slider to make this blue either have more magenta or more green in it. I went towards the green and left it at −0.11.

NOTE As always, only the RGB values affect the image. You just used TMI sliders to set the RGB values in an easier way.

22. Close the Color Wheel and Color Sliders panel (**FIGURE 4.50**).

FIGURE 4.50 The values are always in RGB.

23. You will now increase the highlights a little, so let's start by setting the Contrast to 1.5.

24. To color correct the highlights, first click the 4 icon to enable the Gain slider.

25. Click in the right side of Gain's first field (for the red channel) and use the arrow up and down keys to change the red value. I left it on 0.75 (**FIGURE 4.51**).

FIGURE 4.51 The arrow keys make it easy to nudge values in fields.

26. Leave the next field (green) where it is, but use the arrow keys in the blue field to increase blue. Because I want everything to be a little bluer, I left mine at 1.5.

The first stage of the color correction is finished. Let's bring the rest of the interface back.

27. Close the ColorCorrect1 Properties panel (**FIGURE 4.52**).

FIGURE 4.52 First, close the floating Properties panel.

28. Press the Spacebar to bring back all your panes.

Using the mask input to color correct a portion of the image

Let's say that a movie director asks for the wheels to pop out of the image and have high contrast. To do this secondary color correction, you will need to first define an area to apply the color correction to, then use another Color node and use this area in its mask input.

You haven't learned to create complex mattes yet, but in this case you only really need two radial mattes. You can easily create those using the Radial node in the Draw toolbox.

First, to brighten up the wheels, you will use the Grade node.

1. Select ColorCorrect1 and insert a Grade node after it.

   If you use the Grade node as it is, the whole image will get brighter. You'll need to use Grade1's mask input to define the area to work in.

2. With nothing selected, create a Radial node from the Draw toolbox (**FIGURE 4.53**).

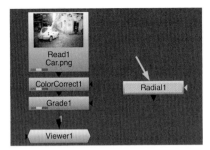

FIGURE 4.53 Creating an unattached Radial node.

3. View Radial1.

   It creates a radial, see? I told you. By moving the edges of the radial box, you can change its shape and location.

4. View Grade1.

5. Drag Radial1's edges until it encompasses the back wheel (**FIGURE 4.54**).

FIGURE 4.54 Radial1 encompasses the back wheel.

You'll need another Radial node to define the second wheel. (You can add as many Radial nodes as you need. Everything in Nuke is a node, remember?)

6. With Radial1 selected, insert another Radial node after it.

7. Adjust Radial2 to encompass the front wheel (**FIGURE 4.55**).

8. To make use of the radials, you will take the mask input for Grade1 and attach it to the output of Radial2, as in **FIGURE 4.56**.

FIGURE 4.55 Using Radial nodes to create masks for color correction

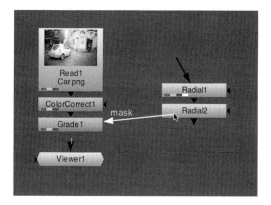

FIGURE 4.56 Attaching the mask input to the mask image.

This means whatever you now do in Grade1 will affect only where the radial's branch is white.

9. Increase the whites by bringing the Whitepoint property for Grade1 down to around 0.51.

10. Some of the deep blacks have become a little too gray, so decrease a little on the Blackpoint property. I left mine at 0.022.

At this point, the grading is finished. Mask inputs can be very important in color correction because a lot of times you only want to color correct an area of the image. But remember not to confuse mask inputs with mattes or alpha channels. The use of the mask input is solely to limit an effect—not to composite one image over another or copy an alpha channel across.

2D TRACKING

This chapter explains how to 2D track in Nuke. *Tracking* means following a group of pixels around from frame to frame and gathering their location on each frame. Tracking makes it possible to gauge how much movement is taking place from frame to frame. You can use this movement information either to cancel that movement out by negating it—called *stabilizing*—or to transfer that movement to another element, called *match-moving*. The way you track in Nuke is via (big surprise here) the Tracker node.

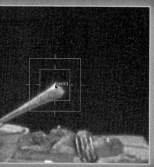

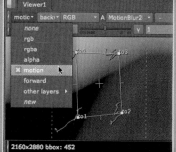

By 2D tracking, I refer to the kind of data you can extract from the image. Because you are following a 2D image, an image projected on the flat screen, you can really only follow the position of pixels as they move around it. The screen and the image have no depth—remember, they are flat. This situation results in nothing but 2D data and 2D transformations, much like the kind of transformation you can create using the Transform node. So you can move in X and Y, but Z doesn't exist. You can scale up and down, and you can rotate around the screen—but not *into* the screen. These are 2D transformations.

3D tracking, also called camera tracking, is the process of extracting the camera information from the image, resulting in 3D transformations. Although 3D tracking uses some of the same initial concepts of 2D tracking, 3D tracking is used in a very different way. (Chapter 10 covers 3D tracking.)

TRACKER NODE BASICS

Nuke's Tracker node is designed to do the two parts of tracking: *accumulating* position data and *applying* position data. The Tracker node is open enough, though, so that you can use the accumulated data in many other nodes by using a linking expression.

In most applications, including Nuke, a tracker point is built out of a tracking anchor, a pattern box, and a search area box. The *tracking anchor* is a single point that collects the position data for the pattern box. The *pattern box* defines the group of pixels to follow from frame to frame. The *search area box* defines where to look for those pixels in the next frame. The tracker point's controls that define these three elements are shown in **FIGURE 5.1**.

FIGURE 5.1 Tracker point anatomy

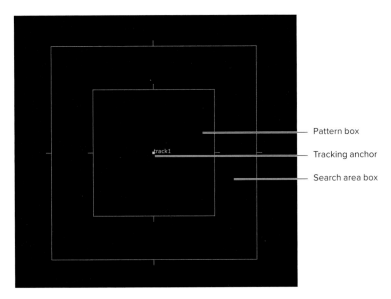

Pattern box

Tracking anchor

Search area box

To track, you need to choose a well-defined pattern—one that has different colored pixels that don't look like other things close to it in the frame—and set the pattern box to engulf that pattern. Then you gauge how far the pattern is moving from frame to frame and set the search area box to cover that part of the image. The tracking anchor is normally automatically set.

You start with a simple exercise in the next section.

STABILIZING A SHOT

In this first exercise you will track a shot in order to stabilize it, meaning stopping it from moving. To give you something to stabilize, bring a sequence in from the disk.

1. Using a Read node, load the sequence named stabilize.####.tif, from the chapter05 directory, and view it in the Viewer.

2. Load Read1 into Framecycler by clicking Read1 and pressing Alt/Option-F. (If you are using the PLE version of Nuke, simply click Play in the Viewer.)

3. Zoom in close to the area in the image where the spoon is, place your mouse pointer over the edge of the spoon handle, and don't move it (**FIGURE 5.2**).

   Notice how much *film weave* there is in this plate. Film weave is the result of the celluloid moving a little inside the camera when shooting on film. You will fix that weave and add some flares to the candle flames.

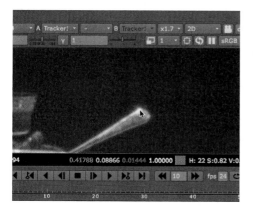

FIGURE 5.2 Placing the mouse pointer and not moving it is a good way to gauge movement.

4. Quit Framecycler, or press Stop in the Viewer.

5. Select Read1 and attach a Tracker node to it from the Transform toolbox.

6. Make sure you're viewing the output of Tracker1 in both the Viewer and frame 1.

   The Tracker node's Properties panel loads into the Properties Bin and looks like **FIGURE 5.3**. Using these controls and the on-screen controls, you can track a feature in the image by defining the pattern box and using the Properties panel.

FIGURE 5.3 The Tracker node's Properties panel.

Tracking buttons

Clear tracking data

Trackers

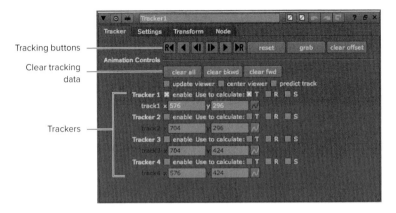

7. In the Viewer, click the center of the tracker point, where it says track1, and move it to the edge of the spoon handle (**FIGURE 5.4**).

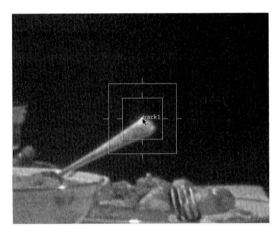

FIGURE 5.4 Placing the tracker point on a good tracking location.

8. In Tracker1's Properties panel click the forward play–looking button, which is the Track Forward button (**FIGURE 5.5**).

Track forward

Track frame forward   Track range forward

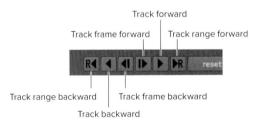

Track range backward   Track frame backward

Track backward

FIGURE 5.5 Pressing the Track Forward button will start tracking to the end of the clip.

The Tracker node starts to follow the pixels inside the pattern box from frame to frame. A Progress Bar displays showing you how long before the Tracker (shorthand for Tracker node) finishes. When the Tracker finishes processing, the tracking part of your work is actually finished. Anything beyond this is not really tracking—it's applying a Tracker's result. You can see the Tracker-accumulated tracking data in the track1.x and track1.y fields in the Properties panel as keyframes (**FIGURE 5.6**).

FIGURE 5.6 The Tracker's accumulated data is held in these fields as animation keyframes.

9. Move back in the Timebar using the left arrow key.

    Look at the track1.x and track1.y fields and how they change to reflect the position of the pattern box in each frame.

    If you subtract the X and Y values in frame 1 from the X and Y values in frame 2, the result will be the movement you need to match the tracked movement. If you take that number and invert it (5 becomes –5), you will negate the movement and stabilize the shot. You can do that for any frame. The frame you are subtracting—in this example, it is frame 1—is called the *reference frame*.

Now that you've successfully tracked the position of the spoon from frame to frame, you probably want to use this to stabilize the shot. This is done in another tab in the Tracker Properties panel.

10. In Tracker1's Properties panel, click the Transform tab.

11. Choose Stabilize from the Transform drop-down menu (**FIGURE 5.7**).

FIGURE 5.7 Using the tracking data to stabilize.

NOTE The Transform tab holds the properties with which you can turn the tracked data into transformations.

    This is all you need to do to stabilize the shot. To make sure the shot is now stabilized, compare it in the Viewer to the unstabilized shot.

12. Select Read1 in the DAG and press 2 on your keyboard.

13. In the Viewer change the center control in the Viewer Composite Control drop-down menu from – to Wipe.

14. Reposition the axis from the center of the frame to just above the spoon handle.

    Notice that Tracker1's transform controls are in the way. You need to get rid of this to see the Viewer properly.

15. Close all Properties panels by clicking the Empty Properties Bin button at the top of the Properties Bin.

16. Press Play in the Viewer and look at both sides of the wipe (**FIGURE 5.8**).

    You can clearly see the stabilization working.

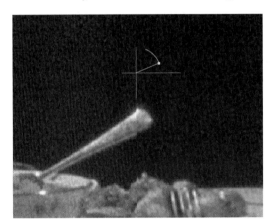

FIGURE 5.8 Wiping between the stabilized and jittery versions of the sequence.

17. Press Stop and change the center control in the Viewer Composite Control drop-down menu back to –.

18. Click Tracker1 and press the 1 key to make sure you're viewing that part of the branch.

Creating an image that is absolutely still is one reason to stabilize a shot. Another reason is to have an easier life when compositing. Instead of match-moving each element (as you do in the next exercise), you can stabilize the shot, comp it, and then bring back the motion using the tracked data you already accumulated. You do this to make compositing a lot easier and so your shot doesn't stand out from the rest of the movie for being absolutely steady.

NOTE The Flare node is a great, very broad tool for creating various types of flares and lighting artifacts.

For this shot, the director asked to "bloom" each candle flame a little. You will add a flare to each candle flame using a node called, you guessed it, Flare from the Draw toolbox.

19. Select Tracker1 and from the Draw toolbox add a Flare node (**FIGURE 5.9**).

20. Drag the center of the flare on the center of the right-most candle flame using the on-screen controls, as shown in **FIGURE 5.10**.

I don't have room to explain every property for the Flare node. It's a very involved and very artistic—hence subjective—tool, which makes it difficult to teach. And let's face it, it has a lot of properties. I encourage you to play with it and see its capabilities, but as far as it applies to tracking, you'll copy some numbers from the list in the next step.

FIGURE 5.9 A new node, Flare1, is inserted after Tracker1.

FIGURE 5.10 Placing the center of the flare on the center of the flame.

21. Copy the following values into the corresponding properties one by one and see what each does. When you're done copying, if you want you can change them to suit your taste:

- Radius = 0, 0, 50

- Ring Color = 1, 0.8, 0.3

- Outer Falloff = 2.3, 2.65, 2.65

- Chroma Spread = 0.1

- Edge Flattening = 6

- Corners = 12

The result of the Flare node should look a lot like **FIGURE 5.11**.

FIGURE 5.11 The flare after treatment.

Now use this Flare to place three more flares in the shot.

22. Copy Flare1 by clicking it and pressing Ctrl/Cmd-C.

23. Make sure Flare1 is still selected and paste another flare by pressing Ctrl/Cmd-V.

You want to move the location of Flare2 to the second candle from the right. This can get confusing because when you paste a node, its Properties panel doesn't automatically load into the Properties Bin, so moving the on-screen control now moves the position for Flare1. You have to be careful which on-screen control you're using.

FIGURE 5.12 Four Flare nodes inserted one after the other.

24. Close Flare1's Properties panel.

25. Double-click Flare2 to load its Properties panel.

26. Move Flare2's position to the second candle.

27. Repeat the process twice more for the other two candles.

Your image should have four flares on it—one on each candle. Your tree should look like **FIGURE 5.12**.

What's left to do now is to bring back the film weave you removed in the first step. You already have all the tracking data in Tracker1. You can now copy it and insert it at the end of the tree to bring back the transformation that you removed before.

28. Copy Tracker1, click Flare4, and paste.

Tracker2 is then inserted after Flare4.

When you return a composited shot, it's important to return it exactly as it was provided—except for making the changes requested. Your shot, remember, is often just one in a sequence.

NOTE Keep in mind that every time you move an image around, some filtering occurs. Filtering means a kind of little blur that degrades the image a little. Moving an image twice like this creates two levels of filtering. Doing that a lot will in effect soften your image. On occasion this is a must, but in general you should avoid it. Here it served as a good way to show both stabilizing and match-moving together.

29. Double-click Tracker2 to open its Properties panel.

30. Click the Transform tab and choose Match-move from the Transform drop-down menu.

31. Make sure you're viewing Tracker2 in the Viewer.

32. Click Play in the Viewer.

You can see that the motion data was returned as it was before, except now it has flares, which are weaving just like the rest of the picture.

33. Save your project in your student_files directory with a name you find fitting.

34. Press Ctrl/Cmd-W to close the Nuke script and create a fresh one.

Next you will go deeper into tracking.

TRACKING FOUR POINTS

In this section you track more than a simple 2D position. How and what do I mean by that? Read on.

Understanding tracking points

In the preceding section you only dealt with movement in the horizontal and vertical position axes. There was no rotation and no scale. That means that every pixel in the image was moving in the same way as its neighbor. This situation doesn't happen very often. Usually elements on-screen move more freely and tend to at least rotate (meaning around the screen's axis) and move towards or away from the camera—thus scaling. So aside from position, there is also rotation and scale. All these are strictly 2D movements (movements you can find in Nuke Transform node, for example) because the element is always facing the camera. There are movements that include changing the angle an element has to the camera. I call this *perspective movement*.

To track rotational value, scaling, or perspective movement, you need more than one tracking point. Using just one tracking point, as you did in the preceding section, can only produce 2D position data. However, using more tracking points (or more track-ers, though I don't want to confuse this term with the Tracker node) and calculating the relationship between their positions you can also figure out rotation, scale, and even limited perspective movement. Traditionally there are three types of tracking:

- One point tracking: This can produce movement in the horizontal and vertical positional axes only.

- Two point tracking: This can produce movement in the same way as one point tracking, but can also produce 2D rotation and scale.

- Four point tracking: This kind of track combination produces *perspective movement*—movement in the pseudo third dimension (not really 3D but looks like 3D). In other words, you can produce things that are turning away from the camera.

By tracking the right number of points, you can tell Nuke to create the right kind of movement using the Tracker node—be it stabilizing or match-moving that movement. You do this by activating move tracks, tracking each one in turn, and then using the T, R, and S check boxes, shown in **FIGURE 5.13**, to tell Nuke to use a track to create T (transform), R (rotation), and S (scale) movement.

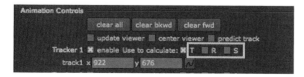

FIGURE 5.13 These three check boxes tell Nuke what kind of movement to create.

Another way to produce complicated movement is to use the Tracker node to accumulate position data on several points and then copy the data to other nodes and use them however needed. It's important to understand that, foremost, tracking data is simply *positional* data, and you can use it in whatever creative way you can think of.

Tracking a picture in the frame

You are now going to track four points and then take the tracking information outside of the Tracker node. For that, you need to start with something to track.

1. Using a Read node from the chapter05 directory, double click frame.####.png.

2. Save this Nuke script to your student_files folder and call it frame_v01.

3. Make sure you are viewing Read1 in the Viewer and press the Play button to watch the clip (**FIGURE 5.14**). Remember to stop playback when you're done.

FIGURE 5.14 A picture frame on a table.

What you are seeing is a picture frame on a table with a handheld camera going around it. You need to replace the picture in the frame. The movement happens in more than two dimensions (though, of course, as far as the screen is concerned everything is moving just in two dimensions). The picture changes its perspective throughout the shot. That means you will have to track four individual points, one for each corner of the frame, to be able to mimic the movement.

The Tracker node has the ability to track up to four tracking points.

4. Insert a Tracker node after Read1.

5. Turn on all four tracking points by checking the boxes to the left of Tracker 2, 3, and 4. The one next to Tracker 1 is checked by default (**FIGURE 5.15**).

6. Make sure you're viewing Tracker1 in the Viewer and that you are on frame 1 in the Timebar.

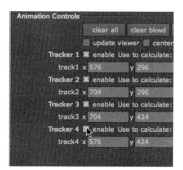

FIGURE 5.15 Activating all four tracking points.

7. In the Viewer, drag the four tracking points to the four corners of the frame, as in **FIGURE 5.16**.

8. Now resize the pattern boxes so they're a lot smaller, and the search area box so it's bigger, similar to **FIGURE 5.17**.

FIGURE 5.16 Locations to place the 4 trackers.

FIGURE 5.17 Adjusting the reference and search areas.

9. Click the Track Forward button and hope for the best.

Chances are it didn't work on the first go. Trackers, even Nuke's very good ones, aren't magicians. You need to give them a good pattern to follow, and even then they can fail.

Here's a list of things to do to improve your tracking:

- Don't track more than one tracking point at a time, as you just attempted now. It makes things more difficult. Turn off all the trackers but one, focus on that tracker until you have a good track for it, then move on.

It's all about the pattern and search areas. Select good ones and you're home free. A good pattern has a lot of contrast in it, is unique in that it doesn't look like anything around it, and it doesn't change much in its appearance except its location from frame to frame.

If you try once, it doesn't work, and you have to go back, go back to the last good frame and click the Clear Fwd button (short for forward) to delete the keyframes already generated (**FIGURE 5.18**). You can click Clear All to clear everything, and Clear Bkwd (short for backward) if you are tracking backwards.

FIGURE 5.18 The clear buttons.

TIP To stop a track, click the Cancel button on the Progress Bar. It's the only way to stop the tracker from working.

View the result of your track in the Curve Editor. It's a handy way to see if you have a good track or not. Simply right-click (Ctrl-click) the Animation menu for that tracker and choose Curve Editor (you learn more about the Curve Editor in Chapter 6).

Changing the Tracker settings

The Tracker Settings tab has properties that change the way the Tracker performs its tracking operation. The following list covers a few things in the Settings tab that can help you with your tracking (**FIGURE 5.19**).

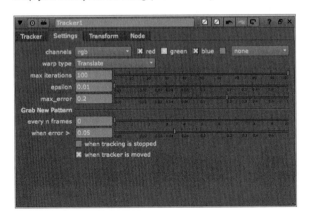

FIGURE 5.19 Tracker1's Settings tab.

You don't have to track on all channels. Sometimes the best reference is only on, say, the green channel. There are many reasons for choosing different channels and you will learn this as you gain experience. For example, the blue channel usually has a lot of noise in it, which can create a jerky track. Turning the blue channel off might help smooth the track a little.

The Epsilon parameter stands for how accurate a track needs to be (I'm sure if they'd put their thinking caps on they could have found a slightly friendlier term).

By default, Epsilon is set to 99%—or 1% wrong. This means that if the tracker found the pattern in the next frame with 99% accuracy, it won't bother looking to see if there's a better match elsewhere. If you know your pattern changes dramatically from frame to frame, this might need to be reduced. If you want a more precise track, you might want to increase the Epsilon property.

▓ Max_error means in what level of accuracy the track will fail. By default, an error rate of 20% and above will stop the tracker.

▓ Changing the Grab New Pattern every *n* frame to something beyond 0 causes the pattern area to update according to the value set in the field. A value of 2 means that a new pattern is grabbed for matching every two frames. This is good for patterns that change dramatically from frame to frame, due to light fluctuations, distortion, or even simple scaling. Notice that the second property in that section means that if the quality of the track falls below 95% accurate (or 5% wrong) a new pattern is grabbed anyway.

Now that I explained the different options you have for tracking with the Tracker node and gave you some tips, I will leave it up to you to get a good track for each of the points. The most important thing, in this case, is to track each tracking point individually. By the way, I'll tell you a secret: I got a good track without changing anything in the Settings tab—just getting a good pattern is enough. Try one pattern, and if it doesn't work, clear the track and try something else. In this exercise a good pattern means, for example, not to include the white part of the wall for the top-right point, because that will change and move in a different way to the picture frame you are tracking.

1. Use the preceding tips to track the image precisely on all four tracks. Keep the four trackers on the four corners of the frame, though.

2. When you're finished, make sure all the tracker check boxes are on (**FIGURE 5.20**).

FIGURE 5.20 After you turn on all the tracker check boxes, your frame should look like this.

NOTE If you fail to track, gave up after 10 seconds, or can't be bothered, you can import a Nuke script called good_track.nk from the chapter05 directory. This is the successful result of the track I did, and you can use it or use yours, it's up to you. If you want to use this script, first delete the Tracker1 node. Then import this script with File > Import Script. A new Tracker node will appear in your DAG. Connect its input to Read1's output. View Tracker1 and double-click it to load it into the Properties Bin.

Using the Tracker node, choose Match-move from the Transform drop-down menu in the Transform tab to apply the tracking data. However, I'd like you to broaden your horizons, so in the example in the next section you don't use the Tracker node to apply the movement. Instead you use another tool and some simple expressions to *link* the properties together.

Replacing the picture

You need a picture to place in the frame.

1. From the chapter05 directory, bring in the file called statue.jpg with a Read node and view it in the Viewer (**FIGURE 5.21**).

    You will insert part of this Buddha image into the frame.

FIGURE 5.21 One little Buddha soon to be placed in a frame.

2. Select Read2 and from the Draw toolbox insert a Rectangle node.

    This node creates, as you might guess, rectangular shapes. In this case, you only want to create the shape in the alpha channel.

3. From Rectangle1's Output drop-down menu, choose Alpha. Make sure you are viewing Rectangle1 in the Viewer.

    To create a nice framing for the statue, use the on-screen controls to move the rectangle until you are happy with how it looks.

4. Drag the rectangle or enter values in the Properties panel to frame the image. The Area property will show values similar to: 500, 790, 1580, 2230 (**FIGURE 5.22**).

FIGURE 5.22 The edges of Rectangle1's on-screen controls will end up being the edge of your picture in the frame.

5. You now need to multiply the RGB with the alpha to create a premultiplied image. Attach a Premult node from the Merge toolbox after Rectangle1.

Because you're not going to use the Tracker node to move the picture around, you will need another transformation tool. CornerPin is specifically designed for this kind of perspective operation, so you will use it in this exercise. CornerPin moves the four corners of the image into new positions—exactly the data the Tracker node accumulates.

6. Attach a CornerPin node from the Transform toolbox after Premult1 (**FIGURE 5.23**).

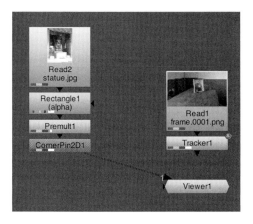

FIGURE 5.23 Your tree should look like this now.

Now that you set up most of the tools, you need to copy the tracking information into the CornerPin node. You'll do that with expressions.

Expressions might sound scary to some, but many others already use them. You also used expressions in Chapters 3 and 4.

The Tracker and CornerPin nodes were created to work well together. You'll see why in a moment.

7. Close all Properties panels and then double-click CornerPin2D1 and Tracker1—in that order—to load both of them into the Properties Bin.

8. Ctrl/Cmd-drag from the track1 Animation menu to CornerPin2D1's To1 Animation menu. Only release the mouse button and keys when you reach the destination (**FIGURE 5.24**).

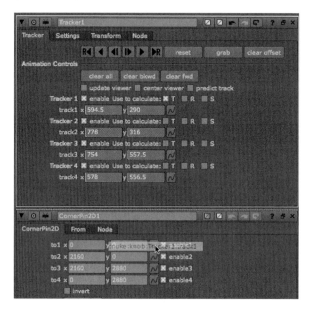

FIGURE 5.24 Dragging from the Animation menu while holding Ctrl/Cmd creates a linking expression.

The color of CornerPin2D1's To1 Property field turned a light blue. This indicates animation (**FIGURE 5.25**).

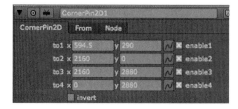

FIGURE 5.25 A light blue color in the field indicates animation.

So how come, all of a sudden, you have animation in this property? You haven't created any keyframes. Let's see…

9. Choose Edit Expression from CornerPin2D1's To1 Animation menu; this opens the Expression panel (**FIGURE 5.26**).

FIGURE 5.26 The Expression panel.

The Expression panel shows a simple expression that points the current property to "look" at the values of another property. It calls for the node (Tracker1) and then the property itself (track1). The word *parent* is not a necessity and can be dropped (if you want you can delete it and the dot after it). Also, there is no need to specify X and Y for horizontal and vertical movement, because Nuke is smart enough to work that out itself in this case. Nuke does this by matching the X value at source to the X value at destination and then doing the same for Y. You can link any kind of property to any kind of property; it doesn't have to be positioned as it is here. You can connect the Gain property of a Grade node to the Size property of a Blur node. If the source destination had only one value or values that were named differently than X and Y (like W and H, for example for Width and Height values), then you would have to specify X and Y (or whatever it needed to be—W, for example).

A green line appears in the DAG showing that a property in CornerPin2D1 is following a property in Tracker1 (**FIGURE 5.27**).

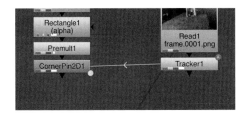

FIGURE 5.27 The green line indicates a linking expression.

Let's have you write an expression yourself next.

10. Don't close the Expression panel. Make sure the top row is highlighted and copy the text with Ctrl/Cmd-C.

11. Click Cancel.

12. Click CornerPin2D1's To2 Animation menu and choose Edit Expression.

13. In the Expression panel that opens, paste the copied expression into the X property field.

14. You don't want to copy data from track1 now, so change the last digit to 2, so you'll have parent.Tracker1.track2.

15. Do the same for the Y expression.

    You have now written an expression. How liberating!

16. Perform the same steps, choosing your favorite method, on the other two proper-
    ties: To3 and To4 for track3 and track4 respectively.

The Viewer should now display an image that looks like **FIGURE 5.28**.

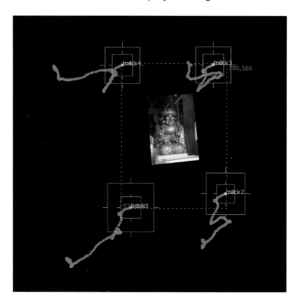

FIGURE 5.28 The CornerPin node positions the edges of the frame by default.

Adjusting the source pins

Look carefully in the Viewer and you can see that the edges of the frame moved rather than the edges of your rectangle or your new masked picture. To fix that, you need to specify source corners. Nuke's CornerPin node allows for that.

1. In CornerPin2D1's Properties panel, switch to the From tab.

2. Close Tracker1's Properties panel and view Premult1 in the Viewer.

3. Move the four From pins (from1, from2, from3, and from4) to the edge of the image. It's easier to do while viewing the alpha channel.

4. View CornerPin2d1's output in the Viewer (make sure you are viewing RGB) and switch back to the CornerPin2D tab in CornerPin2D1's Properties panel.

    You can see here that the To points are sitting on the edges of the image, which is what you were after (**FIGURE 5.29**).

TIP If you change the source pins while viewing CornerPin2D1, you will find adjusting the pins impossible because you'll keep changing what you are viewing, creating a kind of feedback. This is why it is important to view the preceding node—Premult1.

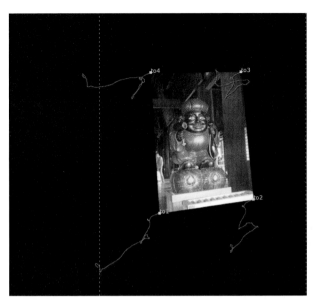

FIGURE 5.29
Adjusting the From
pins made the To pins
move to the correct
place.

You need to now place the new, moving image on top of the frame background.

5. Select CornerPin2D1 and press the M key to insert a Merge node after it.

6. Attach Merge1's B input to Read1 (**FIGURE 5.30**).

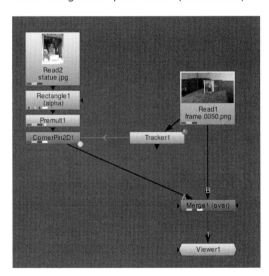

FIGURE 5.30 Merging
the foreground and
background branches.

7. View Merge1 in the Viewer (**FIGURE 5.31**).

    Sits beautifully, snug, in the frame, doesn't it? Too snug maybe.

FIGURE 5.31 The picture now sits in the frame, but it can use some more work.

8. Double-click Rectangle1 to load its Properties panel into the Properties Bin.

9. Set the Softness value to 20.

You also need to blur the image a little—it was scaled down so much by the Corner-Pin node that it has become too crisp and looks foreign to the background.

10. Attach a Blur node to CornerPin2D1 and set its Size value to 2.

You have now added motion to an image that didn't used to have it. When that happens outside the computer, the image gets blurred according to the movement. Doing it after the fact on the computer is called adding *motion blur*. It is important to add motion blur to movements generated inside Nuke to make them more real look-ing; the next section happens to be about just that.

Adding motion blur

Here we will look at two of the several ways to add motion blur. In every motion-gen-erating node there's a motion blur property you can turn on. Although that's a rather taxing option on the ol' processor, it is sometimes used. **FIGURE 5.32** shows the three motion blur properties.

FIGURE 5.32 Motion blur properties.

The three properties are explained here:

- Motionblur is the quality of the motion blur applied. A higher number results in a slower render, but produces a better result. A value of 1 is adequate.

- Shutter is how long the motion blur will be. The default 0.5 mimics normal real-world camera settings, and if you are familiar with real-world film cameras, equals a camera shutter angle of 180 degrees.

- Shutter Offset defines how the blur behaves in relation to the current frame. The blur can precede the motion, come after it, be centered around it (the default), or follow any custom in-between.

The second motion blur method involves generating motion vectors. Nuke has the ability to turn the movement values it is generating within the system into motion data and then use that data to motion blur the image. *Motion vectors* are defined as color values for each pixel in the image representing movement in X and Y. Here's how it's done.

1. Select Blur1 and connect a MotionBlur2D node to it from the Filter toolbox.

2. Connect MotionBlur2D1's second input, called "2D transf," to CornerPin2D1 (**FIGURE 5.33**).

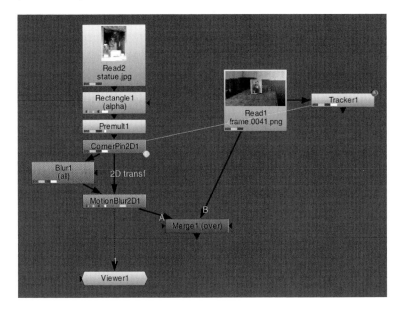

FIGURE 5.33 Connecting the MotionBlur2D node.

MotionBlur2D takes the motion data from the transformation input (that has to be a 2D transformation node) and adds it as a separate channel set to the stream connected to MotionBlur2D1's first input. You can then use the colors in this new channel set to create motion blur.

3. Go to frame 50 in the Timebar.

4. While viewing MotionBlur2D1, switch the channel you are viewing in the Viewer (top left of the Viewer) from RGBA to Motion (**FIGURE 5.34**).

   The red-green image you see is a color representation of the movement the CornerPin node is creating. These are the motion vectors mentioned earlier.

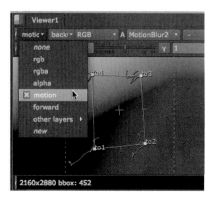

FIGURE 5.34 Viewing a channel set other than RGBA for a change.

5. Switch back to viewing the RGBA channel set.

To actually have motion blur, you need to use a filter node called VectorBlur. Vector-Blur knows how to take motion vector images, like the ones created by MotionBlur2D or rendered out of 3D applications, and turn them into motion blur.

6. Attach a VectorBlur node from the Filter toolbox after MotionBlur2D1.

7. Set the UV Channels property for VectorBlur1 to Motion.

   Because you created the motion vector data in the motion channel set, you are calling for it here as well.

8. Increase the Multiply property to a value of 100 or so, just to see how the direction of blur matches the direction of motion. View Merge1 (**FIGURE 5.35**).

FIGURE 5.35 The VectorBlur node blurs in the direction of the motion.

9. Bring the Multiply value back to 1.

Now with motion blur added, you can view your final composite in Framecycler (or the Viewer).

10. Select Merge1 and press Alt/Option-F to view the final output in Framecycler.

11. When the render finishes click Play and have a look (**FIGURE 5.36**).

FIGURE 5.36 This is what the final result should look like.

One thing is missing: some kind of reflection. You will take care of that in Chapter 10.

12. Close Framecycler.

13. Save your script. This is very important because you will need it again for Chapter 10 (**FIGURE 5.37**).

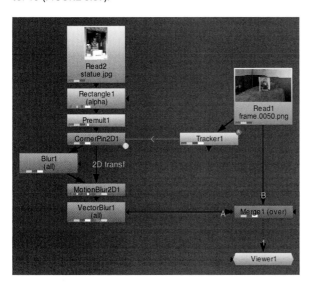

FIGURE 5.37 The final Nuke tree should look like this.

ROTOPAINT

Roto and *paint* are two tools I thought would be long gone by now. In fact, I thought that back in 1995 when I started compositing. Nowadays I realize these tools are always going to be with us—at least until computers can think the way we do. Fortunately, the tools for roto and paint are getting better and better all the time and are used more and more often. Learning how to use these two techniques is even more important today than it used to be.

Roto, short for *rotoscoping*, is a technique in which you follow the outline and movement of an object to extract it from the shot, usually with some kind of shape-generation tool. Normally, that tool is called a *spline*, which generates a *matte* that you use to extract the object from the scene. Because a spline is designed to generate shapes, there is nothing stopping you from using it to generate any kind of shape for whatever purpose.

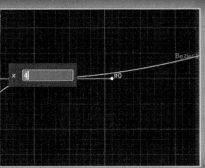
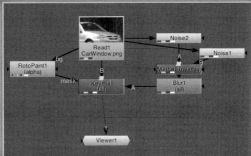

Paint is simply a way to paint on the frame using brushes and similar tools we've all grown accustomed to, such as a *clone* tool (sometimes called a *stamp* tool). This tool is rarely available in a compositing system as a way to paint beautiful pictures, but rather to fix specific problems such as holes in mattes and or spots on pretty faces and to draw simple, but sometimes necessary, doodles (I can't really call them paintings).

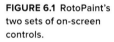

NOTE Up to version 6, when RotoPaint was introduced, two separate tools served these functions. One was called Paint and the other called Bézier. They are still available (although hidden) in Nuke for backwards compatibility.

In Nuke, roto and paint are combined in one tool that can generate both roto shapes and paint strokes as well as handle a few other tasks. I therefore sometimes refer to this single node as a system (the RotoPaint system), because it is more than just a simple node, as you will soon find out.

INTRODUCING ROTOPAINT'S INTERFACE

Nuke's RotoPaint node is a full-blown manual matte extraction and touchup tool designed to do everything from rotoscoping, fixing little problems in mattes, and cleaning hairs from dirty film plates to making shapes, creating simple drawings, and so on. Keep in mind that although RotoPaint is versatile, it's not a replacement for Adobe Photoshop or Corel Painter. You won't draw your next masterpiece on it. Not that I haven't tried.

Go ahead and load a RotoPaint node; it makes it a lot easier to learn its interface.

1. With a new script open in Nuke, create a RotoPaint node by clicking it in the Draw toolbox (or pressing the P key).

2. View RotoPaint1 in the Viewer.

In the Viewer, you will see a third line of buttons (the Tool Settings bar) at the top and a new line of buttons (the Toolbar) on the left (**FIGURE 6.1**).

FIGURE 6.1 RotoPaint's two sets of on-screen controls.

In the Toolbar at left, you can choose from the various tools that display and click each icon to display a menu of more tools (**FIGURE 6.2**).

The Tool Settings bar at the top lets you define settings for the selected tools. This bar changes depending on the tool you choose (**FIGURE 6.3**).

FIGURE 6.3 These are the Selection tool's settings.

The first two tools in the Toolbar on the left are the Select and Point tools, which enable you to select and manipulate shapes and strokes.

The rest of the tools are the actual drawing tools and are split into two sections: shape-drawing tools (the roto part) and stroke-drawing tools (the paint part). The shape-drawing tools are listed in **TABLE 6.1**.

FIGURE 6.2 RotoPaint's Toolbar.

TABLE 6.1 Shape-Drawing Tools

Icon		Tool Function
	Bézier	Creates Bézier shapes. Bézier shapes are defined by using Bézier handles.
	B-Spline	Creates B-Spline shapes. These shapes are defined using points with variable tension.
	Ellipse	Creates an ellipse-shaped Bézier.
	Rectangle	Creates a rectangle-shaped Bézier.

The stroke drawing tools are listed in **TABLE 6.2**.

TABLE 6.2 Stroke-Drawing Tools

Icon		Tool Function
	Brush	Allows for paint strokes in various colors.
	Eraser	Erases previous paint strokes and shapes.
	Clone	Copies pixels from one location in the frame to another. Can copy from different frames as well.
	Reveal	Copies pixels from one image to another.
	Blur	Blurs the image where you draw.

continues

TABLE 6.2 Stroke-Drawing Tools (continued)

Icon		Tool Function
	Sharpen	Sharpens the image where you draw.
	Smear	Smears the image along the direction of your paint stroke.
	Dodge	A brush stroke that brightens the image you are painting on.
	Burn	A brush stroke that darkens the image you are painting on.

Painting strokes

Try drawing something to get a feel for how this node works. Start by drawing some paint strokes.

1. Make sure you're viewing RotoPaint1 by clicking it and pressing the 1 key (so far the Properties panel was open, so you were seeing the on-screen controls in the Viewer, but you weren't actually viewing the output of RotoPaint1 in the Viewer).

2. Select the Brush tool at the left of the Viewer.

   At the top of the Viewer you will see the Tool Settings bar change to reflect your selection. You now have controls for the Brush tool, including opacity, size, color, and more (**FIGURE 6.4**).

FIGURE 6.4 The Tool Settings bar reflecting the Brush settings.

3. With the Brush tool selected, start painting on-screen. Create a few strokes. Change the brush size, color, and opacity. (Use the Color Picker button to change the color.)

   The settings from the Tool Settings bar are mirrored in the Properties panel. You can find generic controls, such as color and opacity, for all shapes and strokes for RotoPaint at the center of the Properties panel (**FIGURE 6.5**).

TIP In addition to using the Tool Settings bar to resize the brush, you can also Shift-click-drag on the Viewer to scale the size of the brush.

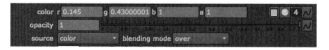

FIGURE 6.5
General properties.

4. Switch to the Stroke tab (**FIGURE 6.6**).

   Here you can find other controls applicable only for strokes, such as brush size, hardness, spacing, and more.

   You can play with all those controls for as long as you like (**FIGURE 6.7**).

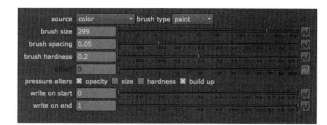

FIGURE 6.6 Stroke-specific properties.

FIGURE 6.7 Can you tell I didn't even use a tablet to draw this?

5. Switch back to the RotoPaint tab.

6. Move one frame forward in the Timebar.

All the strokes you drew have disappeared. The Tool Settings bar now allows you to specify the length of strokes using the last unlabeled drop-down menu on the right. The menu shows Single, meaning just a single-frame stroke. The good thing is, though, that you can change stroke time lengths after you draw them.

Editing strokes

In a tree-based compositing application—and in Nuke specifically—creating paint strokes is done with timing in mind. Sometimes you need to create a stroke that will last only a frame, sometimes it's an *infinite* stroke (one that lasts throughout the whole length of the composition and beyond). Sometimes you need a stroke to start at a specific frame and go all the way to the end of the composition, and sometimes you just need it to appear in a specific range.

You can change the length of strokes using the Lifetime Type property in the Lifetime tab (**FIGURE 6.8**), the drop-down menu, or the buttons (the functionality is the same). The options are:

- **All Frames:** Meaning all frames, beyond your composition, to infinity and beyond.

- **Start To Frame:** From the beginning of the sequence to the current frame.

- **Single Frame:** Just the current frame.

- **Frame To End:** From the current frame to the sequence end.

- **Frame Fange:** A defined start and end.

FIGURE 6.8 Lifetime properties.

Now, click the All Frames button. Your last stroke now exists throughout the clip and beyond—infinitely. Even if you now make your comp longer, the stroke will be there, no matter long you make the composition.

Painting in vectors

You can do changes on the fly in Nuke because the RotoPaint system is *vector* based. In other words, pixels aren't *really* being drawn by your mouse strokes. When you "draw" a stroke, a path is created called a vector, which mathematically describes the shape of the stroke. You can then use this vector to apply a paint stroke in any number of shapes and sizes, and, for that matter, functionality. This means you can change your paint strokes after you draw them, which is very powerful and saves a lot of time.

To be able to change stroke settings after they have been created, you need a way to select strokes. You do that in the Stroke/Shape List window, also called the Curves window (**FIGURE 6.9**).

FIGURE 6.9 The Stroke/Shape List window.

1. Click the second-to-last stroke you created in the Stroke/Shape List window.

2. Click the All Frames button again.

   Your second-to-last stroke now exists infinitely. Now for the rest of the brush strokes.

   TIP You can make your Stroke/Shape List window bigger by dragging the bottom-right corner of the Properties panel.

3. Select all the brush strokes by clicking the topmost one, scrolling down, and Shift-clicking the last one.

4. Click the All Frames button again.

   Now your whole picture is back as it exists infinitely. How exciting!

5. Select a stroke in the list and switch to the Stroke tab.

6. Practice changing the stroke's properties such as opacity and size.

7. Click the Select tool—the arrow-shaped tool at the top of the RotoPaint Toolbar.

8. To select stroke points, you need to select the Allow Paint Selection check box on the Tool Settings bar (**FIGURE 6.10**).

FIGURE 6.10 Turn on Allow Paint Selection to change a stroke's vector.

9. Now select a stroke on-screen by marqueeing some points together and move them around. The box that displays around the selected points allows for scaling and rotation (**FIGURE 6.11**).

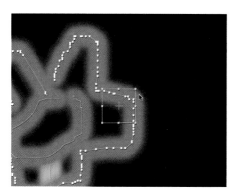

FIGURE 6.11 The box around selected vector points allows for greater manipulation.

Erasing and deleting strokes

Say I drew a lovely picture, but made a mistake. What if I want to erase or delete something?

1. Double-click the Paint tool to access the Eraser tool, and then draw on-screen where you drew before.

   The Eraser erases previous paint strokes. It does *not* erase the image (if you have one connected in RotoPaint's input) in any way, and it's a paint stroke just like any other.

2. Switch back to the Select tool and click to select a stroke to delete.

3. Notice that the selected stroke is highlighted in the Stroke/Shape List window. Click it there as well.

4. Press Backspace/Delete to delete the stroke.

OK, that's enough editing of brush strokes for now.

NOTE The Stroke/Shape List window also allows you to change the order of your strokes. Simply select a stroke and drag it up or down and let go.

NOTE Because Roto-Paint is vector based, you can also edit strokes by changing the vector that draws them.

NOTE If you happened to click the actual name of the stroke, then pressing the Backspace/Delete key will just delete the name. You need to click the icon to the left of the name.

Drawing and editing shapes

It's time to start practicing drawing shapes. For that you will need a new RotoPaint node.

1. Clear the Properties Bin.

2. With nothing selected in the DAG, press the P key to create another RotoPaint node, RotoPaint2.

3. View RotoShape2 in the Viewer. You're going to focus on drawing Béziers.

4. Choose the Bézier tool by clicking it on the RotoPaint Toolbar, or hovering in the Viewer and pressing V on the keyboard.

5. Start drawing a curve by clicking in the Viewer. Make whatever shape you like. A simple click will result in a linear key for the shape, whereas a click and drag will create a smooth key. It is important you finish drawing the curve by clicking the first point again.You can continue adding points after you draw the shape.

6. To add points after the curve is finished, Ctrl-Alt/Cmd-Option-click.

7. Switch back to the Select tool by clicking it in the Toolbar.

You can now keep changing and editing the shape. You can move points around, change what kind of point you have, delete points, or add points.

You can choose a point and right-click (Ctrl-click) to display a contextual menu (**FIGURE 6.12**) with all sorts of editing options, or you can use hot keys. **TABLE 6.3** lists some hot keys to use with selected Bézier points.

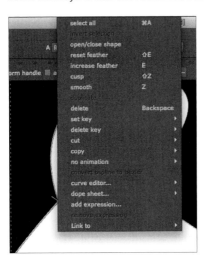

FIGURE 6.12 Right-clicking/ Ctrl-clicking a point on a shape opens the contextual menu.

TABLE 6.3 Bézier Hot Keys

Hot Key	Function
Z	Make tangent handles horizontal on selected points (smooth).
Shift-Z	Make selected points linear (cusp).
Ctrl/Cmd-click-drag	Break tangent handles for selected points. Click handle.
Delete	Remove selected control point.
Ctrl-Alt/Cmd-Option-click	Create points on an existing curve.

8. Go ahead and play with the points and tangents, using the hot keys to move your shape around.

9. You can also click and drag points together to create a marquee and then use the box that pops up to move points around as a group (**FIGURE 6.13**).

   You can blur the whole spline from the Properties panel.

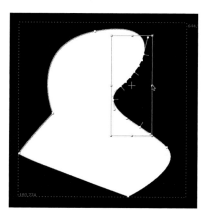

FIGURE 6.13 Transforming a group of points together.

10. Click the Shape tab then display the Feather property's slider to blur outside the spline. You can also reduce the slider to below 0 to blur within the spline.

    The Feather Falloff property lets you choose how hard or soft the feathering will be (**FIGURE 6.14**).

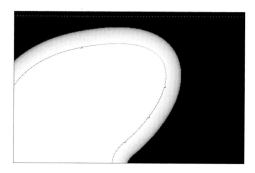

FIGURE 6.14 A high Feather setting with a low Feather Falloff setting.

The default Feather Falloff value of 1 is a linear gradient. Values above 1 are a harder falloff, and values below 1 are a softer falloff.

11. Reset the Feather Falloff property to 1 and the Feather property to 0.

You can also create specific feathered areas instead of feathering the whole shape. I sometimes call these *soft edges*.

12. Pull out a soft edge from the Bézier itself by holding Ctrl/Cmd and pulling on a point or several points (**FIGURE 6.15**).

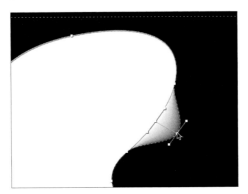

FIGURE 6.15 Pull out a soft edge by holding Ctrl/Cmd.

NOTE You don't have to remember all these hot keys. You can see all of them in the contextual menu by right-clicking/ Ctrl-clicking a point.

13. To remove a soft edge (and bring back the secondright-click (Ctrl-click)right-click/ Ctrl-click a point and choose Reset Feather from the drop-down menu.

Animating a shape

Now you will try animating a shape.

1. Advance to frame 11 in the Timebar and with the Select All tool click a point to move your Bézier around a little and change the shape.

2. Move the Timebar from the first keyframe to the second keyframe and see the shape animating from one to the other.

Keyframes are added automatically in RotoPaint due to the Autokey check box being checked in the Tool Settings bar (**FIGURE 6.16**).

The Autokey check box is checked by default, meaning the moment you start drawing a shape, a keyframe for that shape is created and gets updated on that frame as you are creating the shape. Moving to another frame and changing the shape creates another keyframe and thus creates animation. If, before you start drawing, you uncheck the Autokey check box, drawing will not create a keyframe. If you then move to another frame and change the shape, no keyframe will be created either, and neither will animation. Having a keyframe and then

FIGURE 6.16 Changing the shape will result in a keyframe for which the Autokey check box is checked.

unchecking the Autokey check box, and then changing the shape will only do those things temporarily—if you move to the next frame, the shape will immediately snap to the last available keyframe. You have to turn on the Autokey check box if you want to keep the new shape after changing it.

3. Go to frame 4 in the Timebar and move the spline again to create another keyframe.

4. Move the Timebar to see the shape animating between the three keyframes.

You can also animate other things for the shape, such as its overall feather.

5. Go to frame 1. In the Shape tab click the feather's Animation menu, and choose Set Key (**FIGURE 6.17**).

The color of the Feather field changes to bright blue, indicating a keyframe.

FIGURE 6.17 Setting a keyframe for a Shape property.

6. Go to frame 11.

The color of the numeric box is now light blue to indicate there is some animation associated with this property, but no keyframe at this frame.

7. Change the Feather property to 100.

The color of the box changes to a bright blue.

8. Go to frame 4 and change the Feather value to 70.

Using the Animation menu, you can add and delete keyframes. But you need greater control over animation. Sure you can add keyframes as you have been doing, but what about the interpolation between these keyframes? What kind of interpolation are you getting? And what about editing keyframes? You know how to create them, but what about moving them around in a convenient graphical interface? This is what the Curve Editor is for.

THE CURVE EDITOR

As you add keyframes to a property, you create a *curve*. The curve represents the value of the property over time. You can see this curve in the Curve Editor panel, where each value (the Y axis) is plotted as it changes over time (the X axis). You can add keyframes, delete keyframes, and even adjust the interpolation between key-frames without ever looking at this curve. However, as the animation grows more com-plex, you may find it easier to edit the animation by manipulating this curve directly.

In most nodes in Nuke, right-clicking/Ctrl-clicking the Animation menu gives you an option called Curve Editor, as seen in **FIGURE 6.18**, but this functionality has been removed from the RotoPaint node. In RotoPaint, because all properties are linked to a stroke or a shape, all curves are associated with a stroke or a shape as well. Simply selecting a shape or stroke and switching to the Curve Editor panel shows their asso-ciated properties.

FIGURE 6.18 There is usually a Curve Editor option, but that is not the case with RotoPaint.

1. Click the Curve Editor tab in the Node Graph pane to switch to it (**FIGURE 6.19**).

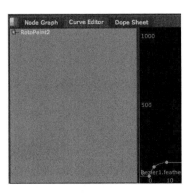

FIGURE 6.19 The Curve Editor as you first see it.

In the Curve Editor shown in Figure 6.19, the window on the left shows the list of properties (I call it the Properties List window), whereas the window on the right shows the actual curves for the properties as they are being selected. I call that the Graph window.

At the moment, all you see is the name of the node with a little plus sign at its left. Clicking that plus sign reveals more.

2. Click the plus sign to the left of the RotoPaint2 text (**FIGURE 6.20**).

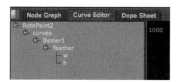

FIGURE 6.20 More is revealed in the Curve Editor's Properties List window.

You can now see that a few sub-elements have opened in the Properties List window. The first one we'll talk about is called Bezier1. If you have more than one shape or stroke drawn, and you select them in the Stroke/Shape List window in the Properties panel, they will display here instead of Bezier1. Under Bezier1, you have the name of the property that has animation in it—Feather, and under that you have W and H, for Width and Height. True, you only operated the Feather property with one slider, but these are actually two properties grouped together, one for Width and another for Height.

Here, I will show you how to load these curves into the Graph window on the right and what to do with them there.

3. Select both the W and H Feather properties by clicking the first and then Shift-clicking the second. Click the Graph window on the right to select that window.

4. Press Ctrl/Cmd-A to select all keyframes and then press F to fit the curves to the window (**FIGURE 6.21**).

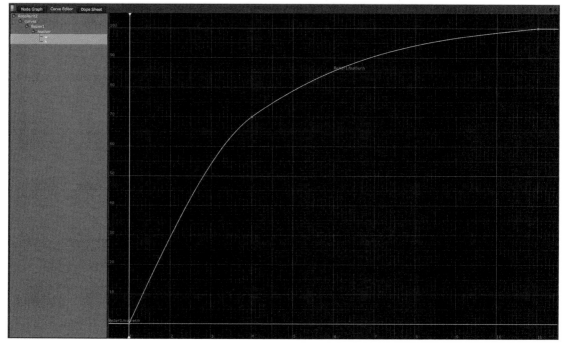

FIGURE 6.21 Two identical curves in the Curve Editor.

The Curve Editor now shows two curves and all the keyframes for both curves are selected. You have selected two curves that are exactly alike, which is why it appears that you are seeing only one curve.

5. Click an empty space in the Curve Editor to deselect the keyframes.

One thing you can do in the Curve Editor is change the interpolation of a keyframe. You can switch between a smooth keyframe and a horizontal one, for example.

6. Select the middle keyframe on the curve and press the H key to make the point a horizontal one (**FIGURE 6.22**).

TABLE 6.4 lists some hot keys for different types of interpolation on curves.

FIGURE 6.22
Making a point on a
curve horizontal.

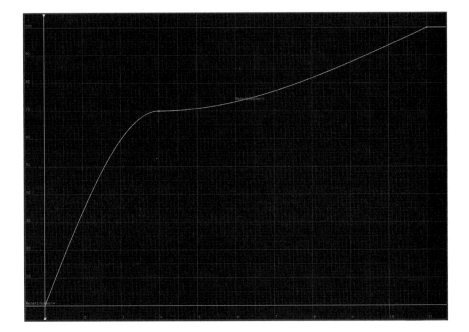

TABLE 6.4 Curve Interpolation

Hot Key	Function	Description
H	Horizontal	Makes the tangents horizontal, making animation slow down to a stop at the keyframe.
L	Linear	Produces sharp velocity changes at keyframes and straight lines between them.
Z	Smooth	Smooths out the interpolation between the keyframes.
K	Constant	Forces a constant value after each selected point.
X	Break	Adjusts the two tangents of a selected point independent of each other.

You can move around in the Curve Editor in the same way that you move around in other parts of the application. You use Alt/Option-click-drag to pan around. Use + and – to zoom in or out, or use the scroll wheel to do the same. You can also use Alt/Option-middle-button-drag to zoom in a non-uniform way. Pressing the F key will frame the current curve to the size of the window.

You can create more points on the curve by Ctrl-Alt/Cmd-Option-clicking just as you do when drawing shapes in the RotoPaint node.

7. Select the middle keyframe by clicking it (marqueeing won't do).

    Three numbers display: an X, a Y, and a ø. The X and Y are obvious, but the ø is the angle of the tangents. At the moment it's set to 0 because you told this key-frame to be horizontal.

8. Double-click X to activate its field and increase or decrease by 1, then press Enter/Return (**FIGURE 6.23**).

    This makes editing locations of points on a curve very easy. Sometimes it is easier to edit the location of points numerically, and it's nice to have this available.

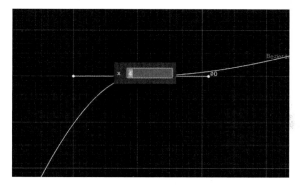

FIGURE 6.23 Numerically changing the location of points.

Many other functions are available in the Curve Editor, but I won't cover them all now. Here's one last function that enables you to edit the whole curve using simple math.

9. Drag to select the whole curve (or Ctrl/Cmd-A to select them all).

10. Right-click (Ctrl-click) and then choose Edit/Move (**FIGURE 6.24**).

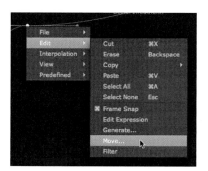

FIGURE 6.24 You can access more features through the contextual menu.

FIGURE 6.25
Manipulating the curve function.

11. In the Move Animation Keys dialog box that opens, enter **x+5** in the X field to move your curve 5 frames forward (**FIGURE 6.25**).

12. Click OK.

Watch your curve move five frames forward. What happened here is you asked to move all X values by the current X value plus five. So the whole curve moved five frames forward.

Let's try another function.

13. Select your curve again, right-click (Ctrl-click), and choose Edit/Move again.

14. This time enter **x/2** in the X field and press Return/Enter.

Watch your curve shrink. This is because you asked all X values to be half their current value. Because X is time, your animation will now be twice as fast.

These examples and the other features in the contextual menu enable you to manipulate your curve in many ways.

15. If you want to save this project, do so. Otherwise, press Ctrl/Cmd-W to close this project and create another one. If Nuke quits altogether for some reason, just start it again.

This concludes the introduction to both the Curve Editor and the RotoPaint node. That's enough playtime! Let's move on to practical uses.

PAINTING IN PRACTICE

I would like you to start practicing with a simple and common example: Painting to remove things you don't want in the image. Let's load some footage to practice on.

1. Bring in KnifeCU.####.png from the chapter06 folder with a Read node.

2. Click the newly imported Read node, and then press Alt/Option-F to view it in Framecycler or simply view it in the Viewer and click Play (**FIGURE 6.26**).

FIGURE 6.26 The wire holding the knife in place is visible and needs to be removed.

In this shot, a wire holding the knife in place needs to be painted out and the little white hairs that display here and there on the negative need to be removed as well.

Using Paint for wire removal

Start with painting out the wire. You will use a brush you haven't practiced with before: the Clone brush. This brush uses pixels from one location in the frame and copies them to another, allowing you to copy areas.

1. Make sure Read1 is selected and attach a RotoPaint node to it. Make sure you are viewing RotoPaint1.

2. From RotoPaint1's toolset, choose the Clone brush.

3. Because you want the wire to be gone for the whole duration, change the Lifetime Type drop-down menu from Single to All in the Tool Settings bar (**FIGURE 6.27**).

NOTE It doesn't matter which frame you are on when painting because you are painting on all frames.

FIGURE 6.27 Changing the Lifetime Type setting before drawing a stroke.

The Clone brush copies from one location in the image to another. You set it up by Ctrl/Cmd-clicking the point you want to copy from and then, without letting go, dragging to the point where you want to copy to.

4. Make sure you're zoomed in nicely (by using the + and – keys) to the area where you want to work and Ctrl/Cmd-click the area to the right of the wire and at the top of the frame. Then, without letting go, drag toward the wire and then release (**FIGURE 6.28**).

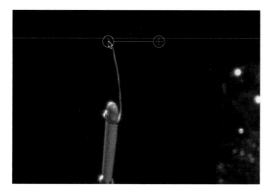

FIGURE 6.28 Setting up the Clone brush.

FIGURE 6.29 First pass clone operation.

5. You can now paint the top bit of the wire up to the handle very easily. Notice that your paint strokes are now copying grain and all other texture from your source area. I ended up with the image shown in **FIGURE 6.29**.

FIGURE 6.30 Aligning the Clone brush with the handle.

FIGURE 6.31 Some bad strokes remain at the top right of the handle.

FIGURE 6.32 The cleaned-up knife handle.

FIGURE 6.33 Creating two RotoPaint nodes in succession.

Cleaning up the actual handle is going to be a tad more difficult as there is more texture there and hard lines you need to follow.

6. Align your brush with the angle of the handle, as in **FIGURE 6.30**.

7. Once the brush is aligned, start carefully cloning.

8. You can align the brush with other source areas according to your need until you have a cleaned-up handle (**FIGURE 6.31**).

As shown in Figure 6.31, I drew some strokes that made the top of the handle look wrong. You can use the Eraser tool to paint them out.

9. Select the Eraser and paint out any problem areas.

10. Repeat the process until you are happy with the results. Remember that you can change properties as well—such as Size and Opacity—that might help (**FIGURE 6.32**).

11. Click RotoPaint1 and press Alt//Option-F to view your work in Framecycler. Alternatively, click Play to watch your work play in the Viewer.

12. When you're finished, quit Framecycler or press Stop in the Viewer.

13. If you are not happy enough with your result, fix it and repeat the viewing until you are pleased with it.

I'm pleased with my work, so I'm moving on.

Dust removal with Paint

Now that you fixed the wire, there's only the dust to remove. I'm sure you noticed while looking at the clip that there is dust on it. You need to clean this up.

You can use the same RotoPaint node for this purpose, but I like to keep things separate. After all, that's the good thing about the node tree. You use another RotoPaint node instead for painting out the dust. You also use another little trick to quickly and easily clean the dust up:

1. Click RotoPaint1 and insert another RotoPaint node by pressing the P key (**FIGURE 6.33**).

2. Clear the Properties Bin and then double-click RotoPaint2 to open just that node's Properties panel.

    NOTE On-screen controls display for each node that has controls associated with it and for which its Properties panel is loaded in the Properties Bin. This can get very confusing and clutter the screen, so it's good practice to close Properties panels when you're not using them.

To make it easy to paint out the dust, you are going to reveal back to the next frame using the Reveal brush in hopes that the speckle of dust won't appear in the same location frame after frame. This is faster than performing cloning on each frame, but it only works if there is no movement in the clip or if the movement in the clip has been stabilized beforehand.

First, let's see which frames have dust.

3. Click Read1 and press Alt/Option-F to load it into Framecycler (as always, you can press Play in the Viewer instead).

4. If you're using Framecycler, change the Origin field on the right, above the timeline, from 0 to 1 (**FIGURE 6.34**). This makes Framecycler start counting from frame 1 rather than 0, just like your Nuke timeline.

FIGURE 6.34 By default, Framecycler starts to count frames from 0, while Nuke starts to count from frame 1.

5. Take a pen and paper and start writing down which frames have dust. Here's the list I made for the first 20 frames. You should find all the rest of the frames that have dust in them and write them down. 2, 8, 10, 13, 14, 16, 19.

6. Close Framecycler when you're finished (or press Stop in the Timebar, if that's what you were using).

As mentioned earlier, you will use the Reveal brush. You will now set up the Reveal brush and reveal one frame forward from the current frame.

7. Select the Reveal brush from RotoPaint2's toolbar in the Viewer. The Reveal tool is the second tool in the Clone tool's menu (**FIGURE 6.35**).

8. Once the Reveal brush is selected, choose Single from the Lifetime Type dropdown menu in the Tool Settings bar.

The magic of this setup will happen in the Reveal's Source Time Offset property (**FIGURE 6.36**), which will determine what offset should be given for the clip from which you reveal. You are revealing from the background—the same source as you are painting on—however, you want to reveal to one frame forward.

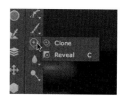

FIGURE 6.35 The Reveal brush is hidden under the Clone tool's menu.

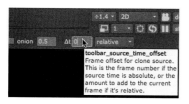

FIGURE 6.36 The Source Time Offset field.

9. Change the Source Time Offset field at the top of the Viewer from 0 to 1. This is the field represented by the Δt label.

10. Change the drop-down menu to the left of Δt from Bg1 to Bg to reveal back to the original image (**FIGURE 6.37**).

FIGURE 6.37 Choosing a reveal source from the drop-down menu.

You are now ready to start painting.

11. This kind of work is easier done with a big screen, so hover your mouse pointer over the Viewer and press the Spacebar briefly to maximize the Viewer. In case you need to go back, press the Spacebar again.

12. Zoom in so the image fills the frame by pressing the H key.

13. Go to frame 2 and paint over the dust speckle to reveal back to the next frame and, in effect, remove the speckle.

14. Repeat this process for every frame on your list.

15. When you're finished, load your work into Framecycler, or play it in the Viewer, to make sure you didn't miss anything. If you did, repeat.

16. Save your Nuke project in the student_files folder and restart Nuke with a new empty project.

There's more work with RotoPaint in the next example.

SPLIT-SCREENING TWINS WITH ROTO

Let's save on idle chatter and load some images so you have something to look at as I explain.

1. From the chapter06 directory, bring in fg##.png and bg##.png.

2. Go to frame 51 in the Timebar and view both Read nodes in the Viewer, one after another (**FIGURE 6.38**).

   Both images have the same actor. What you need to do is create one shot that has the same actor twice in it! How novel!

FIGURE 6.38 I'm seeing double. Are you seeing double?

To see the overlap a little better, use a handy tool called the Dissolve node.

3. Select the fg##.png Read node and insert a Dissolve node from the Merge toolbox.

4. Connect the input called 1 to the bg##.png Read node's output (**FIGURE 6.39**).

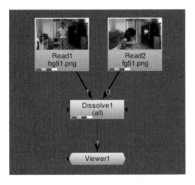

FIGURE 6.39 Your tree should look like this.

5. Set the Which property to 0.5 to blend evenly between the foreground and background (or in this case inputs 0 and 1).

6. View Dissolve1 in the Viewer.

7. To see it playing, either press Alt/Option-F to load the sequence into Framecycler, or press Play in the Viewer (**FIGURE 6.40**).

FIGURE 6.40 There is still substantial overlap between the characters.

It's clear what needs to be done in this composite. In most of the frame, there is no overlap between the characters, and so this can be solved with a simple split screen—a non-animating shape that defines what part of the final image to take from which Read node. However, the foreground actor's head does go on top of the background actor, and this will need to get properly extracted with a roto. Obviously this calls for the prowess of RotoPaint!

8. Close Framecycler or press Stop.

9. Make sure no node is selected and press the P key to create a RotoPaint node.

10. Make sure you're on the last frame (frame 51) of the comp.

11. Choose the Bézier tool from the toolbox and draw a spline that includes the area on the left—except for the person standing.

    You should have something that looks like **FIGURE 6.41**.

FIGURE 6.41 A simple split-screen shape.

12. Drag a soft edge from the points on the right side of the shape to smooth that part of the transition by holding down Ctrl/Cmd and dragging (**FIGURE 6.42**).

FIGURE 6.42 Make sure the elbow stays outside the shape when pulling a soft edge.

You now need to create another Bézier for the part of the person on the left screen that overlaps the person on the right screen. You'll use another shape in the same node.

13. Select the fg.png Read node and press the 1 key to view it.

14. Select Dissolve1 and press the 2 key (**FIGURE 6.43**).

Having Viewer inputs 1 and 2 set up like this lets you see the area you need to roto clearly in buffer 1 and where it overlaps in buffer 2.

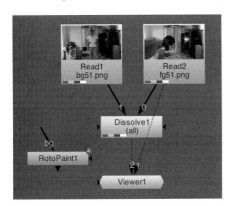

FIGURE 6.43 Connecting up two Viewer inputs.

15. To avoid accidentally moving the first shape you drew, lock it by clicking the Lock icon in the Shape/List Window in RotoPaint1's Properties panel (**FIGURE 6.44**).

FIGURE 6.44 Click the Lock icon to prevent shapes from changing.

16. While viewing Viewer input 1, select the Bézier tool and follow the actor's head from the end back to when he leaves the frame. Start by drawing the shape in frame 51.

17. Keep switching between buffer 1 and 2 to make sure you're covering everything you need to, without doing unnecessary work. The curls at the back of the actor's head, for example, are something you don't have to worry about as there is no overlap (**FIGURE 6.45**).

FIGURE 6.45 The second Bézier shape on frame 51.

TIP If the shape is ever in the way of seeing where you want to draw, you can turn it off by hovering the mouse pointer over the Viewer and pressing the O key. Press O again to display the overlays again.

18. Take your time and go over the whole clip, changing the shape and adding key-frames as you go.

When you're finished, pat yourself on the back. You now just need to use the matte you created to place the foreground actor on top of the background actor. If you can work it out yourself, I urge you to try, or continue following the instructions to finish this comp. Even if you do it yourself, you should probably read the rest of this section, as there are things you might want to learn about.

19. To use the matte you created, select the fg.png Read node and press Shift to branch out a ShuffleCopy node from the Channel toolbox (**FIGURE 6.46**).

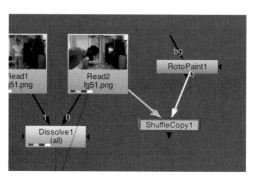

FIGURE 6.46 Make sure to branch the ShuffleCopy.

20. Attach ShuffleCopy1's input 1 to the output of RotoPaint1.

The ShuffleCopy node is a really handy tool for this kind of stuff (see Chapter 3 for more on this). ShuffleCopy's default setup lets you simply copy the alpha channel from input 1 and copy the RGB channels from input 2.

21. Because this procedure creates an RGBA image that is not multiplied, insert a Premult node after ShuffleCopy1.

Now that you have a premultiplied foreground, you can use a Merge node to connect the foreground and background together.

22. While Premult1 is selected, press the M key to create a Merge node.

23. Connect Merge1's B input to the output of the bg.png Read node (**FIGURE 6.47**).

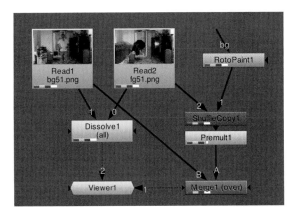

FIGURE 6.47 Your tree should look like this.

24. Look at your final result in the Viewer by making sure you are viewing Merge1.

25. A little bit of blur on the matte is probably in order, so insert a Blur node after RotoPaint1 by selecting RotoPaint1 and pressing the B key.

26. Increase Blur1's Size property. I left it on 3.

This is pretty much it. To make sure your work is completed to a high standard, watch this thing playing. I will remind you how to render.

27. Select Merge1 and press W on the keyboard.

28. In Write1's Properties panel, click the Folder icon next to the File property to open a File Browser (**FIGURE 6.48**).

FIGURE 6.48 Clicking the File icon to launch a File Browser.

29. Navigate to your student_files folder and name your sequence: SplitScreen.####.png.

30. Click OK.

31. Click the Render button in Write1's Properties panel.

32. In the Render dialog box that displays, make sure the frame range is set to 1-51 and click OK (**FIGURE 6.49**).

FIGURE 6.49 The Render dialog box.

33. When the render is finished, select Write1 and press Alt/Option-F to load your rendered clip into Framecycler to view it. If you're using the PLE, load the rendered clip into a new Read node and view it in the Viewer.

You might have noticed that your render did not have any motion blur in the matte (**FIGURE 6.50**), especially around frame 22 or so. This is easily fixed as Nuke can create motion blur for any motion generated inside Nuke. You will simply make changes to the tree and render again.

FIGURE 6.50 An obvious lack of motion blur in the matte.

34. When you're finished, quit Framecycler or click Stop in the Viewer.

35. Choose Bezier2 from the Stroke/Shape List window in RotoPaint1's Properties panel and navigate to the Shape tab.

36. To the right of the Motion Blur property there's an On check box. Check it to activate motion blur for this shape (**FIGURE 6.51**).

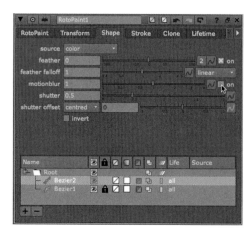

FIGURE 6.51 This elusive check box is in charge of turning on motion blur.

37. Render your project again and view it again to make sure you're happy with the motion blur settings.

38. When you are happy with your work, save your project.

39. Press Ctrl/Cmd-W to clear the current script and open a fresh script.

I would like to take you through just one more example, which involves both strokes and shapes.

COMBINING PAINT, ROTO, AND ANIMATION

The following little exercise is simple enough, but I will overcomplicate it a little so I can teach you more stuff. How's that for overachieving?

1. In a new project, bring in an image called CarWindow.png from the chapter06 folder with a Read node (**FIGURE 6.52**).

FIGURE 6.52 This is the single image this production provided to you.

For this shot, you have been asked to dirty up the windshield and write "CLEAN ME" on it, as some people do when they walk past a dirty car. The magic is going to be that it needs to appear as if it's being written on with an invisible hand.

The first stage will be to create a dirty image to use on the windshield. You will use two Noise nodes from the Draw toolbox to make the noise image appear more interesting.

2. While Read1 is selected, create a Noise node from the Draw toolbox.

I don't want you to create the noise function on top of the car; I just asked you to con-nect it to the car so you'll have the same resolution as the car. You now need to ask the Noise node to replace the car color channels.

3. Check the Replace check box at the top middle of Noise1's Properties panel (**FIGURE 6.53**).

FIGURE 6.53 The Replace option tells Draw functions to replace rather than blend with the above nodes.

4. Change the X/Y size property to 1.

5. While Read1 is selected, branch out another Noise node.

6. Again check the box for Noise2's Replace value.

7. Select Noise2 and press the M key to insert a Merge node after it.

8. Connect the B input to Noise1.

9. Change Merge1's Operation to Overlay.

10. Change Merge1's Mix value to 0.65.

NOTE In a Merge node, the B input always stays 100% opaque and the A input changes according to the Mix property's value.

11. Add a Blur node after Merge1 by pressing the B key.

12. Change the Blur Size to 2 (**FIGURE 6.54**).

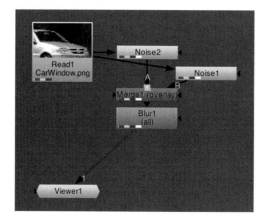

FIGURE 6.54 Your tree should look like this.

TIP I find the Noise function in Nuke very useful. I make a lot of things with it—from moving texture, to clouds, smoke, and even simple noise effects. Try it sometime, it is very useful.

This long list of steps created the noise image you needed. There are a lot of other ways to get something like this, but this will do here.

You now need to create a matte for the windshield.

13. Select Read1 and press Shift-P to branch out a RotoPaint node.

Since you only want to create the Bézier on the alpha channel, uncheck the Red, Green, and Blue boxes at the top of RotoPaint1's Properties panel (**FIGURE 6.55**).

FIGURE 6.55 You can create images in any combination of channels.

14. Make sure you are viewing RotoPaint1. Select the Bézier tool and start drawing to trace the edges of the windshield (**FIGURE 6.56**).

15. Refine your shape by changing the Bézier handles and moving things around until you've created a matte you're happy with.

FIGURE 6.56 My Bézier shape for the windshield.

16. Hover your mouse pointer over the Viewer and press the A key to view the alpha channel.

You have now created your first matte!

17. Press the A key again to view the RGB channels.

Compositing with the KeyMix node

You will use another type of layering node than the usual Merge node here, just to spice things up. The KeyMix node has three inputs: a foreground, a background, and a matte. Unlike the Merge node, the KeyMix node accepts a non-premultiplied (unpremultiplied) image as its foreground image. It's very convenient to use the Key-Mix node to mix two images that have no matte. It would have been perfect for the split-screen exercise you did earlier, although I wanted you to try both options. But you would save two nodes using a KeyMix, as you wouldn't have to use a Shuffle-Copy or a Premult node. You will use KeyMix now instead.

1. Select Blur1 and from the Merge toolbox click KeyMix.

2. Connect KeyMix1's B input to Read1, and the Mask input to RotoPaint1 (**FIGURE 6.57**).

TIP For fine-tuning, select a point and use the number pad on your keyboard to move the point around. NUM2 is down, NUM7 is diagonal left and up, for example. Holding Ctrl/Cmd reduces the move by a 10th, and holding Shift increases by 10.

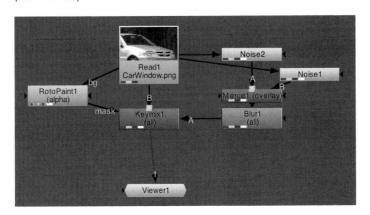

FIGURE 6.57 Connecting KeyMix's three inputs.

3. View Keymix1.

4. I don't want this much noise, so change Keymix1's Mix property to 0.2.

5. The matte you created is a bit sharp, so select RotoPaint1 and press the B key to insert a Blur between RotoPaint1 and Keymix1.

6. Change Blur2's Size value to 2.

7. Close all Properties panels by using the Clear All Properties button at the top right of the Properties Bin.

You finally have a dirty car window (**FIGURE 6.58**). Now to punch a hole in the matte by writing "CLEAN ME" on it. You'll use RotoPaint1 to create the hand-drawn text "CLEAN ME."

FIGURE 6.58 A dirty car window.

8. Double-click RotoPaint1 to load its Properties panel.

Working with the Stroke/Shape List window

To make sure things are tidy, you will create a folder in RotoPaint1's Stroke/Shape List window. You can use folders there to group things together and separate different elements. Also, the group has settings of its own, including an axis, which can be used to move the content of the folder around. This comes in really handy sometimes.

1. Create a new folder in the Stroke/Shape List window by clicking the + button at the bottom left of the window (**FIGURE 6.59**). If the button is grayed out, click anywhere in the window to activate it.

FIGURE 6.59 Use the + button at the bottom of the Stroke/Shape List window to add folders.

2. Rename the new folder (Layer1) by double-clicking the name and typing **CLEAN ME** (an underscore will be added automatically) (**FIGURE 6.60**).

FIGURE 6.60 Renaming the folder to keep things even tidier.

3. To see what you're doing, temporarily hide Bezier1 by clicking the Eye icon to the right of the name Bezier1 (**FIGURE 6.61**).

FIGURE 6.61 The Eye icon controls visibility.

4. Select the Brush tool and hover your mouse pointer over the car window.

5. Make sure your newly created folder is selected in the Stroke/Shape List window.

6. Make sure you're drawing on all frames by choosing All from the drop-down menu in the Tool Settings bar.

7. Write CLEAN ME on the window. It took me 16 strokes (**FIGURE 6.62**).

FIGURE 6.62 I wrote this with a trackpad. Don't blame me.

8. Turn Shape1 back on by clicking to bring back the Eye icon in the Stroke/Shape List window to the right of the name Bezier1.

You won't see the writing anymore. This is because both the shape and the strokes draw in white. However, RotoPaint is a mini-compositing system in its own right. You can tell all the strokes to punch holes in the shape just as you can with a Merge node.

TIP The Stroke/Shape List window can become very cramped very quickly. You can make the whole panel bigger by dragging the bottom-right corner. This will make the Stroke/Shape List window grow in size, too.

9. Select all the strokes called Brush# by clicking the first and then Shift-clicking the last in the Stroke/Shape List window (**FIGURE 6.63**).

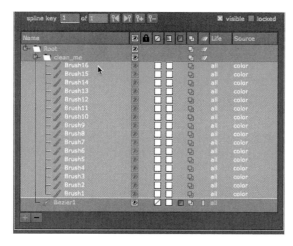

FIGURE 6.63 Selecting in the Stroke/Shape List window.

10. Change the Blending Mode drop-down menu from Over to Minus (**FIGURE 6.64**).

You can now see your writing (**FIGURE 6.65**)!

The only thing left to do is animate the writing of the words. For that, you will use the Write On End property in the Stroke tab and the Dope Sheet.

FIGURE 6.64 Changing the Blending Mode property.

FIGURE 6.65 Your car should look something like this.

USING THE DOPE SHEET

The Dope Sheet is another panel that helps to control timing in your tree. It's an easier way to change the timing of keyframes than the Curve Editor, and it can also change the timing of Read nodes in your tree.

To get started with a Dope Sheet, the first thing to do is create two keyframes for all the brush strokes on the same frames. You will then stagnate the keyframes using the Dope Sheet so the letters appear to get drawn one after the other.

1. All the brush strokes that draw the text should already be selected in the Stroke/ Shape List window. If they aren't, select them again.

2. Go to frame 1 in the Timebar. This is where the animation will start.

3. Click the Stroke tab in RotoPaint1's Properties panel.

4. Change the Write On End property to 0.

5. Right-click (Ctrl-click) the field and and choose Set Key from the contextual menu (**FIGURE 6.66**). This will set keyframes for all the selected brush strokes.

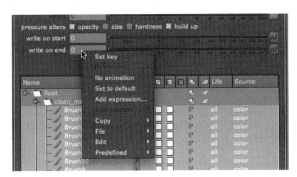

FIGURE 6.66 Setting a keyframe using the Write On End field.

Now for the second keyframe.

6. Go to frame 11 in the Timebar.

7. Bring the Write On End property to 1.

8. Click Play in the Viewer.

At the moment, all the letters are being written at once. You can stagger this so that the first letter is written first and so on.

9. In the bottom left pane, switch from the Node Graph tab to the Dope Sheet tab.

   What you should be seeing is something similar to **FIGURE 6.67**.

FIGURE 6.67 The Dope Sheet.

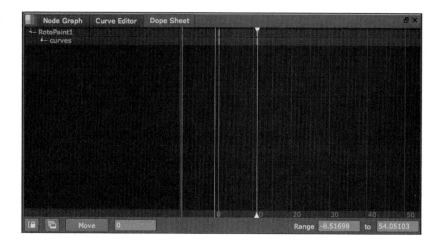

This is the Dope Sheet. It is very similar to the Curve Editor, but its function is the timing of keyframes rather than their value and interpolation. You can change the timing of keyframes in the Curve Editor as well, but it is a lot more convenient here. Another function the Dope Sheet serves is changing the timing of Read nodes—meaning clips in the timeline. (You will learn this in Chapter 8.)

The window on the left shows the list of properties open in the Properties Bin, which I call the Properties List window. The window on the right will show the actual keyframes for each property, which I call the Keyframe window.

The Properties List window is hierarchical, meaning it shows the tree as submenus within submenus. This lets you move groups of keyframes together, which is very convenient when doing animation-based work.

At the moment, you are only looking at the Properties List window, RotoPaint1—the only node that is loaded into the Properties Bin. Under that you can see the submenu Curves, representing all the animation curves available, in the same way as it was presented in the Curve Editor. Let's see what else is in there.

10. Click the little + symbol to the left of the Curves submenu in the Dope Sheet's Properties List window.

11. Do the same for the folder clean_me.

    You now see the list of brush strokes you added keyframes to (**FIGURE 6.68**).

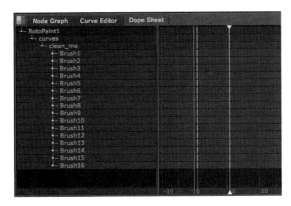

FIGURE 6.68 The list of brushes displays in the left window.

Each of these strokes has keyframes associated with it—in your case, keyframes for the actual shape that was drawn and two keyframes for the Write On End property you animated.

12. Click the little + symbol to the left of the Brush1 property (**FIGURE 6.69**).

FIGURE 6.69 This shows the two properties that Brush1 has keyframes in.

I really only want to stagger the Write On End property. If I move the stroke's drawing keyframe it won't have any effect on the animation or the shape. As it's easier to move both of them as one entity that's what you will do.

13. Click the − symbol to the left of the Brush1 property.

It is a little hard to see the keyframes on the Keyframe window because you are zoomed out quite a bit. The Keyframe window is set at the moment to show you frames 1 to 100. You can navigate in the Keyframe window in the same way that you navigate the Viewer and the Curve Editor. However, you can also zoom it in using two fields at the bottom of the window. Zoom in to view frames 0 to 20.

14. Using the Range fields at the bottom right of the Dope Sheet, frame the Keyframe window between 0 and 20 (**FIGURE 6.70**).

FIGURE 6.70 This is a very convenient way to frame the Keyframe window.

You can now see the keyframes more clearly (**FIGURE 6.71**). Each vertical box represents a keyframe.

FIGURE 6.71 The Key-frame window shows the keyframes more clearly now.

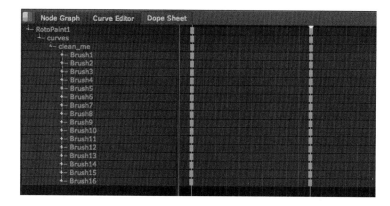

15. Click Brush2 in the Properties List window.

Dragging the box that displays around the keyframes, you can move them in unison. You can also use the box to scale the animation by dragging on its sides. Of course, you can also move each keyframe individually (**FIGURE 6.72**).

FIGURE 6.72 The box allows you to control keyframes together.

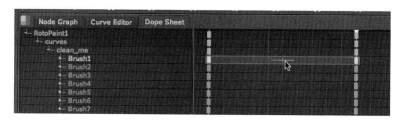

16. Click the center of the box and drag the keyframes until the first one is at frame 6. You can see the frame numbers at the bottom (**FIGURE 6.73**).

FIGURE 6.73 Using the box to offset your animation.

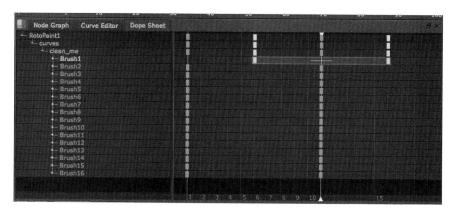

So you are starting to do what you set out to do: stagnate the animation. You need to keep doing this for every subsequent brush stroke by a further five frames. Here's another way to do this.

17. Select Brushes three until the end by clicking Brush3 and then Shift-clicking the last Brush stroke, in my case, Brush16 (**FIGURE 6.74**).

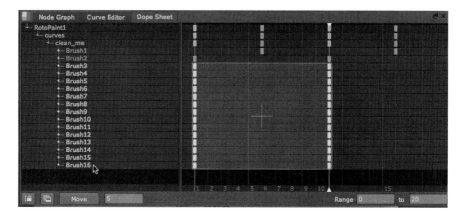

FIGURE 6.74 You can also change a whole bunch of properties' keyframes in one step.

At the bottom of the Dope Sheet window there is a Move button and next to it a field (**FIGURE 6.75**). You can use this button to change the location of keyframes without needing to drag.

FIGURE 6.75 The Move button.

18. Enter **5** in the field.

19. Click the Move button twice to move all the keyframes selected by 10 frames (**FIGURE 6.76**).

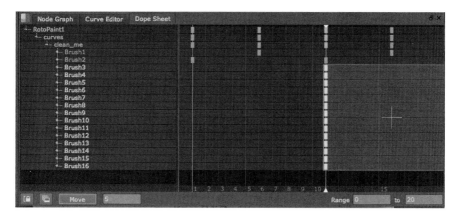

FIGURE 6.76 Moving all the selected keyframes by 10 frames.

Next time you click Move, you don't need to move Brush3 anymore, so you'll need to deselect it before clicking. Then again without Brush4, then again without Brush5, and so on.

20. Deselct Brush3 by Ctrl/Cmd-clicking it.

21. Click the Move button.

It is probably getting hard to see what you are doing, because as you are pushing keyframes forward they are going off screen. You need to reframe your Dope Sheet again.

22. Set the Range fields to run from 0 to 100.

23. You now need to keep offsetting the keyframes five frames at a time, while deselecting another and another property.

When you are finished, the Dope Sheet should look like **FIGURE 6.77**.

FIGURE 6.77 The staggered staircase of keyframes in the Dope Sheet.

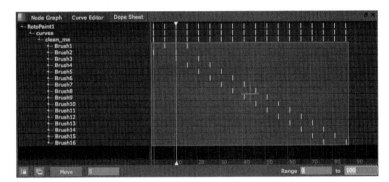

This concludes the animation creation stage. All you have to do now is sit back and enjoy this writing-on effect you made.

24. With Keymix1 selected, press Alt/Option-F to load it into Framecycler.

25. Since this composite started with a single frame, the Frame Range is set to 1-1. Change the Frame Range property to 1-100 and click OK (**FIGURE 6.78**).

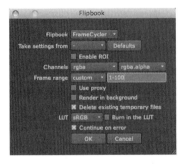

FIGURE 6.78 Setting the Frame Range in the Flipbook panel.

The RotoPaint node is indeed very powerful and you should become good friends with it. I hope going through these examples helped.

KEYING

Keying is the process of creating a *matte* (an image that defines a foreground area) by asking the compositing system to look for a range of colors in the image. This is also sometimes called *extracting a key*. It's a procedural method, which makes keying a lot faster than rotoscoping, for example. However, it has its own problems as well.

You have to shoot specifically for keying because you have to place the foreground object in front of a single-color screen. The color of the screen can't include any of the colors of the foreground object because the computer will be asked to remove this color. Usually this is done with either a blue or green backing—called a *bluescreen* or *greenscreen*, respectively. The color you choose usually is related to the colors in the foreground object. If it's an actor wearing blue jeans, a greenscreen is used. If it's a green car, go with a bluescreen.

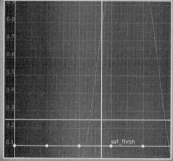
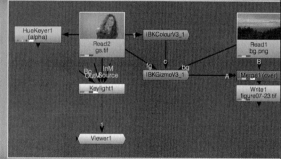

Because you want the computer to *remove* a color from the image (blue or green, normally) you want the screen to be lit as evenly as possible to produce something close to a single color. This is, of course, hard to do and rarely successful. Usually what you get is an *uneven screen*—a screen that has many different shades of the screen color.

Because you have to shoot especially for keying and you can't shoot on location, you have to do a lot of extra work to make a shot like this work. Extracting a key is not an easy process, and problems of holes in the matte and fine edges such as hairs are always a problem. Also, standing an actor in the middle of a green-painted studio means the actor will have a strong green discoloration (called *spill*) that will have to be removed somehow—a process called *spill suppression* or just *spill* for short.

But still, keying is very often the better method of working, and is used extensively in the VFX (visual effects) industry.

Most applications try to create a magic keying tool that gets rid of the screen with a couple of clicks. However, this hardly ever works. Most likely, you have to create a whole big composition just for extracting the matte. Nuke's tree-based approach makes it easy to combine keys, mattes, and color correction together to reach a better overall matte and corrected (*spill suppressed*) foreground.

BASIC KEYING TERMS

There are four basic types of keying techniques. Without going into a complete explanation of the theory of keying, here are the four techniques:

- Luma-keying uses the black and white (called *luminance* in video terms) values of the image to extract a matte.

- Chroma-keying uses the hue and saturation (called *chrominance* in video terms) values of the image to extract a matte.

- Different-keying comprises the difference between an image with a foreground element and another image with that foreground element taken away (also called a *clean plate*).

- Color difference-keying utilizes the difference in color between the three color channels to extract a matte. Spill suppression is a side effect of this technique.

INTRODUCING NUKE'S KEYING NODES

Nuke has many keying nodes, but I only have room to cover a few of them in detail. Here is a a rundown of the options in Nuke's Keying toolbox:

- **Difference:** This undocumented node is rarely used. It is a simple difference key node that creates a matte for the difference between two images. It has very little control over the matte and no control for spill (**FIGURE 7.1**).

FIGURE 7.1 The Difference node's Properties panel.

- **HueKeyer:** This is a simple yet very handy and easy to use chroma keyer. It lets you choose a range of hues and saturation to extract (*key out*) in a very handy user interface (**FIGURE 7.2**).

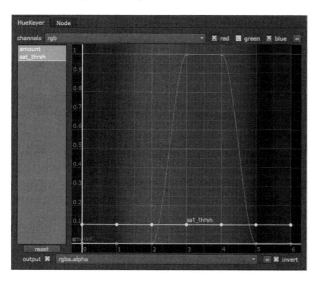

FIGURE 7.2 The HueKeyer's Properties panel.

- **IBK:** The Image Based Keyer (IBK) was first developed at Digital Domain, which also originally developed Nuke itself. This keyer is designed to work with uneven green- and bluescreen elements. So instead of having one blue or green shade, you have many. The IBK, which consists of two nodes—IBKColour and IBKGizmo—creates a color image representing all those different screen colors (but without the foreground element), and then uses that to key instead of a single color (**FIGURE 7.3**).

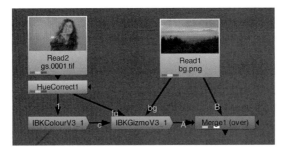

FIGURE 7.3 A basic IBK tree that includes the two IBK nodes.

- **Keyer:** This is a basic keyer, mainly used for luminance-based keying or *luma keying* (**FIGURE 7.4**).

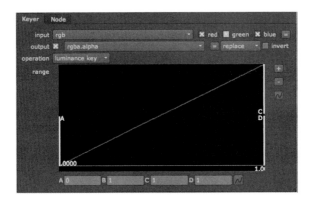

FIGURE 7.4 The Keyer node's Properties panel.

- **Primatte:** This plug-in from Imagica Corp. is bundled with Nuke. It is one of three industry-leading keying plug-ins available. (Primatte, Keylight, and Ultimatte all come with Nuke.) This is a great keyer that can key any color and reach very high levels of detail and control. It has control over matte, edge, transparency, and fill. Primatte is not available in the PLE version of Nuke.

- **Keylight:** This plug-in from The Foundry is included free with Nuke. It only keys blue and greenscreen—and it does the job very well, producing results I find unprecedented.

- **Ultimatte:** This plug-in from Ultimatte is also bundled with Nuke. Yet another great keyer, it has control over the matte, edge, transparency, and spill.

Now, let's jump right in and try a few of these keying nodes.

1. Go to your chapter07 directory and bring in bg.png and gs.tif.

2. Select Read2 (this should be the greenscreen element) and view it in the Viewer.

This is a pretty flat greenscreen element. Then again, even if it is, as always, it will still pose all sorts of problems. There are a lot of wispy hairs that can hopefully be retained, and also a fair amount of green spill on the white areas in the woman's shirt and the dark midtones of her skin tone that will need to be fixed.

HUEKEYER

The HueKeyer is a straightforward chroma keyer. It has one input for the image you want to key. HueKeyer produces an alpha channel by default, and does not premultiply the image.

Let's connect one HueKeyer node.

1. Select Read2 and insert a HueKeyer node from the Keyer toolbox after it (**FIGURE 7.5**).

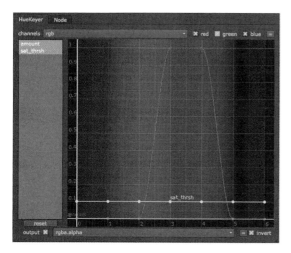

FIGURE 7.5 Again, for reference, here is the HueKeyer's Properties panel.

HueKeyer's interface consists of a graph editor where the X axis represents hue, and the Y axis represents amount to be keyed. By creating a point on the graph at a certain hue and pulling the graph up to a value of 1, you tell HueKeyer that this hue should be 100% gone.

2. Make sure you are viewing the output of HueKeyer1. Switch to viewing the alpha (**FIGURE 7.6**).

FIGURE 7.6 HueKeyer's default alpha channel.

You can see that already there's some kind of alpha in there. This is because, by default, it's designed to key out a range of greens and cyans. This greenscreen is, surprisingly, a more yellowish rather than a true green or a cyan green.

3. Switch back to viewing the color channels.

4. Hover your mouse pointer over the greenscreen area and look at HueKeyer1's graph (FIGURE 7.7).

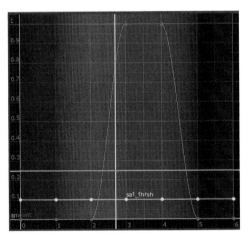

FIGURE 7.7 The yellow line in the graph represents the hue of the color that the mouse pointer is hovering over.

You can see by the yellow line that's moving about that the greenscreen sits somewhere around 2.5 on the hue, or X axis. The girl's hair sits somewhere around 1.5, by the way.

You are now going to edit the curve in the graph by moving some of the points that are already there. You can do it by hand, but I'll start you off by typing numbers instead.

5. View the alpha channel.

FIGURE 7.8 Clicking a curve in the list selects only that curve.

6. In the Curve List window, click the Amount curve so you only see that curve in the graph (FIGURE 7.8).

The other curve controls the amount of saturation, which can be edited in the same way. However, it has little effect in this case, so you don't need it.

7. Click the point in the graph that's at X = 2, Y = 0 (FIGURE 7.9).

8. Double-click the X value next to the point itself. This displays an input field.

9. Change the value from 2 to 1.5, which will tell the keyer not to key out the hair. Press Enter/Return (FIGURE 7.10).

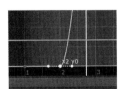

FIGURE 7.9 Clicking a point in the graph allows you to numerically edit it.

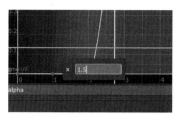

FIGURE 7.10 Changing a point on a graph numerically using the input field.

10. Select the point at X = 3, Y = 1 and drag it to the left until it reaches somewhere around 2.5 on the X axis.

    Notice that when you start to drag in one axis, the movement is already locked to that axis. This is very convenient as it allows you to change only what you want to change without having to hold any modifier keys (**FIGURE 7.11**).

FIGURE 7.11 HueKeyer's results in the Viewer.

Surprisingly, this is not a bad key for such a simple keyer. Although some keying nodes can only extract green or blue screens, you can use the HueKeyer to extract a key from any range of colors. The downside to the HueKeyer is that it can't key different amounts of luminance, for example (although the sat_thrsh curve, or saturation threshold, does give control over saturation). It doesn't have fine-tuning capabilities.

Put the HueKeyer aside for now and we'll move on to another keying node.

THE IBK: IMAGE BASED KEYER

The IBK consists of two nodes: The first is the IBKColour node and the second is the IBKGizmo node. IBKColour is designed to turn the screen element into a complete screen image—removing the foreground element and essentially producing what's called a clean plate. (*Plate* is another word for image, and *clean plate* means an image without the foreground object.) By this I mean, it gets rid of the foreground elements and produces only the screen colors, green or blue. The IBKGizmo takes this clean plate, by connecting the IBKColour's output to the IBKGizmo's c input, and uses that to create a key, including fine detail adjustments and, if you connect a background image as well, some smart spill suppression. The great thing about this method is that for each pixel in the screen element you will have a corresponding clean plate pixel. So it doesn't matter how uneven the screen is, as you are giving a different color for every part of the image using the clean plate.

Incidentally, if you have a clean plate that was shot—as in, you asked the actors to clear out of the frame and took a picture—you can connect the IBKGizmo's c input to that instead of the IBKColour's output. This is even better as it really gives you the best source to work with.

The screen element you have is pretty flat, but still, the IBK can give a great result here as well, especially on fine hair detail.

1. Select Read2 and hold Shift to branch an IBKColour node from the Keyer toolbox.

2. Select Read2 again and branch an IBKGizmo node from the Keyer toolbox.

3. Connect IBKGizmoV3_1's c input to the output of IBKColourV3_1.

4. Connect IBKGizmoV3_1's bg input to the output of Read1.

   You are connecting the background image to the Keyer so that the spill suppression will factor in the background colors.

   Your tree should now look like **FIGURE 7.12**.

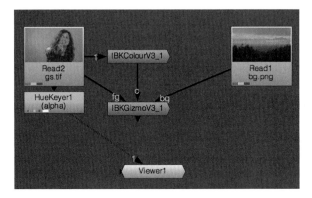

FIGURE 7.12 Setting up an IBK tree.

The first thing you need to do is set up the IBKColour node to produce a clean plate. When that's done you will set up the IBKGizmo node to produce a key.

5. View IBKColourV3_1 in the Viewer. Also make sure that its Properties panel is open in the Properties Bin.

You should be seeing black. The first thing to do when adjusting the IBKColour node is state which kind of screen you have: green or blue.

6. Change the first property, Screen Type, to Green.

   You will now see the greenscreen image with a black hole where the girl used to be (**FIGURE 7.13**).

FIGURE 7.13 This is the beginning of producing the clean plate.

The main things left to remove are the fine hair details around the edges of the black patch. If you leave them there, you will actually be instructing the IBKGizmo to get rid of these colors, which is not what you want to do.

The next step will be adjusting the Darks and Lights properties. For a greenscreen element, you adjust the G (green) property. For a bluescreen, adjust the B (blue) property.

7. Click to the right of the 0 in the Darks G property (**FIGURE 7.14**).

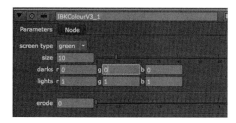

FIGURE 7.14 Place the cursor to the right of the available digits.

To change really fine values, you'll need another decimal digit.

8. Enter **.0**. That's a dot and then a 0 (**FIGURE 7.15**).

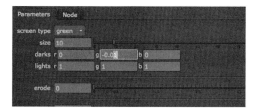

FIGURE 7.15 Using the arrow keys to nudge values is a convenient way to do fine adjustments.

Your cursor is now to the right of the 0 you just entered. Using the Up and Down Arrow keys, you can now nudge the value in hundredths.

9. Decrease the value by pressing the Down Arrow key slowly. You are looking for the magic value that will not bring in too much black into the green area, but will still reduce the amount of hairs visible on the edge of the black patch. Nudge the value down to −0.05 (**FIGURE 7.16**).

FIGURE 7.16 Having all those black holes around the edges of the image is not good.

You have actually gone too far. You should not have these black holes around the edges. A few will be OK, but not big patches. You need to go back a little.

10. I ended up moving the cursor again to the right and adding another digit (the thousandth) and my final value is −0.035. Anything else started producing blacks at the bottom-right corner. Find your magic value.

    You should now do the same with the Darks property. Slowly bring it down. But I tried it already. Moving it even by 0.001 will bring in unwanted black patches. So leave it as it is.

The next property to adjust is the Erode property. This will eat in further from the black patch and reduce the amount of hair detail you have. It might also introduce some unwanted black patches, so be careful.

11. Start dragging the slider to increase the Erode property value. It's OK to let a few little black patches appear, but not too much. I left mine at 1.5 (**FIGURE 7.17**).

FIGURE 7.17 The result so far.

Finally you need to adjust the Patch Black property until all your black patches are filled.

12. Bring up the Patch Black property until all your black areas are filled with green. The slider goes up to 5, but you need 10 to get the result you're after. To do this, you can enter 10 in the field (**FIGURE 7.18**).

FIGURE 7.18 A complete green image—the clean plate.

Now that you have a clean plate, you need to adjust the IBKGizmo settings to get a nice-looking key. Let's move over to the IBKGizmo then.

13. Double-click IBKGizmoV3_1 to load its Properties panel into the Properties Bin.

14. View IBKGizmoV3_1 and its alpha channel in the Viewer.

Again, the first thing to take care of here is setting the screen color.

15. Change the Screen Type property to C-green.

You can already see that the alpha has some really good things happening in it. First, the whole foreground (where the girl is) is indeed white. Also, all the fine hair detail is preserved beautifully. There is just the noise in the black areas that needs to be cleaned up.

The other properties (**FIGURE 7.19**) worth mentioning include:

▧ **Red Weight:** This property changes the density of the generated matte by adding or subtracting the red areas of the image.

▧ **Blue/Green Weight:** This property changes the density of the generated matte by adding or subtracting the blue or green areas of the image. If you're keying out blue, then it's the green channel that is being used. If you're keying out green, then it's the blue channel.

▧ **Luminance Match:** This property first needs to be turned on with the check box. Once it is on, the Screen Range slider will affect light areas and firm up the matte there.

▧ **Luminance Level:** This property has no effect anymore and will be removed in the next version of the software.

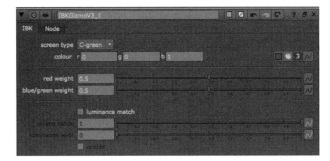

FIGURE 7.19
The IBKGizmo's
properties.

To properly see the adjustments as you change property values, you should actually be looking at a composite. This means you need to place the keyed foreground on top of your background image.

16. Select IBKGizmoV3_1 and insert a Merge node after it by pressing the M key.

17. Connect Merge1's B input to Read1's output (**FIGURE 7.20**).

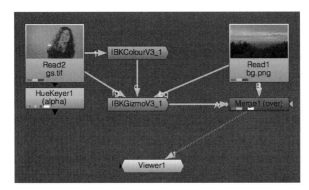

FIGURE 7.20 Your tree
should look like this
after adding the Merge
node.

18. Make sure you are viewing the RGB channels of Merge1 in the Viewer.

Notice the green coloration of the hair on the left—you will remove this. You can get rid of it by using the Red Weight and Blue/Green Weight properties (**FIGURE 7.21**).

FIGURE 7.21 This green
can be removed with the
Weight properties.

19. While looking at your screen, adjust the Red Weight and Blue/Green Weight properties until you get rid of the green color in the hair. Don't go too far or you will compromise the density of the inside of your matte. I ended up with 0.455 for the Red Weight and 0.47 for the Blue/Green Weight.

To get a little more hair detail, check the Luminance Match box and then move the slider a little.

20. View the alpha channel in the Viewer.

21. Check Luminance Match.

    You can see that only a few hairs were added to the matte.

22. Move the Screen Range property a little so that you reduce the amount of noise on the background a little—without changing the foreground. I left mine at 0.9.

It doesn't seem like this property did any good to the overall key, so you should turn it off.

23. Uncheck Luminance Match.

This is as far as you can get the matte. It is hardly perfect, but for this greenscreen element it is the best you can do. You will get to use this matte later, using another technique. For now, you can still adjust the spill a bit more.

The IBKGizmo has some controls remaining at the very bottom for edge correction. These properties are Screen Subtraction, Use Bkg Luminance, and Use Bkg Chroma. Let's see what these do (**FIGURE 7.22**).

FIGURE 7.22 The bottom three properties for the IBKGizmo node.

24. Switch to viewing the RGB channels of Merge1.

25. Screen Subtraction is checked by default in IBKGizmov3_1. Uncheck and check it again to see what it does. Leave it on.

    This property subtracts the original greenscreen element from the result. This reduces spill on the edges of the matte, and it does a very good job at that.

26. Use Bkg Luminance is unchecked by default. Check it to see its effect, but leave it unchecked when you're finished.

    This property uses the background's luminance to color correct the foreground around the edges of the matte. In this case, its effect isn't helpful.

27. Use Bkg Chroma is unchecked by default. Check it to see its effect, and leave it on when you're finished.

This property uses the background's chroma to color correct the foreground around the edges of the matte. In this case it creates a better composite, and so you should leave it on (**FIGURE 7.23**).

FIGURE 7.23 The final composite as it stands at this stage.

Even though the matte is very noisy, the final compositing still looks pretty good. You know it is not perfect, but it holds this still frame pretty well. You will learn to make this look even better later in this chapter. For now, move on to the third, and last, keying node: Keylight.

KEYLIGHT

Keylight, like the IBK earlier in this chapter, is a bluescreen and greenscreen keyer. It is not designed to key out any color, just green and blue screens. It does that job very well, and many times all you have to do is choose the screen color and that's it. Keylight also tackles transparencies and spill exceptionally well.

Let's start by branching it out from the greenscreen element.

1. Select Read2 and Shift-click the Keylight icon in the Keyer toolbox on the left (**FIGURE 7.24**).

2. Make sure you are viewing the output of Keylight1, and viewing the RGB channels.

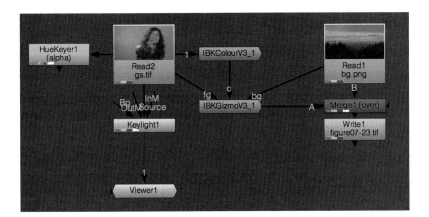

FIGURE 7.24 Branching out a Keylight.

Keylight has four inputs (**FIGURE 7.25**):

■ **Source:** The first and main input—often the only input you will use. This is where the element to key should go in. This input should already be connected to your greenscreen element.

■ **Bg:** You can connect a background image here. Because Keylight also suppresses spill, it can use the color of the background for that suppression (and it does so by default if the input is filled). Keylight can also actually composite over the background, although this is rarely done.

■ **InM:** Stands for *inside matte* (also called *holdout matte*). If you have a black-and-white image (roto or other rough key), you can use it with this input to tell Keylight not to key out this area. This can also be called a *core matte*.

■ **OutM:** Stands for *output matte* (also called *garbage matte*). If you have a black-and-white image (again through a roto or a rough key), you can use it with this input to tell Keylight to make all this area black.

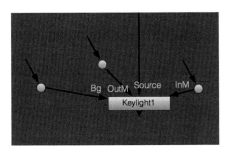

FIGURE 7.25 Keylight's four inputs (marked with dots so you can see them).

When using Keylight, the first thing to do is connect the background if you have it.

3. Connect Read1 to Keylight1's Bg input.

Now you can begin keying by choosing the screen's main green pigment.

4. Click the sample color from the Viewer button for the Screen Colour property to activate it (**FIGURE 7.26**).

FIGURE 7.26 Turning on the Screen Colour property's sample color from the Viewer button.

NOTE Remember, when capturing colors from the screen, holding down Ctrl/Cmd activates the actual selection. Adding Alt/Option chooses colors from the input of the node, rather than the output. And adding Shift lets you pick several pixels and then average between them.

5. Now, while holding down Ctrl-Alt-Shift/Cmd-Option-Shift, click and drag on-screen to find the best screen color. Look at **FIGURE 7.27**—the red line shows where I ended up dragging. If you drag exactly like my red line the rest of the exercises in the chapter will work smoother for you.

This is what I have set for Screen Colour property: 0.0712, 0.1452, 0.0478.

FIGURE 7.27 The red line signifies where to drag.

This drag action is a very important one. It is the basis for all other operations that come later. Try several different colors first, and then choose the best one. Every time you release the mouse button and click again, you are changing the selected color.

TIP It is very important to remember to uncheck color pickers. If you leave them on and then click on-screen, you will change the selected color.

6. Uncheck the sample color from the Viewer button to turn off Viewer sampling.

7. You can look at the alpha channel now by hovering the mouse pointer over the viewer and pressing the A key. The matte won't be perfect, but it should look something like **FIGURE 7.28**.

You can now start to tweak the matte. Keylight has a lot of different properties, but the main one is Screen Gain. This is a multiplier, which hardens the matte. By *harden* I mean that it pushes the contrast up—the dark grays towards black and the light grays towards white.

FIGURE 7.28 The starting matte for Keylight1.

8. Change the Screen Gain property to 2 (**FIGURE 7.29**).

   As you can see, the background part of the matte is completely black now. However, that's been achieved at the expense of the fine detail in the hair. This value should be used with a lot of caution and should rarely ever reach these high values.

FIGURE 7.29 Fine hair detail is lost when Screen Gain is pushed too hard.

There are controls similar to Screen Gain that are a little finer. Find them under the Tuning submenu below Screen Gain.

9. Bring back the Screen Gain parameter to 1.1 or so.

10. Click to twirl down the triangular arrow in order to display the Tuning submenu (**FIGURE 7.30**).

FIGURE 7.30 The Tuning submenu.

Here you see four properties. The bottom three are Gain controls for the three dynamic ranges: shadows, midtones, and highlights. The first property defines where the midtones are—if this were a generally dark image, the midtones would be lower.

NOTE If your matte looks different than mine, that means you picked different colors for the Screen Colour property. That's OK. But you'll have to play around with the Shadow Gain, Midtones Gain, and Highlights Gain properties to make the foreground areas white and the background areas black. The Screen Matte properties, which I explain in the next step will also need to be adjusted in a different way.

11. Bring up the Shadow Gain property to about 1.1. This should eliminate most of the grays in the background area.

Keylight offers a lot of additional controls. Under the Screen Matte submenu you find properties that control the matte after its keying process creation. I call these the *post key* operations, as they are actually operations that happen on the produced matte rather than using any keying process.

12. Click the arrow next to Tuning to hide those controls, and then click the arrow next to Screen Matte to display those options instead (**FIGURE 7.31**).

FIGURE 7.31 The Screen Matte options.

You can adjust the Clip Black property to remove any remaining gray pixels in the background area. If you lose too much detail, you can use the Clip Rollback property to bring back fine detail.

13. Adjust Clip Black and Clip Rollback to get rid of all the gray pixels in the background area. I ended up with 0.02 in the Clip Black property and 0 in Clip Rollback, which is the default value.

14. If you have any holes in the white foreground area that need filling you can use the Clip White property to fill those in.

The View drop-down menu at the top of the Properties panel will change the output of the Keylight node to show one of several options. The important ones to note are:

▪ **Source:** Shows the source image as it came in.

▪ **Final Result:** Shows a premultiplied foreground image with its matte. This is normally how you would output the result of this node.

▪ **Composite:** Creates a composite over whatever is in the Bg input of the Keylight node. You will normally not use the Keylight node to composite the foreground over the background, but it is convenient while keying to see your final composite and see what other work is left to be done.

▪ **Status:** Shows a black, gray, and white representation of the keying process, where white represents complete foreground pixels, black represents complete background pixels, and a 50% gray represents transparent or spill suppressed pixels. This is a handy tool to see the status of your matte and pinpoint problematic areas (**FIGURE 7.32**, next page).

FIGURE 7.32 Choosing output mode in the View property.

15. To see the final result with the background, change the View property to Composite.

16. Change the View property back to Final Result.

    Here you can see your greenscreen element composited over the background. It is not bad at all (**FIGURE 7.33**).

FIGURE 7.33 The final output of the Keylight node.

Using post key operations, as you did before using the properties in the Screen Matte submenu, usually significantly degrades the matte. Edges start to *bake* and *wiggle* (two terms describing a noisy matte that changes in an unnatural way from frame to frame), and the level of detail starts to deteriorate. A good way of getting a better key is to use the tree itself to build up a series of keys together that produce the best result.

This is really where node-based compositing systems, and Nuke in particular, shine. Being able to easily combine mattes using the tree can result in a very good key and can utilize several keyer nodes together, taking the best from each.

COMBINING KEYER NODES USING THE TREE

In my opinion, the IBK produced a far superior result compared to the other two keyer nodes discussed in the previous section. The hair detail was really fine, and the edges were great. The main problem, however, was that the area that's supposed to be background wasn't black in the matte. After all, edges are really what keying is all about. It is very easy to draw a shape with the RotoPaint node and fill in things that are supposed to be white in the center (or core) of the matte, and it is very easy to do the same for areas that are supposed to be black (also called *garbage*). But the actual edge, that's what you are looking for when keying.

The result of the Keylight node was OK, but not great. On the other hand, playing with the Screen Gain property for the Keylight node produces a very hard matte with well-defined white and black areas. Maybe you can use the Keylight node together with the IBK nodes to create a perfect key.

First let's use Keylight1 to create a garbage matte—a matte that will define unwanted areas.

1. You might want to save this Nuke script and then save it again with a different name. You are going to degrade the key your Keylight node is producing, so you might want to keep it for posterity looking the way it does now. I saved mine as chapter07_v01 and chapter07_v02.

2. Increase Keylight1's Screen Gain property to something like 1.5. This should make the matte a perfect black on the outside and white on the inside. The hair detail will still be gray, which is fine.

3. If increasing Screen Gain isn't enough, you can change the Clip Black and Clip White properties in the Screen Matte area as you did before. I brought down the Clip White property to 0.1 to get rid of some gray patches on the side of the girl's arm and really whiten up the hair (**FIGURE 7.34**).

FIGURE 7.34 A crunchy matte made up of mainly black and white.

Now what you have in front of you is a hard matte, or *crunchy* matte, and you can use it for two things: a garbage matte and a core matte. You don't need a core matte, because the core of the IBK is fine. You do need a garbage matte because the outside of the IBK matte is a big mess of gray noise. However, if you use the matte as it is now, you will lose a lot of the fine detail the IBK produced. You need to make the matte you have here bigger and then you can use it to make the outside area black. For that you will need to use one of three tools: Erode, Dilate, and Erode (yes, really, keep reading).

Erode, Dilate, and Erode

There are three tools in Nuke that can both *dilate* (expand) or *erode* (contract) a matte. Their names are confusing and, since they all have two sets of names, it gets even more confusing. They are called one thing in the Filter toolbox, where you can find them, but once you create them they are called something else in the interface. Yes, it is that crazy. I do wish they would simplify this little source of confusion. Here's the rundown:

- **Erode (Fast):** A simple algorithm that allows only for integer dilates or erodes. By *integer* I mean it can dilate or erode by whole pixel values. It can do 1, 2, 3, and similar sizes , but it can't do 1.5 pixel width, for example. This makes it very fast, but if you animate it you see it jumping from one size to another. Once created, the control name becomes Dilate.

- **Erode (Filter):** A more complex algorithm that uses one of four filter types to give more precise control over the width of the Dilate or Erode operation. This allows for *subinteger* (or subpixel) widths. Its name changes to FilterErode when created.

- **Erode (Blur):** Another type of erode algorithm. This one creates a harsh black-and-white matte and then gives control over blurring. Called Erode when created.

Right now you will use the Erode (Fast) node.

1. Select Keylight1 and insert an Erode (Fast) from the Filter toolbox after it (**FIGURE 7.35**).

2. You will also need a Blur node, so insert one after Dilate1 (the Erode you just created).

3. View Blur1 in the Viewer and make sure you are viewing the alpha channel (**FIGURE 7.36**).

FIGURE 7.35 The node is named Erode (Fast) in the Filter toolbox.

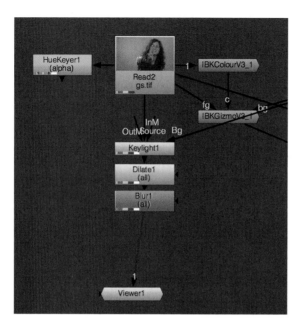

FIGURE 7.36 In the Node Graph, the new Erode node is labeled Dilate1.

Now you can see what you are doing and have full control over the size of your matte. You can increase the Dilate Size property to expand the matte. And then you can increase the Blur Size property to soften the transition.

4. Increase Dilate1's Size property to 40.

5. Increase Blur1's Size property to 25 (**FIGURE 7.37**).

FIGURE 7.37 An expanded matte.

The matte defines areas that need to remain as part of the foreground rather than be thrown out, as usually it's the white areas that define a shape and not the black areas. If you invert this image, it will then define the areas that are garbage.

6. From the Color toolbox, insert an Invert node after Blur1.

Now the garbage matte and the matte coming out of the IBK need to be combined. You will use a regular Merge node for that.

7. Click Invert1 and then Shift-click IBKGizmoV3_1. The order is important as it defines which will end up being the A input and which the B.

8. Press the M key to insert a Merge node (**FIGURE 7.38**).

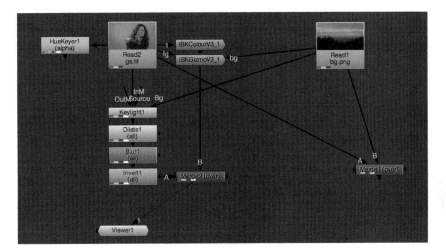

FIGURE 7.38 The Merge node is supposed to be connected like this.

9. In Merge2, choose Stencil from the Operation drop-down menu (**FIGURE 7.39**).

FIGURE 7.39 Changing the Operation from Over to Stencil.

This removed all the gray noise in the background. It did, however, produce a gray noise halo around the girl's head—but that won't be noticeable in the final result, and can be tweaked by changing the properties in the Dilate and Blur nodes (**FIGURE 7.40**).

FIGURE 7.40 Using the garbage matte has cleaned up most of the black area in the matte.

Spill suppressing with HueCorrect

So you built a little tree to create a better matte. In general, you will make another tree to create a better *fill* as well. The fill consists of the RGB channels, so you will remove any kind of spill you can find in the RGB. Some keyers take care of that, some don't—but even the ones that do handle it don't always give you the same control as a tree built in Nuke where everything is something you chose.

A good node for removing spill is the HueCorrect node. HueCorrect is another very useful tool for color correcting in Nuke. HueCorrect allows for changes according to the hue of a pixel, mixing together the color weights for that hue.

1. Select Read2 and Shift-click to branch out a HueCorrect node from the Color toolbox (**FIGURE 7.41**).

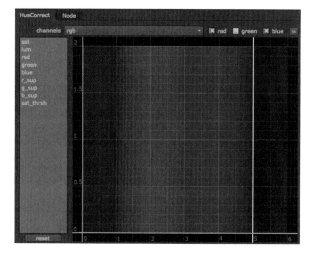

FIGURE 7.41 The HueCorrect's interface is very similar to that of the HueKeyer.

HueCorrect has several functions, all of them having to do with selecting a hue and moving a point on the graph. The curves you can manipulate include saturation, luminance, red, green, blue, red suppression, green suppression, and blue suppression. The difference between changing green and suppressing green is that changing simply multiplies the amount of green, and suppressing reduces the amount of green so that it's not higher than that of the other two channels.

To reduce the amount of green in the brown color of her hair and face, you first need to find out where that color is in the graph. This works in a similar way to the HueKeyer node.

2. While viewing the RGB channels of HueCorrect1 in the Viewer, hover your mouse pointer around the hair and face areas.

The resulting yellow line in the graph shows a hue at around 1.5. This is the area where you need to suppress green. To suppress the green color, you will use the G_sup curve in the Curves List window on the left.

3. Click G_sup in the Curves List window.

4. Ctrl-Alt-click/Cmd-Option-click the curve at about 1.5 to create a new point there.

5. Bring down the point you just made to somewhere closer to 0 on the Y axis.

6. To get rid of more spill, also bring down the point at the X value of 2 to something closer to 0 on the Y axis. Then click it again and drag it to the right so it's at about 2.8 on the X axis.

    The resulting curve should look something like **FIGURE 7.42**.

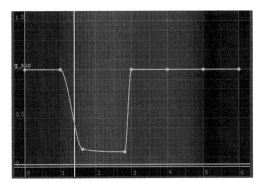

FIGURE 7.42 Suppressing green from various hues in the image using the G_sup curve.

This has taken care of the spill on her face and in her hair. Now you have a branch for the matte, ending with Merge2, and a branch for the fill, ending with HueCorrect1. You need to connect them. Here's how:

7. Click HueCorrect1 and insert a ShuffleCopy node after it.

8. Connect ShuffleCopy1's 1 input to the output of Merge2 (**FIGURE 7.43**).

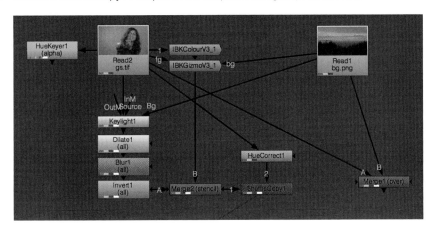

FIGURE 7.43 Connecting the two branches with a **ShuffleCopy** node.

This now copies the alpha channel from the matte branch to the RGB channels from the HueCorrect branch, which is exactly what you need.

The result of the ShuffleCopy node, though, is an unpremultiplied image. You need this image to be premultiplied before you can composite it over the background.

9. Click ShuffleCopy1 and insert a Premult node after it.

Now you can use the output of Premult1 as the A input for Merge1.

10. Grab the top part of Merge1's A pipe and drag it to Premult1's output (**FIGURE 7.44**).

FIGURE 7.44 Moving an existing pipe from one place to another.

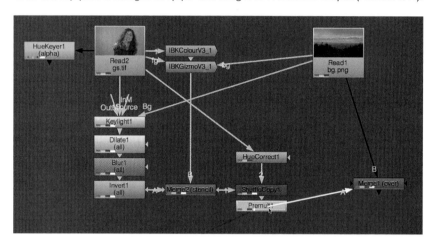

11. View the output of Merge1 (**FIGURE 7.45**).

FIGURE 7.45 The final result of the keying tree.

You now have a tree consisting of three keyers, but only two of them are used for output. You have one branch for the matte and another for the fill. Though no one keyer gave you a perfect result, the tree as a whole did manage that. If you needed to further tweak the matte, you would do so in the matte branch using eroding nodes, blurs, and merges. If you needed to further correct the color of the foreground image, you'd do so in the fill branch and add color-correcting nodes there. If you needed to move the foreground element, you'd do so after the keying process was done, between Premult1 and Merge1. The same goes for filtering, such as blur.

Working in this way gives a great amount of control over your matte. Now that you see your final composite, it is very easy to change it and make it better. It is all accessible and open to you for manipulation.

8

COMPOSITING HI-RES STEREO IMAGES

In this chapter you complete a stereoscopic, film resolution composite. A lot of problems are associated with stereo work and hi-res images, and this chapter explains how to deal with those problems in Nuke. This chapter also covers parts of the interface that haven't been discussed yet.

So far you've been using Nuke easily enough, but you might have noticed some things were missing—things you might be accustomed to from other applications. For example, you haven't once even set the length, size, or fps speed (frames per second) of a project. In many other applications, these are some of the first things you set.

In Nuke, doing that stuff is not necessary—but it is still possible. In the following sections, you will learn why.

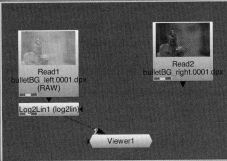

USING THE PROJECT SETTINGS PANEL

Each Nuke project has settings associated with it. You aren't required to set any of them, but sometimes they make things easier. You haven't touched these settings so far, but now let's take a look at them.

1. Make sure you have a fresh script open in Nuke.

2. Hover over the DAG and press the S key.

The Project Settings panel displays in the Properties Bin. The bottom part of the Root tab is filled with goodies (**FIGURE 8.1**).

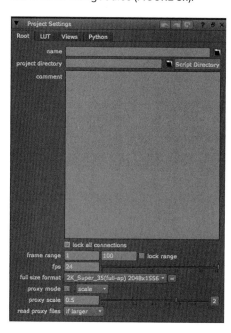

FIGURE 8.1 The Project Settings panel.

The Root tab

The two Frame Range fields control the frame range of your Viewer as well as the Frame Range fields in the panels that appear when you launch flipbooks or click Render. Nuke automatically sets this range to the length of the first Read node you create, which is why you haven't had to set it until now.

With the Lock Range box checked, the Frame Range property stays as it is. If it isn't checked, bringing in a longer Read node updates the Frame Range fields to accommodate.

The FPS (frames per second) field determines the speed at which the project is running: 24 is for film, 25 for PAL (video standard in Europe), 30 is for NTSC (video standard in the United States). This has very little meaning in Nuke—Nuke only cares about individual frames. It doesn't care if you later decide to play these frames at 25fps or 1500fps. Setting the FPS field just sets the default fps for newly created Viewers and for rendering video files such as Quicktime and AVI.

The Full Size Format drop-down menu sets the default resolution for creating images, such as Constant, Radial, and RotoPaint nodes, from scratch. You can always set the resolution in other ways as well, including using Format drop-down menus in the node's Properties panel or connecting the input to something that has resolution (such as a Read node). You have done that several times up until now, but setting the resolution means you don't have to worry about it.

The next four properties—Proxy Mode check box, Proxy Mode drop-down menu, Proxy Scale and Read Proxy File—control proxy settings that are discussed later in this chapter.

Nonlinear images and lookup tables (LUTs)

More settings are available in the LUT tab of the Project Settings panel.

1. Click the LUT tab at the top of the Project Settings panel (**FIGURE 8.2**).

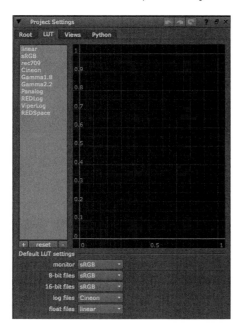

FIGURE 8.2 The Project Settings panel's LUT tab.

This area is where Nuke's color management happens. Color management is a topic that can—and does—fill entire books. Here, I only have room to explain how Nuke deals with it.

As mentioned in Chapter 4, Nuke is a 32-bit float *linear* compositing system. However, most of the images you will work with won't be linear images. Most images are made with color correction built into them automatically in the form of color management to compensate for other external problems that make them nonlinear.

Review two main nonlinear color spaces, sRGB and log, and understand why they exist.

- sRGB shows the reverse of what the nonlinear monitor you're using is displaying (yes, that means all your monitors, even that really good new Apple LED cinema monitor, even that one). sRGB is applied to show you the real image on the nonlinear monitor. You can click the sRGB curve in the Curves List window on the left to see the color correction that will be applied to an sRGB image. This curve will be used just like in a ColorLookup node.

- Log (sometimes called Cineon) is there to compress and better mimic that large abundance of colors found on a celluloid negative. It's used when scanning film to digital files. You can click the Cineon curve in the Curves List window on the left to see the color correction that will be applied to a log image.

When you bring an image into Nuke, Nuke needs to convert it to linear so that all images that come in are in the same color space, and so that mathematical operations give you the results you are looking for (a blur on a log image gives very different results than a blur on a linear image). To convert all images to linear, Nuke uses lookup tables (abbreviated LUTs). *LUTs* are lists of color-correcting operations similar to curves in the ColorLookup node. Nuke uses these LUTs to correct an image and make it linear and then convert it back to whatever color space it came from or needs to be for display or render.

The LUT tab is split into two areas, the top and the bottom. The top area is where you create and edit lookup tables. The bottom part sets default LUTs for different image types.

2. Click Cineon at the top left list of available LUTs to see the Log Colorspace graph (**FIGURE 8.3**).

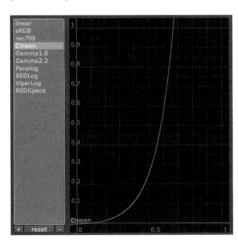

FIGURE 8.3 Select a graph in the list at left to display it at right.

What you see now is a standard log curve. Studios that have their own color pipelines can create other LUTs and bring them in here to better customize Nuke and make it part of their larger-scale pipeline (**FIGURE 8.4**).

FIGURE 8.4 Nuke's default LUT settings.

By default, Nuke assumes that all images that are 8 and 16 bit were made (or captured) on a computer and have the sRGB color space embedded. It assumes that log files (files with an extension of cin or dpx) are log or Cineon, and that *float files* (files that were rendered on a computer at 32-bit float) are already linear. Also it rightly assumes that your monitor is sRGB, and sets all Viewers to sRGB as well.

These settings are fine for most purposes, but you can always change a specific Read node's color space independently. In fact, you'll do that later in this chapter.

The Views tab

Click the Views tab at the top of the Project Settings panel (**FIGURE 8.5**).

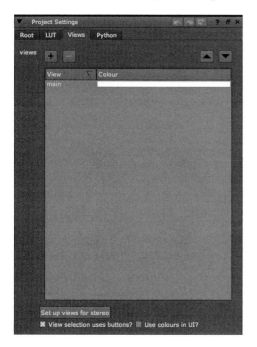

FIGURE 8.5 The Views tab.

This tab manages views, which let you have more than one screen per image. This can be used for multi-screen projects, like big event multi-screen films, but it is usually used for stereoscopic projects. *Stereoscopic* projects are done with two views, one for each eye—you've seen this effect in films such as Pixar's *Toy Story 3* and James Cameron's *Avatar.*

The Views tab lets you set up as many views as you like. The button at the bottom is a quick way to set up two views called Left and Right for a stereo workflow (**FIGURE 8.6**).

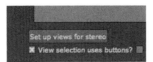

FIGURE 8.6 The Set Up Views For Stereo button creates Left and Right views.

Throughout this chapter you will use various controls in the Project Settings panel, so get used to pressing the S key to open and close it.

SETTING UP A HIGH-RES STEREO SCRIPT

OK, it's time for a little project. Start as you normally do, by bringing in images from disk.

1. Press the R key and navigate to the chapter08 directory.

   You should see a BulletCG and BulletBG directories.

2. Navigate inside BulletBG to the full directory. There are two image sequences in the full directory: bulletBG_left.####.dpx and bulletBG_right.####.dpx. These are a stereo pair of sequences. One represents what the left eye will see and the other what the right eye will see.

3. Bring in both sequences.

   You now have two Read nodes. Read1 is the left sequence, and Read2 the right sequence.

4. Click Read1 and press the 1 key to view it in Viewer input 1. Then click Read2 and press the 2 key to view it in Viewer input 2.

5. Hover your mouse pointer over the Viewer and press the 1 and 2 keys repeatedly to switch between the two views.

   You should see a woman holding a gun in front of her (**FIGURE 8.7**). Switching between the two inputs is like shutting one eye and then the other eye—one is supposed to look like it was shot from the direction of the left eye and the other like it was shot from the direction of the right eye.

FIGURE 8.7 A woman with a gun.

6. Stay on Viewer input 1. Have a look at the bottom right of the image (**FIGURE 8.8**).

What you see in that corner is the resolution of the image you are viewing. This is a log scanned plate from film with a nonstandard resolution of 2048x1240. Normally a 2K scanned plate will be a resolution of 2048x1556. (*Plate* is another word for image used mainly in film.)

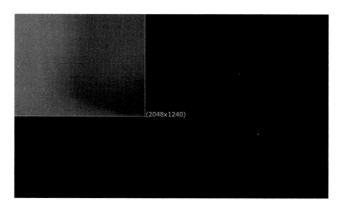

(2048x1240)

FIGURE 8.8 The image's resolution.

Setting formats

Now you need to define the resolution you are working in so that when you create image nodes they will conform to the resolution of the back plate. You will give this resolution a name, making it easier to access.

1. Double-click Read1 to make sure its Properties panel is at the top of the Properties Bin.

2. Click Read1's Format property and review the options in the drop-down menu (**FIGURE 8.9**).

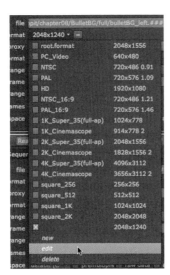

FIGURE 8.9 The Format drop-down menu.

The Format drop-down menu lists all the defined formats available. The image you brought in doesn't have a name, just a resolution: 2048x1240. You can add a name to it, and by that define it. As it is selected already, you can choose to edit it.

3. Choose Edit from the Format drop-down menu (**FIGURE 8.10**).

FIGURE 8.10 The Edit Format dialog box.

NOTE This shot is taken from a film called This is Christmas by Alex Norris, with support from the North London Film Fund.

4. Enter **Christmas2k** in the Name field. (This is an arbitrary name; you could have called it anything.)

The File Size W and Full Size H fields represent the resolution of the image, which should already be set for you. The pixel aspect at the bottom is for non-square pixel images, such as PAL widescreen and anamorphic film.

5. Click OK (**FIGURE 8.11**).

FIGURE 8.11 The format has been defined and is now presented in the Viewer as well.

NOTE For some formats, a value called pixel aspect ratio is needed for the display to show the image in the correct width. This is simply a way for older formats to present widescreen images while still using 4:3 technology. Using this value in the Format panel makes the Viewer show the correct image. Nuke can't correctly compensate for pixel aspect ratio in a composite. If you need to combine images with different pixel aspect ratios, you need to use the Reformat node (covered in Chapter 10) to change the resolution and pixel aspect ratio of one of the images.

If you look at the bottom-right corner of the image in the Viewer, you will see that it now says *Christmas2k* instead of *2048x1240*. You have now defined a format. You can set the Full Size Format property in the Project Settings panel to the newly defined format as well.

6. Hover over the DAG and press the S key to display the Project Settings panel.

7. Make sure the Root tab is displayed.

8. Choose Christmas2k from the Full Size Format drop-down menu.

Now when you create a Constant node, for example, it will default to the above format and resolution.

Working with LUTs

As mentioned earlier, Read1 and Read2 are log scanned plate from film. Meaning this image was shot on film, scanned using a film scanner, and saved to disk. During the conversion from film, the colors of this image were changed to preserve more dark colors than bright colors (due to our eyes' increased sensitivity to darker colors). This was done using a logarithmic mathematical curve, hence it is called a log image. Let's look at the image as it was scanned.

1. Double-click Read1 to load its Properties panel into the Properties Bin.

2. At the bottom right of the Properties panel, check the Raw Data box (**FIGURE 8.12**).

FIGURE 8.12 The Raw Data check box.

This property asks the Read node to show the image as it is, without any color management applied. The image looks washed out and is lacking any contrast (**FIGURE 8.13**).

FIGURE 8.13 The raw log image.

So how come you saw it looking better before? This is where Nuke's color management comes in. Every Read node has a Colorspace property that defines what LUT to use with an image to convert it to a linear image for correct processing (**FIGURE 8.14**).

This still isn't the image you saw in the Viewer before, though. The image you saw in the Viewer before was corrected a second time, to show you the correct image for your sRGB screen. This setting is in a drop-down menu in the Viewer, and unless you are fully aware of what you are doing, should remain set as it is (**FIGURE 8.15**).

FIGURE 8.14 The Colorspace drop-down menu.

FIGURE 8.15 The Colorspace drop-down menu set to sRGB.

The log image you now see is also corrected by the Viewer—otherwise you won't see a real linear image.

3.   Press the S key to display the Project Settings panel.

4.   Click the LUT tab.

I mentioned the default LUT settings before, and here they are again at the bottom of this tab. When you imported this file, Nuke knew (because of its dpx extension) that it was a log Cineon file, so it automatically assigned it the Cineon LUT. Now that Raw Data is checked, Nuke is no longer using this LUT to do the color conversion.

Another way to convert the image from log to linear is by not using Nuke's color management and instead doing the correction yourself.

Before changing the Color Management setup, let's save a copy of the color managed image so you have something to compare to.

5.   Select Read1 and press the 2 key to load it into Viewer1's second buffer.

6. In Read1 properties, uncheck the Raw Data box.

7. Click the Pause button at the top right of the Viewer to disable any updating on Viewer1's 2nd buffer (**FIGURE 8.16**).

8. While hovering over the Viewer, press the 1 key to view the first buffer.

9. In Read1's Properties panel, check the Raw Data box.

Now that you have the uncorrected, unmanaged log image, let's see the alternative method for applying color space conversion.

FIGURE 8.16 Pausing the Viewer means it won't update unless you click the Refresh button on its left.

10. Make sure Read1 is selected in the DAG and from the Color toolbox insert a Log-2lin. Log2Lin converts log images to linear images.

11. Hover over the Viewer and press the 1 and 2 keys to compare between the two types of color management you used.

The images look the same. These two different ways to color manage produce the same result. The first method is quicker and uniform. The second method is more customizable, but means more work because you need to apply this to every Read node (**FIGURE 8.17**).

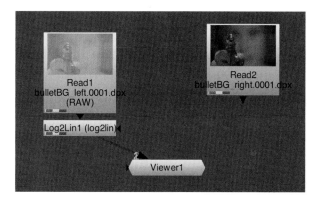

FIGURE 8.17 Your tree should look like this at this point—but not for long.

12. Delete Log2Lin1.

13. Uncheck the Raw Data box for Read1.

14. Switch to Viewer1's second buffer and uncheck the Pause button.

Stereo views

You have two Read nodes in the DAG, both representing the same image, but through a different eye. For the most part, everything you will do to one of these images you will also do to the other. For the illusion to work, both eyes need to feel like they are indeed images seen from the audience's left and right eyes. Hence color correction applied to one eye should also be applied to the other eye, for example.

Doing this can be very annoying, though, because you have to keep maintaining two trees and copying nodes from one to the other—or it would be so if Nuke didn't have its Views system.

Using Views, you can connect two Read nodes into one multi-view stream and from then on build and manipulate only one tree. If you do need to work on just one view, you will be able to do so per node—or if needed, split the tree in a specific point to its two views and join them again later.

Let's connect the two Read nodes into one stream. But before that, you need to define this project as a stereo multi-view project.

1. Press the S key to display the Project Settings panel.

2. Click the Views tab (**FIGURE 8.18**).

FIGURE 8.18 The current list of available views.

At the moment, only one view displays in the Views list: Main. That's normally the case, but now you will replace that with two views called Left and Right. You can do that manually using the + (plus) and – (minus) buttons at the top of the list. However, since Left and Right views are the norm, a button at the bottom of the list enables that as well.

3. Click the Set Up Views For Stereo button (**FIGURE 8.19**).

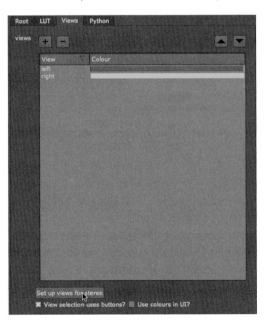

FIGURE 8.19 The Main view was replaced with Left and Right views.

After clicking this button, your Views list should change to display Left and Right instead of Main. At the top of the Viewer there are also two new buttons that allow you to switch between the two views you created, as shown in **FIGURE 8.20**.

FIGURE 8.20 The Views buttons in the **Viewer.**

In the Project Settings Views tab, notice the red-colored box next to the Left view and a green-colored box next to the Right view. These colors are reflected in the Views buttons in the Viewer and, if you check the Use Colors In UI box, they will be used to color the pipes connecting left and right specific parts of your trees.

Now that you've set up the multi-view project, you can proceed to connect your two Read nodes together into one multi-view stream.

All view-specific nodes are held in the Views toolbox in the Node toolbar. You use the node called JoinViews to connect separate views into one stream.

4. With nothing selected in the DAG, click JoinViews from the Views toolbox to create one.

5. Connect JoinViews1's left input to Read1 and the right input to Read2 (**FIGURE 8.21**).

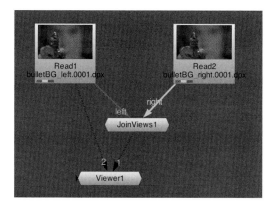

FIGURE 8.21 Connecting two streams into the beginnings of a multi-view tree.

NOTE Figure 8.21 shows the pipes colored red and green. This mirrors the colors of the views in the Views tab. I colored the pipes by selecting the Use colours in UI check box at the bottom of the Views tab.

6. Make sure you are viewing JoinViews1 in the Viewer and use the Left and Right buttons to switch between the views.

You can see the two Read nodes' output in the Left and Right views now instead of through separate Viewer inputs. This is the beginning to working with views. Later in this chapter you will do more.

For now, there is just one more thing to set up so that you can work quickly with such large-scale images.

Using proxies

Working in 2K (over 2000 pixels wide, that is) can become very slow, very quickly. Because compositing software always calculates each and every pixel, giving it more pixels to work with dramatically increases processing times, both for interactivity and rendering.

For example, a PAL image of 720x576 has 414,720 pixels, which is seven times fewer than a normal 2K frame of 2048x1556 with 3,186,688 pixels! So it's that much slower to work with.

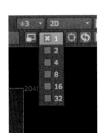

FIGURE 8.22 The Viewer's Downscale Resolution drop-down menu.

Nuke has a few ways to make working with hi-res images faster. First, there is the Viewer Downscale Resolution drop-down menu (**FIGURE 8.22**). This menu lets you scale down the display resolution. Input images are scaled down by the selected factor, then scaled up in the Viewer by the same factor. This creates a speedier workflow with just a quality difference in the Viewer.

1. Choose 32 from the Viewer's Downscale Resolution drop-down menu.

2. Move the Timebar one frame forward.

    You can see the apparent change in quality. The first time you load a frame it will still take a little longer as it still needs to access the full-resolution image.

3. Move back one frame.

    This time around it took Nuke no time at all to show this frame. From now on, working with both frames 1 and 2 will be very quick as you will be working with 1/32nd of the resolution. Note that if you are using a very fast system with a fast hard drive this change in speed might be negligible.

4. Switch the Viewer Downscale Resolution drop-down menu back to 1.

    This is a useful function to quickly switch to a faster way of working. This also offers a good way to have just one Viewer show a lower-resolution image while another Viewer shows a full-res image.

But this is just the tip of the proverbial iceberg. Nuke has a full-blown Proxy System that handles the switch between low-res and hi-res images for the whole project.

5. Press the S key again while hovering over the DAG to make sure your Project Settings panel is at the top.

The way Nuke's Proxy System works is by taking care of everything related to changes of resolution. The Proxy System is split into three areas.

▪   The first area is the Read node. All images coming in through a Read node are scaled down by a scale ratio. The Proxy System takes care of that. A Proxy Scale of 0.5, for example, halves the resolution of all images.

▨ The second area concerns all pixel-based properties. Blurring a 500-pixel wide image by a value of 50 pixels is a 10% blur, whereas blurring a 50-pixel wide image by a value of 50 pixels is a 100% blur—to keep the same level of blur you would blur by only 5 pixels. The same goes for transforms and every other pixel-based property. When using the Proxy System, Nuke takes care of that. And if your Proxy Scale is half, asking for 100-pixel blur actually shows you half a resolution image with half, or a 50-pixel, blur in the Viewer.

▨ The third area is the Viewer. It's inconvenient that anytime a Proxy Scale changes, the Viewer shows images at a different size. Because of this the Proxy System scales up the Viewer to compensate for the change of resolution. All this is done automatically and controlled using one of two ways to define the change of scale (**FIGURE 8.23**).

FIGURE 8.23 The two types of Proxy Modes.

The drop-down menu for the Proxy Mode property shows two types of proxy: Format and Scale. Format lets you choose another defined format for the size of the proxy. On the other hand, Scale allows you to choose a ratio to scale the image down by, as a derivative of the Full Size Format dimensions.

By default, the Scale option is selected and under it the Proxy Scale property lets you choose the ratio to scale everything by (**FIGURE 8.24**).

FIGURE 8.24 The Proxy Scale property.

6. Under the Root tab in Project Settings, choose Format from the Proxy Mode drop-down menu.

Now that Format is selected, the Proxy Scale property is replaced by a Proxy Format property. You can now use that to define the format proxy images will be scaled to (**FIGURE 8.25**).

FIGURE 8.25 The Proxy Scale property is replaced with the Proxy Format property.

Let's use the Proxy System to make working with this project faster. You will use the Scale property rather than Format, and you will scale down to a third of the original resolution.

7. Choose Scale from the Proxy Mode drop-down menu.

8. Change the Proxy Scale to 0.333.

9. To activate the Proxy System, check the box next to the Proxy Mode property to turn it on (**FIGURE 8.26**).

FIGURE 8.26 Turning on the Proxy System using the Proxy Mode check box.

FIGURE 8.27 The Proxy Mode button in the Viewer is set to on.

You don't have to load the Project Settings panel every time you want to turn on Proxy Mode. To toggle Proxy Mode on and off, you can also either use the Proxy Mode button in the Viewer, as shown in **FIGURE 8.27**, or press the hot key Ctrl/Cmd-P.

Now that Proxy Mode is on, what happens is that, much like the Viewer Downscale Resolution you used before, images are read in and scaled down, the Viewer scales the images back up, and all pixel-based values are changed to reflect the smaller resolution.

As shown before when using Downscale Resolution, there is still some processing done on the full-resolution image. Nuke has to read in the whole image to scale it down. It does this on the fly, without your needing to do anything else. However, this stage, too, can be removed.

Instead of using on-the-fly proxies as you are doing now, you can be reading smaller-resolution images directly from a specified location on the disk. This way the images are already there and will always be there, and no processing ever needs to be done to them—resulting in a quicker workflow throughout.

Let's generate some proxy images. These are sometimes called *pre-rendered proxies* because they are not rendered on the fly.

10. Create an unattached Write node and connect its input to Read1.

11. Click the little folder button beside the Proxy property (**FIGURE 8.28**).

FIGURE 8.28 This time you should use the Proxy property instead of the File property.

12. Navigate to the BulletBG directory inside the chapter08 directory. Create a new directory here called **third** (if it doesn't already exist).

13. Name your sequence the same as the full resolution one: **bulletBG_left.####.dpx** and press Enter/Return.

This is a pretty standard way to work with pre-rendered proxies—have a directory with the name of the element. Inside it, have a directory for each resolution and then keep the sequence name the same.

Just like in the Read node, there is a Colorspace property here as well. As the tree itself is in linear color space, the image needs to be reconverted to sRGB so it will be like the image that came in. All this is set by default in the Views tab in the Project Settings panel.

14. Make sure Proxy Mode is checked in the Viewer.

15. Click the Render button in Write1's Properties panel.

Since you are rendering Read1 and not a multi-view tree (only after JoinView1 does your tree become a multi-view tree), you need to use the Views drop-down menu in the Render panel to select only the Left view (**FIGURE 8.29**).

FIGURE 8.29 Selecting the Left view to render.

16. In the Render panel that opens, use the Views drop-down menu to uncheck the Right check box and then click OK to start the render.

Because Proxy Mode is on, your image is now being scaled to a third of its size. Nuke is now using the Proxy property in the Write node instead of the File property it usually uses and it's actually rendering third resolution images.

When the render finishes, tell your Read1 node that there are pre-rendered proxies on the disk.

17. Copy and paste the path from the Write1 Proxy field to the Read1 Proxy field.

Copying the file path like you just did doesn't update the Read node. You can easily fix that.

18. To update the Read node, click the folder icon to the right of the Proxy property field, select the sequence that's in there, and then press Enter/Return.

   Make sure the Proxy format has updated to 682x413.

19. Switch Proxy Mode on and off. Now, when you enable and disable Proxy Mode, you actually switch between two file sequences on the disk.

You now need to do the same for the right view, or Read2. You can use the same Write node—just move its input and change some settings.

20. Grab the output side of the pipe connecting Read1 to Write1 and move it to Read2.

21. In Write1's Properties panel, change the proxy file name in the Proxy field so instead of "left" it says "right" (**FIGURE 8.30**).

FIGURE 8.30 It's easy to change the name of the proxy file simply by editing the text itself.

22. Make sure Proxy Mode is on as you want to render the lo-res version of the image.

23. Click the Render button.

In the Render panel that displays, only the Left view should be checked. This is fine, as it doesn't matter which view you are rendering at this point in the tree, just that you are rendering only one. When working with a multi-view project you always have two streams; however, this Read node represents only one of them and will show the same image in both views. As there is no point in rendering the same image twice, checking only one view is enough.

24. Click OK.

When this render finishes, you will have pre-rendered proxy files for both views. You need to tell Read2 to use the files you just generated.

25. Copy and paste the path and file name from Write1's Proxy field to Read2's Proxy field.

26. To update the Read node, click the folder icon to the right of the Proxy field, select the sequence that's in there, and click Enter/Return.

27. You don't need Write1 anymore; you can delete it.

That's that. Both views are now ready.

Creating stereo-view proxies efficiently

You need to bring one more element and perform the same processes on it. It will be a lot quicker now that everything is already set up.

Also, notice you had to run through the proxy-making stages twice, once for the left eye and once for the right eye. This is not strictly necessary. There are other ways to work with Read and Write nodes when it comes to multi-view projects and trees.

Instead of bringing in two separate Read nodes, one for each eye, you can bring in a single Read node and use a variable to tell Nuke that there are both a Left and a Right view. A *variable* is simply a placeholder that tells Nuke to look for something else. In this case, the variable will be %V, and it tells Nuke that it needs to replace this variable with whatever is in the Views list. In this case it looks for Left and Right.

1. Create a new Read node and navigate the File Browser to the chapter08/ BulletCG/full/ directory.

Here you can see there are two sequences. One is called bulletCG_left.####.exr, and the other bulletCG_right.####.exr. Replacing Left or Right with %V will enable you to use only one Read node.

2. Click the first sequence in the list, the one indicating the left eye.

3. In the path bar at the bottom, replace the word "left" with %V and press Enter/ Return (**FIGURE 8.31**).

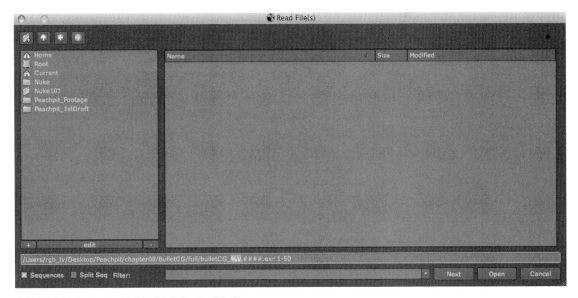

FIGURE 8.31 Replacing "left" with %V in the File Browser.

You now have a single Read node in the DAG: Read3. If you look at it carefully, you can see there is a little green icon with a V in it at the top-left corner (**FIGURE 8.32**). This indicates that this node has multi-views. Let's see this in the Viewer.

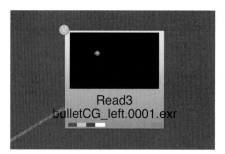

FIGURE 8.32 The green V icon indicates a multi-view node.

4. Look at the newly created Read3 in the Viewer.

5. Go to frame 50 in the Timebar.

6. Switch between viewing the Left and Right views using the Viewer buttons.

   You can see the difference between the two eyes. This bullet is coming right at you. You can see more of its left side on the right of the screen with the left eye, and more of its right side on the left of the screen with the right eye. (Take a pen and hold it close to your face and shut each eye and you can see what I mean.)

7. View the alpha channel in the Viewer, then switch back to the RGB channels. Notice there is an alpha channel here.

Having an alpha channel affects some of what you are doing here. As a rule, you shouldn't color correct premultiplied images without unpremultiplying them first. Having an alpha channel is supposed to raise the question of whether this is a premultiplied image. You can see in the Viewer that all areas that are black in the alpha are also black in the RGB. Black indicates that this indeed is a premultiplied image. Just to make sure, I asked the 3D artist who made this to render out premultiplied images, so I know for a fact that's what they are.

Applying color management on Read3 applies color correction on the image. Because it is premultiplied, you need to unpremult it first. To do that, use the Premultiplied check box next to the Colorspace property (**FIGURE 8.33**) in the Read node's Properties panel. However, because this image is actually a 32-bit linear image, there won't be any color correction applied to it, so this step is not necessary.

FIGURE 8.33 Premultiplied needs to be checked for premultiplied images that are not linear.

Now that you've brought in this stereo pair of images, you can make proxies for them in one go.

8. Connect a new Write node to Read3 by clicking it and pressing the W key.

9. Set the path under the Write2 Proxy field to: chapter08/BulletCG/third/ bulletCG_%V.####.exr. If the third directory doesn't exist, create it.

    Notice that again you are using the %V variable. This means you can render the two views, and the names of the views—Left and Right—will be placed instead of the variable.

10. Because you want to render the alpha channel as well, change the channel set for Write2 from RGB to All to be on the safe side.

This is an EXR file, which has a lot of properties you can change. The original image is 32 bit and you will keep it that way.

11. Choose 32-bit Float from the Datatype drop-down menu.

Again, because there is an alpha channel in these images, color management should normally get considered here, and the Premultiplied check box should be checked. However, because this is a linear image, no color management is applied, and so no change needs to be applied.

Notice that the render range here is only 1-50, whereas the background sequence is 1-60. You'll deal with this later.

12. Click the Render button.

13. In the Render panel, change the Views drop-down menu so that both Left and Right are turned on (**FIGURE 8.34**).

FIGURE 8.34 Turning on both views for rendering.

NOTE Write nodes default to rendering the RGB channels only because usually this is the final render and there's no reason to retain the alpha channel. Keep this in mind— forgetting it will waste render times when you do need an alpha channel.

14. Make sure Proxy Mode is on.

15. Click OK to start the render.

16. When the render is complete, copy and paste the proxy path from Write1 to Read3. Again click the folder icon to the right of the Proxy field, select one of the file sequences that are in there, change the view to %V, and click Enter/Return.

17. Delete Write1.

The proxy setup is ready. You have pre-rendered proxies for all files, individual or dual-view streams. Now you can go ahead and create the composite. This is a very simple composite.

COMPOSITING A STEREO PROJECT

With this composite, the first thing you need to do is deal with the change in length between the two elements. The background is a 60-frame element, whereas the bullet is a 50-frame element. You have several ways of dealing with this, both creatively and technically. Let's look at the options.

Retiming elements

The first creative way to deal with the lack of correlation between the lengths of these two elements is to stretch (slow down) the bullet element so it's 60 frames long. Slowing down clips means that in-between frames need to be invented. You can do that in three ways:

- Copying adjacent frames.

- Blending adjacent frames.

- Using a technology called Optical Flow to really gauge the movement in adjacent frames and create in-between frames by moving and warping groups of pixels.

Several different nodes in the Time toolbox deal with timing. You're going to look at two different options for slowing down elements.

1. Select Read3 and insert an OFlow node after it from the Time toolbox.

    The OFlow (optical flow) node generates high-quality retiming operations by analyzing the movement of all pixels in the frames and then rendering new in-between images based on that analysis. This node is slow.

You can use this node in two different ways—either by stating the speed you want to change to or by keyframing frame locations, which you will do now.

2. In OFlow1's Properties panel, choose Source Frame from the Timing drop-down menu (**FIGURE 8.35**).

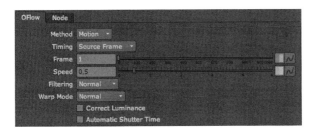

FIGURE 8.35 Retiming an element with OFlow.

3. Go to frame 1 in the Timebar, right-click (Ctrl-click) the Frame field, and choose Set Key from the contextual menu.

4. Go to frame 60 in the Timebar and set the Frame field to 50 (the last frame of the original element you brought in).

5. While viewing OFlow1 in the Viewer, click Play.

   If you look at the sequence frame by frame, you can clearly see that there are some original frames and some newly created frames. Change that by increasing the ShutterTime property in the OFlow node; doing so increases the blending that's happening in-between frames.

OFlow is a very good tool. However, its down side is that it is also very slow. You are working in Proxy Mode at the moment, so things are quick and easy. But when you go back to the full-res image, you will feel how slow it is. Let's try another retiming node.

6. Click Stop when you're done watching.

7. Delete OFlow1.

The next retiming node is simply called Retime.

8. Click Read3 and from the Time toolbox insert a Retime node.

Retime is a handy tool to stretch, compress, or change the timing location of clips. Retime is fast as it doesn't use optical flow technology and either blends between frames or freezes frames to accommodate speed changes. There are many ways to play around with this tool. It can really work in whatever way fits your needs (**FIGURE 8.36**).

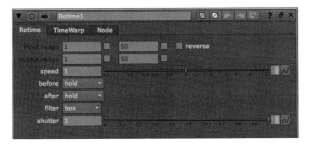

FIGURE 8.36 The Retime node's interface.

You can specify speed using a combination of the Speed, Input Range, and Output Range properties.

9. Check the boxes next to the Input Range and Output Range properties.

10. Enter 60 in the second field for the Output Range property.

    The original 50 frames now stretch between frames 1 and 60.

11. While viewing Retime1 in the Viewer, click Play.

Again, you can see that movement isn't exactly smooth. Retime is set to blend frames at the moment. Setting it to blend or freeze is done in the Filter property. Box means blending, while Nearest means freezing. None means slowing down animation done inside Nuke—keyframes—and will create smooth slow motion for those. None of these three options will produce appealing results. Slowing down crispy, clean movements like the one you have here for the bullet is always a bit difficult and creates jerky movement. Let's delete this retiming node.

12. Click Stop.

13. Delete Retime1.

Notice that the element you were working on was part of a multi-view branch. You didn't even notice. You were only viewing one view—either Left or Right, depending on what your Viewer was set to—but the other view was being manipulated as well. That's the beauty about working in this way.

You're going to solve this problem in a different way, by simply shortening the background element.

First, let's make the project itself only 50 frames long.

14. Display the Project Settings panel.

15. Enter 1 and 50 in the two Frame Range fields (**FIGURE 8.37**).

FIGURE 8.37 Changing the Frame Range in the Project Settings panel.

The longer length of the background element doesn't matter that much anymore. Now you will use the end of the element and trim the beginning, rather than the other way around. You need to shift the position of two Read nodes in time.

16. Clear the Properties Bin.

17. Double-click Read1 and then double-click Read2.

Using the Dope Sheet, you can shift the position of Read nodes in time.

18. Click the Dope Sheet tab in the same pane as the DAG (**FIGURE 8.38**).

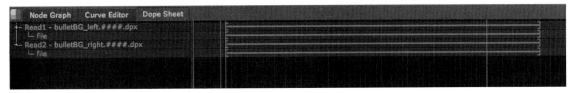

FIGURE 8.38 The Dope Sheet shows the timing of elements.

Using the bars on the right side of the Dope Sheet, one for the first file property and one for the second file property, you can shift the timing of the Read nodes.

19. In the Graph window, click the first file property and move it back (to the left) until your outpoint on the right reaches frame 50 (**FIGURE 8.39**).

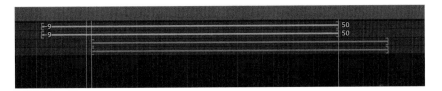

FIGURE 8.39 The numbers on the left and right indicate the new in and out points.

20. Do the same for the second file property.

21. Go back to viewing the Node Graph.

That's it for retiming. You can now proceed to placing the foreground over the background.

Compositing the two elements together

Now to place the foreground over the background—simple stuff you've done several times already. This time you are actually doing it once, but creating two of everything, one for the Left view and another for the Right view.

1. Click Read3 and press the M key to insert a Merge node.

2. Connect Merge1's B input to the output of JoinViews1.

3. View Merge1 in the Viewer.

4. Click Play in the Viewer (**FIGURE 8.40**).

FIGURE 8.40 The slap
comp (a quick, basic
comp). You can see it
needs more work.

At this point, you should be getting pretty good playback speed because of the small proxy you are using. What you see now is the bullet leaving the gun's barrel (the trigger was pulled in a previous shot). The color of the bullet is wrong, and it should start darker, as if it's inside the barrel. Let's make this happen.

5. Insert a Grade node after Read3.

Because this is a premultiplied image, you need to unpremultiply it. You can do that as you did in Chapter 2. However, you can also do it inside the Grade node (or indeed any color correction node).

6. At the bottom of Grade1's Properties panel, choose Rgba.alpha from the (Un)premult By drop-down menu.

    This ensures that the RGB channels are divided by the alpha and then multiplied again after the color correction.

7. Go to frame 20 in the Timebar. It's a good frame to see the color correction needed (**FIGURE 8.41**).

FIGURE 8.41 The difference in color is apparent.

You can see here that the metal of the gun and the metal of the bullet have very different colors. Although they aren't necessarily supposed to be the same kind of metal, it looks at the moment as if there is different-colored light shining on them, and their contrast is very different as well. You will use the Gamma property to bring down the midtones and create more contrast with the bright highlights that are already there and use the Lift property to color the shadows to the same kind of red you can find in the background image.

8. Adjust the Gamma and Lift to color correct the bullet so it looks better. I ended up with Lift: 0.035, 0.005, 0.005 and Gamma: 0.54, 0.72, 0.54.

The bullet should look better now. Now for the animation—but first you will learn what to do if you want to change the color of just one of the views.

Changing properties for a single view

You have two primary options for manipulating just one of the views. The first is to split the whole tree up into two again, and then back to one, using a SplitAndJoin node.

1. Select Grade1 and in the Views toolbox click SplitAndJoin (**FIGURE 8.42**).

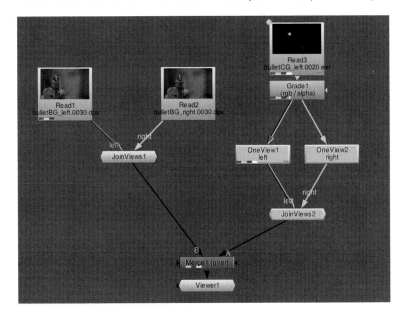

FIGURE 8.42 The SplitAndJoin node is actually several nodes.

You now have three new nodes in your DAG, not just one. SplitAndJoin actually creates as many nodes as it needs to split the number of views out to individual branches—usually two views, with a OneView node—and then connects them up again using a JoinViews node. You can now insert whatever node you want in whatever branch you want. This is one method.

2. Select OneView1, OneView2, and JoinViews2 and delete them.

   The other method is to split just specific properties inside nodes, because you need them.

3. Insert another Grade node after Grade1.

   Look at the Gain property. There's a new button on the right that lets you display the View menu (**FIGURE 8.43**).

FIGURE 8.43 The new View menu.

4. Click the View button to display the View drop-down menu, which allows you to split off one view to be controlled separately.

5. Choose Split Off Left from the View drow-down menu for the Gain property (**FIGURE 8.44**).

FIGURE 8.44 This is how to split a property to control two views independently.

   You now have a little arrow next to the Gain property.

6. Click the little arrow next to the Gain property (**FIGURE 8.45**).

   This reveals the two separate View subproperties.

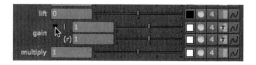

FIGURE 8.45 You now have two properties for Gain, one for each view.

This method lets you manipulate each view separately for this property, and still have overall control over the rest of the properties as well.

You can also reverse this using the View drop-down menu again.

7. Choose Unsplit Left from the View drop-down menu for Gain1.

   You are back where you were before—controlling the two views together.

Now to change the color of the bullet as it's leaving the barrel.

8. Go to frame 10 in the Timebar.

9. Create a keyframe for both the Gain property and the Gamma property.

10. Go to frame 1 in the Timebar.

11. Change these two properties so the bullet looks dark enough, as if it's still inside the barrel. I set the Gain to 0.004 and the Gamma to 1.55, 1.5, 1.35.

This image is still premultiplied, remember? Using the (Un)premult By checkbox in Grade1 earlier only unpremultiplied the image where Grade1 was applied. The output of Grade1 is still a premultiplied image. You need to do the same here, in Grade2.

12. Change the (Un)premult By drop-down menu to Rgba.alpha.

This is all you are going to do at this stage to this composite. It's been a long lesson already.

RENDERING AND VIEWING STEREO TREES

Before you finish this lesson, you will see what you did and learn a couple of things as you do it.

1. Insert a Write node after Merge1.

2. Click the File property's Folder button to load a File Browser.

3. Navigate to your student_files directory and create another directory named **bullet_full**.

4. Give the file to render the name of **bullet_%V.####.png** and click Enter/Return (**FIGURE 8.46**).

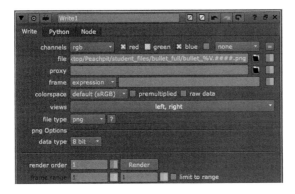

FIGURE 8.46 Notice the Data Type and Colorspace properties.

You now have a Write node set up to render to disk. You haven't set up a proxy file name, just the full-resolution file name. If you render now, with Proxy Mode turned on, the render will fail. You can, of course, create another folder and call it bullet_third if you want to render a proxy. Right now you will render the full-resolution image.

Notice that as you render a PNG file sequence, which is an 8-bit file format, you are rendering it to the sRGB color space. Nuke is taking one of your elements, which is a Cineon color space, and another element which is in linear color space, working with both of them in linear, and then rendering out an sRGB color space PNG sequence. It's all done automatically and clearly presented in front of you.

5. Click the Render button. In the Render panel that displays, make sure the Frame Range property is set correctly by choosing Global from the drop-down menu.

This render might take a little while because of the hi-res images you are using. Good thing you deleted that OFlow node—it would have taken a lot longer with that one.

When the render is complete, bring in the files so you can watch them. You can do it in the Write node.

6. Check the Read File box at the bottom of Write1's Properties panel.

You can now view your handiwork. The thing is, however, that this is a stereo pair of views you have here and you can only watch one eye at a time.

If you have anaglyph glasses (red and cyan glasses, not the fancy kind you find in cinemas), you can use them to watch the true image you are producing. If you don't have 3D glasses, you can buy some online or download instructions on how to make them here: www.peachpit.com/nuke101.

To view stereo with anaglyph glasses, you need your image to be an anaglyph image in the first place. You can do that with the Anaglyph node, found in the Views/Stereo toolbox.

7. Select Write1 and insert an Anaglyph node after it (**FIGURE 8.47**).

FIGURE 8.47 Inserting an Anaglyph node after the Write node.

Your image now looks gray with red and cyan shifts of color on the left and right. This shift in color makes viewing with anaglyph glasses correct in each eye (**FIGURE 8.48**).

FIGURE 8.48 An anaglyph image.

8. Click Play and enjoy the show.

Anaglyph glasses don't give a spectacular stereoscopic experience, I must admit. There are other solutions out there, but they are more professional and a lot more expensive. (If you have one of those solutions, that means you know what you are doing and you don't need instructions from me.)

9

THE NUKE 3D ENGINE

One of the most powerful features in Nuke is its 3D engine. Nuke has an almost fully featured 3D system that enables the compositor to import cameras, create simple objects and import objects, do camera projections, extract various types of 2D data from 3D data, and much more.

An important thing to note is that Nuke's 3D engine isn't there to replace your 3D department. You won't see character animation done in Nuke. You won't see serious lighting and rendering done in Nuke. Although Nuke's 3D capabilities are remarkable for a compositing system, they are still far from replacing full-blown 3D applications.

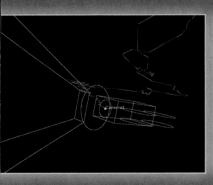
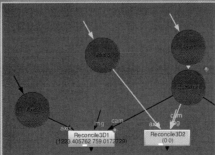

Nuke's 3D capabilities are there to enhance the compositor's abilities and make it easier for the compositor to converse with the 3D department. In addition, with scenes for which 3D data is available—whether from a live shot or generated in a 3D application—there are ways to get other 3D data, such as 3D tracking, and use that in novel ways.

You can use Nuke's 3D engine to more easily generate 2D tracking information, give still frames more life, simplify roto and paint work, and do much, much more.

3D SCENE SETUPS

NOTE Nuke works well with external 3D applications and can exchange data with them using file formats commonly used in 3D applications: obj and fbx. The obj extension is for files that hold geometry. The fbx extension can hold practically anything generated in a 3D scene.

In Nuke, 3D scenes are built out of four main elements: a camera, a piece of geometry, a Scene node (optional), and a ScanlineRender node to render the 3D data into a 2D image.

Let's look at the four elements:

- **Camera:** Through the camera element, the rendering node views the scene. You can also import camera properties from fbx files.

- **Geometry:** The geometry element can be a *primitive* (simple geometry) created in Nuke, such as a card or a sphere, or it can be imported from another application as an obj file, an obj sequence of files (for animating objects), or an fbx file.

- **Scene:** The Scene node connects all the pieces that make up the scene you want to render. This includes all pieces of geometry, lights, and cameras. That means if you have only one element, you don't need this node. By using this node you are saying that all these elements live in the same space.

- **ScanlineRender:** The ScanlineRender node renders the scene. It takes the 3D data and makes a 2D image out of it. Without it, you won't see a 2D image.

Using these nodes together, and some other nodes that are not part of the basic 3D setup, you can do remarkable things. I cover a few techniques in this chapter and the next two chapters (**FIGURE 9.1**).

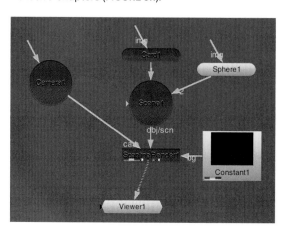

FIGURE 9.1 The basic 3D setup.

You'll find all the tools dealing with the 3D engine in the 3D toolbox. I'm not going to go over everything because it's just too expansive, and I need to leave something for the advanced book, don't I? But you will still get to do some pretty advanced stuff.

MOVING IMAGES WITH A 3D SCENE

A long time ago in a chapter far, far away (OK, Chapter 3), you composited a lemming running towards a car and grabbing on to it with a hook. You were also supposed to render your composite. Whether you did or didn't, I did it for you, and you can find the output of that composite in the chapter09 directory of this book's disc.

1. From the chapter09/chapter03_output/ directory, bring in lemming_v01.####.png.

    Have a look at this. It's been a while after all.

2. Watch the sequence by loading it into Framecycler or playing it in the Viewer.

When the lemming attaches the hook to the latch on the car, the hook doesn't disappear behind the latch. This is a problem, but it is easily fixed in several different ways. Because I am teaching the 3D engine here, I will show you an interesting way to do this involving a 3D setup and some new tools.

The idea is to cut a hole in the render with a matte and use it to show through to the background, which doesn't have the lemming or the hook in it. You'll generate the matte using a RotoPaint node connected to a Tracker node. The Tracker node won't take its data from 2D tracking, but directly from 3D data. Bit by bit I walk you through this process. Fear not.

Setting up a Nuke 3D scene

Because you will also need the original background of this comp, bring that in.

1. Now that you know how to use the Project Settings panel, set up the script by opening the Project Settings panel and changing Full Size Format to HD and Fps to 25. Also change the length of the composite to 1-143.

2. From chapter03/bg/ import bg.####.png.

Now that the background and the render are both in, you can start to create the rest of the comp and step into the 3D engine.

The first element you will be creating is a camera.

3. With nothing selected in the DAG, create a Camera node from the 3D toolbox.

4. With nothing selected, create a Scene node from the 3D toolbox.

5. Select Camera1 and Scene1 and insert a ScanlineRender node from the 3D toolbox. The ScanlineRender node connects itself to the Camera and Scene nodes in the correct inputs (**FIGURE 9.2**).

Eventually you will need some kind of geometry or this setup won't mean much, but there's still time.

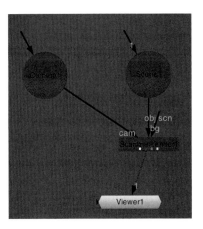

FIGURE 9.2 The beginning of a 3D setup.

6. Select ScanlineRender1 and press the 1 key to view it.

At the moment you don't see much in the Viewer, and you shouldn't. Although you have a camera and a ScanlineRender node, you have nothing to shoot through the camera. You don't see anything in the resulting 2D image. However, in the 3D world, you should be seeing at least a camera. Nuke's Viewer functions as both a 2D and a 3D Viewer. You can easily switch between 2D and 3D viewing modes by hovering the mouse pointer over the Viewer and pressing the Tab key. Alternatively, you can choose 2D or 3D (or other views such as Top and Front) from the View Selection drop-down menu at the top right of the Viewer as seen in **FIGURE 9.3**.

FIGURE 9.3 Changing the View Selection in the Viewer.

7. Hover the mouse pointer over the Viewer and press the Tab key.

You are now in the 3D view, as you can see by looking at the View Selection drop-down menu. You're still not seeing much. Your view's default position is at *world center*, a value of 0, 0, 0 (that's X, Y, Z, if you weren't sure). That's the default position for everything in Nuke's 3D engine, including the camera. So at the moment your view is at world center, and so is the camera, so you can't see it—just as you can't see London when you're standing in the middle of Trafalgar Square. You need to zoom out to see the camera in front of you. And for that you need to know how to navigate the 3D Viewer.

Navigating the 3D world

The following hot keys and techniques are useful for navigating in the 3D view:

- Ctrl/Cmd-click and drag to rotate around the 3D world.

- Alt/Option-click and drag to pan across the 3D world.

- Use the scroll wheel (if you have one) or the + and – keys to zoom in and out.

Now that you know how to move around the 3D world you can use this knowledge to move back a little.

1. Use the scroll wheel or the – key to zoom out until you can see the camera.

    You can see the back of the camera now.

2. Move the camera around by holding Ctrl/Cmd-click and dragging to the left.

    You should see something similar to **FIGURE 9.4**.

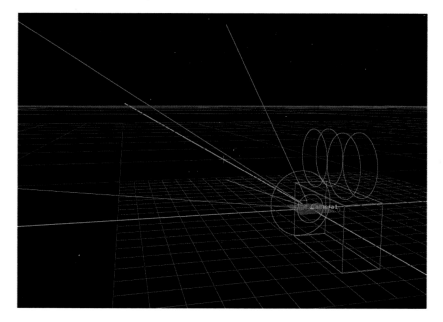

FIGURE 9.4 Viewing Nuke's 3D world and the Camera in it.

Now that you can see the camera, it will be good for you to know how to move it—and by extension, everything else in the 3D world.

You can, of course, use the Properties panel to move the camera, but often this is unintuitive. Instead, you will want to use on-screen control Camera axes. To do that, first select the camera element in the Node Graph.

3. Click on Camera1 in the DAG to select it.

    See how the camera lights up in green in the Viewer. The axes—a colorful red, green, and blue color—display in the center of the camera and let you move it around (**FIGURE 9.5**).

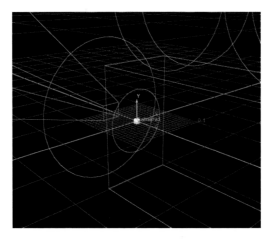

FIGURE 9.5 After selecting Camera1 in the DAG, the camera's axis appears.

Now that you have the axes, you can click them and move the camera around. You can also use an individual axis to move in one direction. The reason the axes are in three colors is to help you figure out which is which. The order of colors is usually: red, green, blue. The order of directions is usually: X, Y, Z. In other words, the red-colored axis controls the X direction, the green one controls the Y direction, and the blue controls the Z. Very convenient and easy to remember.

The same happens with rotation.

4. In the Viewer, hold down Ctrl/Cmd and watch the axes change to show the rotation controls (**FIGURE 9.6**).

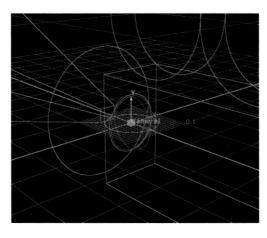

FIGURE 9.6 Holding Ctrl/Cmd lets you control rotation.

The circles that appear on the axis when holding down Ctrl/Cmd allow you to rotate the camera around one of three axes. This is done in the same way as the translation axes: red for X rotation, green for Y rotation, and blue for Z rotation.

These are the basic techniques for moving things around in the 3D viewer. Feel free to play around with the camera and get a feel for it. You will reset it in a minute anyway, so you can really go to town here.

Importing a camera

For this exercise, you will need the 3D camera to act like the camera used to shoot this footage. The method for extracting camera data from an existing moving image, called *3D tracking* or *camera tracking,* is covered in Chapter 10. In this case, you don't have to do the camera tracking yourself because the artist in charge of creating the Lemming's animation already took care of that and has supplied you with a file to import. How convenient. You probably want to learn how to import. Here goes:

1. Double-click Camera1 to display its Properties panel at the top of the Properties Bin.

The top-most property is a little check box called Read From File. Click it to use the File tab, which is where you read the camera location and other properties from a file (**FIGURE 9.7**).

FIGURE 9.7 Checking this box enables the File tab.

2. Check the Read From File check box.

3. Switch to the File tab in Camera1's Properties panel (**FIGURE 9.8**).

FIGURE 9.8 Camera1's File tab.

4. To import the camera file, click the folder icon to the right of the File property to load the File Browser.

5. In the File Browser, navigate to the chapter09 directory and bring in camera.fbx.

6. A dialog box asks if it's OK to destroy the current camera data; click Yes.

An FBX file can hold a lot of cameras' properties in various takes. From the two drop-down menus, you will choose a take name and a node name. These usually include a lot of default presets that you wouldn't normally use, depending on which application you used when exporting the camera file.

7. From the Take Name drop-down menu, choose Take 001. This should be the default.

8. From the Node name drop-down menu choose track:Camera01 (**FIGURE 9.9**). This should also be the default.

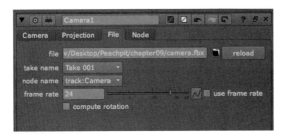

FIGURE 9.9 This is how your File tab should look at this point.

9. Switch to the Camera tab.

You can see that the Translate and Rotate fields are all bright blue to indicate that each one has a keyframe, and it's like that for each and every frame. This is how the animation is carried across.

The camera has disappeared from the Viewer (or at least it did on mine). To see it again, tell the Viewer to frame the selected element.

10. Select Camera1 in the Node Graph again.

11. Hover your mouse pointer over the Viewer and press the F key to frame the Viewer to the selected element (**FIGURE 9.10**).

FIGURE 9.10 The camera after the import.

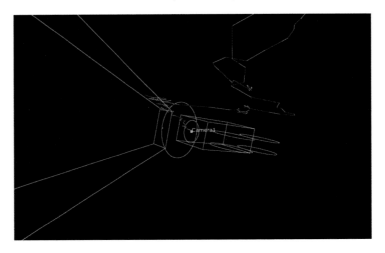

The camera appears to be on its side. There are all sorts of differences between 3D applications that involve scale and rotation. In this case, the world axis (the 3D world's definition of what is up or down and what is right or left) in the application that generated the camera is different than the axis you have in Nuke. This is easily fixed, though. Because the camera has animation on every frame, it's inadvisable to rotate the camera itself. Instead you will use a new node called an Axis node. The Axis node lets you move things around in the 3D world.

12. Make sure nothing is selected and create an Axis node by clicking the 3D toolbox.

13. Connect Camera1's input to Axis1's output (**FIGURE 9.11**).

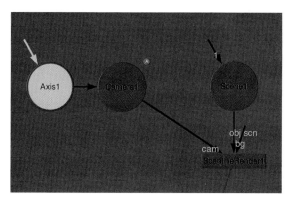

FIGURE 9.11 Connecting an Axis node to the Camera node.

14. In Axis1's Properties panel, change the rotate.x (that's the first field in the Rotate property) to −90 to rotate the camera to its right alignment.

15. The camera is gone again from the Viewer. Select it again in the DAG and press the F key again to frame the Viewer to the camera.

The camera is now straight and ready.

Creating a cube

Wouldn't you like to see if the camera does indeed match the background? For that you need to create a cube, texture it, and place it on the floor of the shot, then see if it stays put.

1. Create a Cube node from the 3D/Geometry toolbox.

For the texture you will use a simple checkerboard.

2. Deselect Cube1 and create a CheckerBoard node from the Image toolbox.

3. View CheckerBoard1 in the Viewer.

4. Press the Tab key while hovering your mouse pointer in the Viewer to switch to the 2D Viewer.

You don't need a full HD texture—something smaller will do.

5. From CheckerBoard1's Properties panel, choose Square_1k from the Format drop-down menu.

This will be your texture. You just need to connect it to the cube geometry.

6. Connect the input (called img) of Cube1 to the output of CheckerBoard1 (**FIGURE 9.12**).

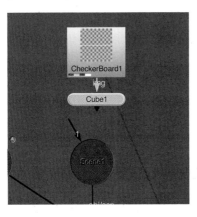

FIGURE 9.12 The texture is normally connected to the img input of the geometry.

7. To see your handiwork, switch the Viewer back to the 3D Viewer by hovering your mouse pointer over it and pressing the Tab key.

8. Select Cube1 and with the cursor over the Viewer press the F key.

The Viewer lets you rotate around the cube to really see all six sides of it, all of them textures with beautiful checkers.

To place the cube on the floor, you need to move it up a little. By default, the cube is created between −0.5 and 0.5. The floor usually is at 0. You need to change the creation location to run from 0 to 1.

9. In Cube1's Properties panel, change the Y and T Cube properties to 0 and 1 respectively (**FIGURE 9.13**).

FIGURE 9.13 Change how the cube is created using the Cube properties.

In relation to the imported camera, the cube, which is a size of 1 now, is pretty small. Let's make it bigger.

10. Change the Uniform Scale property to 10.

To now see the cube over the background, input the original background of the Lemming shot to the "bg" input of the ScanlineRender node.

11. Connect the output of Read2 to the "bg" input of the ScanlineRender1 node.

12. View the output of ScanlineRender1 in the Viewer and make sure you're viewing the 2D Viewer.

You still can't see the cube because it's not connected to the Scene node.

13. Connect Cube1 to Scene1 by dragging from Cube1's output and releasing the mouse button on top of Scene1 (**FIGURE 9.14**).

FIGURE 9.14 The cube composited on the background.

The textured cube now appears to the left of the car. It already looks like it fits in there, because it's already at an angle, just like the floor.

Check out how this plays and see how well the tracked camera fares. The quickest way I like to do that is:

14. Click the Proxy toggle in the Viewer to turn on Proxy mode and scale down the image to half size (**FIGURE 9.15**).

FIGURE 9.15 Turn on Proxy mode for quick playback.

15. Change the Downrez drop-down menu from 1 to 2 to further increase the speed of processing images (**FIGURE 9.16**).

Now that you have slightly poorer quality but a quicker playback, you can play the whole shot. Remember, the first time you play in the Viewer, frames are being rendered and cached to the disk. The second time around, the cached images are being played back, so you don't have to wait for renders.

FIGURE 9.16 Changing the Downrez option reduces the quality by 2.

16. Click Play in the Viewer.

    You can see the cube is sticking to the floor, proving the track is perfect.

17. Click Stop in the Viewer and go back to frame 1.

18. Switch the Downrez drop-down menu back to 1.

19. In the Viewer, click the Proxy button again to turn it off.

You are ready to use the camera to produce a matte for the latch.

RECONCILE3D: TRANSFORMING 3D DATA INTO 2D DATA

Reconcile3D is a great tool for working with 3D renders. It enables the compositor to pick a location in the 3D world and easily convert it to 2D position, just like a tracker, but without actually tracking. You will use this technique here to generate two tracked points in the 2D world, attach them to a Tracker node, and use it to move a RotoPaint shape.

Setting up a Reconcile3D node

For Reconcile3D to work you need three things: a camera, which you now have; a defined resolution, the same as the full-size format in the project's Settings panel; and an Axis for the location of the point you want to track.

1. Clear the Properties Bin to remove all on-screen controls.

2. With nothing selected, create another Axis node.

Where shall you place the axis? The next steps show you a good way to view the 3D scene in context.

3. Make sure you're in 3D view.

4. Select Read1 and press the 1 key to view it.

As you are still viewing the 3D view, you won't see any difference, until…

5. Choose Over from the Viewer Composite Controls drop-down menu (**FIGURE 9.17**).

FIGURE 9.17 Choosing Over for the Viewer Composite.

6. Move the Viewer composite axis all the way to the left so you see the whole shot.

You can now see the 3D world composited over the 2D image. The only thing to do now is to look at the scene through the shot's camera. First you need to load that camera into the Properties Bin.

7. Double-click Camera1 to load its Properties panel into the Properties Bin.

8. On the top right of the Viewer, change the Camera drop-down menu from Default to Camera1 (**FIGURE 9.18**).

FIGURE 9.18 Changing the camera around to view the 3D view.

This setup enables you to view both the shot and the 3D scene that made it, which makes it easy to do things in context (**FIGURE 9.19**).

FIGURE 9.19 Viewing the render in 3D context.

You can now position Axis2.

9. Double-click Axis2.

10. Place your cursor in the Translate.x field, to the left of the 0, and start pressing the Up Arrow on your keyboard. You can see the axis traveling on the floor towards the camera. Stop at 8.

11. Place your cursor in the Translate.y field, to the left of the 0, and start pressing the Up Arrow on your keyboard. You can see the axis traveling up. Stop at 14.

12. Do the same for Translate.z. This time, press the Down Arrow until you reach –26. You can see the axis now sits on the latch (**FIGURE 9.20**).

FIGURE 9.20 The axis is bang on the latch.

NOTE Multiple point tracking is covered in Chapter 5, but here's a short recap: Because the camera in this shot produces a movement that includes translation, rotation, and scale, only one set of X and Y locations won't produce the rotation and scale needed, just translation. Adding another set of X and Y locations will enable calculation of rotation and scale.

Because the motion you have has translation, rotation, and scale, you will need another axis, which will create another point for the tracker.

13. Create another Axis node from the 3D toolbox. Make sure it's not connected to anything.

14. Do to Axis3 the same as you did to Axis2. The Translate.y and Translate.z values should be the same, but the Translate.x value should be different as shown in **FIGURE 9.21**:

- Translate.x = 33
- Translate.y = 14
- Translate.z = –26

As you can see, this should bring your axis on top of the tail pipe.

All that remains now is to connect up all the parts to Reconcile3D nodes, one for each Axis node. But first you need to reset your view.

15. Turn off the Viewer Composite Controls by selecting – from the drop-down menu.

16. Switch to a 2D view by clicking your mouse pointer in the Viewer and pressing the Tab key. Make sure you're viewing Read1.

FIGURE 9.21 The axis is
bang on the tail pipe.

Now for the Reconcile3D part:

17. With nothing selected, create a Reconcile3D node from the Transform toolbox.

18. Attach Camera1 to Reconcile3D1's cam input and Axis2 to Reconcile3D1's axis input (FIGURE 9.22).

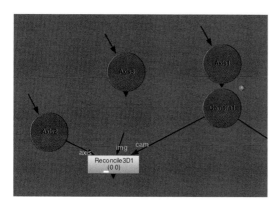

FIGURE 9.22 Reconcile3D's
three inputs, with two
connected.

Normally, you also need to input something into the img input. Reconcile3D needs to know the resolution for the image to be able to extrapolate the 3D to 2D data, as the 2D location depends on the size of the frame. Because you set up your project at the beginning of the lesson to a full-size format of HD, Reconcile3D1 assumes that is the resolution for the img input and you don't actually have to input anything there.

19. Double-click Reconcile3D1 to load its Properties panel to the top of the Properties Bin (FIGURE 9.23).

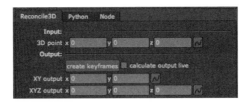

FIGURE 9.23 Reconcile3D1's Properties panel.

20. Click the Create Keyframes button in Reconcile3D1's Properties panel.

21. In the Execute panel that opens, make sure **1-143** is entered and click OK (**FIGURE 9.24**).

FIGURE 9.24 Filling in the Execute panel.

Reconcile3D starts drawing a path in the Viewer. Also, if your machine isn't blazingly fast, a Progress Bar pops up to show progress (**FIGURE 9.25**).

FIGURE 9.25 Reconcile3D at work.

What Reconcile3D did was essentially transfer the 3D information into a 2D location and save these values for every frame in the XY Output property.

Let's do this again for Axis3:

22. With nothing selected, create another Reconcile3D node.

23. Connect Camera1 to Reconcile3D2's cam input.

24. Connect Axis3 to Reconcile3D2's axis input (**FIGURE 9.26**).

25. Click the Create Keyframes button in Reconcile3D2's Properties panel.

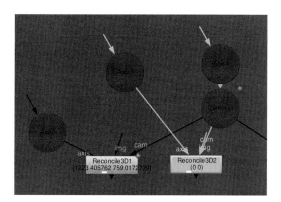

FIGURE 9.26 Setting up the second Reconcile3D node.

26. In the Execute panel that opens, make sure the Frame Range is still 1-143 and click OK.

Wait until Reconcile3D2 finishes processing.

You now have another set of Translate properties (animating location in X and Y) for the second axis held in Reconcile3D2's XY Output property (**FIGURE 9.27**).

FIGURE 9.27 Reconcile3D2's result is held in its XY Output property.

These Translate properties differ from a normal 2D track as they are not based on finding a good reference to track. Rather, they are based on 3D information simply made available as a 2D location.

Using Reconcile3D's output with a Tracker node

You now need to create a RotoPaint node and then use the Reconcile3D data to move it around using a Tracker node.

1. Make sure you're viewing the last frame of the bg that does not include the lemming. That's frame 143 on Read2.

2. Clear the Properties Bin.

3. With nothing selected, create a RotoPaint node by pressing the P key.

4. Draw around the front part of the latch with the Bézier tool (**FIGURE 9.28**).

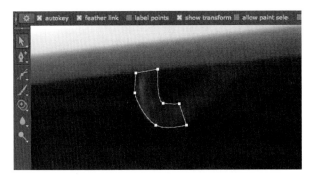

FIGURE 9.28 Drawing a mask for the the latch.

To use all your nicely tracked data, you're going to use a Tracker node to apply the motion.

5. Select RotoPaint1 and insert a Tracker node after it.

6. Close all Properties panels and empty the Properties Bin.

7. Double-click Tracker1 and double-click Reconcile3D1.

You should copy the animation values from Reconcile3D1 to Tracker1's track1 property rather than just link to it, which I would normally do. This is because the Tracker node can be funny about linked data at times.

8. Shift-click and drag from Reconcile3D1's XY Output's Animation menu to Tracker1's track1's Animation menu (**FIGURE 9.29**).

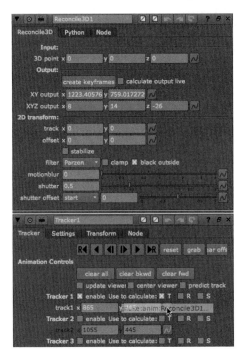

FIGURE 9.29 Copying the animation values from Reconcile3D1 to Tracker1 by holding Shift.

Ctrl/Cmd-dragging creates an expression link, and Shift-dragging copies the curve itself with all its keyframes.

9. Close Reconcile3D1's Properties panel, and then double-click Reconcile3D2 to open its Properties panel.

10. In the Tracker1 node, check the Tracker 2 check box to enable it (**FIGURE 9.30**).

FIGURE 9.30 Turn on Tracker 2 using the check box.

11. Repeat this process between Reconcile3D2's XY output and Tracker1's track2 properties. Remember to hold Shift and not Ctrl/Cmd.

    You now have 2D tracking information in two tracking points without even attempting to set up a single tracking region.

12. To tell Tracker1 to use both tracks for position, rotation, and scale matching, check the check boxes next to Tracker 1 and 2's following three boxes: T, R, and S (**FIGURE 9.31**).

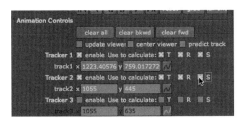

FIGURE 9.31 Using two tracks to match translate, rotation, and scale.

13. Go to the Transform tab of Tracker1's Properties panel and change the Transform property from None to Match-move.

Because you drew the shape on frame 143, you should tell Tracker1 that this is the reference frame.

14. Change the Reference Frame property to 143. If you are standing on frame 143, you can click the Set To This Frame button to do the same (**FIGURE 9.32**).

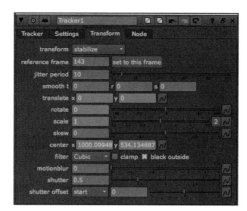

FIGURE 9.32 This is how the Transform tab should look.

You will use a KeyMix node to connect the composited background, the clean background, and your moving matte together.

15. To connect it all, select by Shift-clicking, in this order, Read2 (the original background), Read1 (your composite), and Tracker1.

16. Press the Tab key, enter **keym**, press the Down Arrow on the keyboard, and press Shift-Enter/Return to create and branch a KeyMix node.

    Keymix1 will automatically connect Read1 to its A input, Read2 to its B input, and Tracker1 to its mask input.

17. Close all the Properties panels and view the output of Keymix1.

It is a little hard to see detail in that dark area under the car there. This is what the Display Gain and Display Gamma sliders in the Viewer are for (**FIGURE 9.33**).

FIGURE 9.33 Display Gain and Display Gamma sliders.

Display Gain slider   Display Gamma slider

These Viewer sliders will not affect your final render and will simply let you do quick color correction on your Viewer for exactly such times as you need to see more to check the consistency of your composite. In order to lift dark midtones (as you have here under the car) the Display Gamma slider will be perfect.

18. Using the Display Gamma slider, brighten the image to see how well the composite is going.

    The hook is now where it should be, behind the latch. The matte is just a little harsh.

FIGURE 9.34 This button resets the Display Gamma slider.

19. Reset the Display Gamma slider by clicking the Y button on the left of the slider (**FIGURE 9.34**).

20. Select RotoPaint1 and press B on your keyboard to insert a Blur node.

21. Change Blur1's Size property to 5.

    Your tree should look something like **FIGURE 9.35**.

Notice that there are all sorts of small trees and open-ended branches in the DAG. This is common in tree-based systems.

You can do a lot more to this shot, and by now you have a lot of tools. If you have time, try to remove the red sticker on the bumper of the car. You'll probably need a RotoPaint node to clean one frame, a FrameHold node to freeze that frame, and more Reconcile3D nodes and Tracker nodes to move that frame over time. Good luck.

NOTE Inserting the Blur after the RotoPaint (instead of after the Tracker) means that Nuke only has to render the blur for one frame—as it's a still frame. Adding the Blur after the Tracker means Nuke has to render the blur on each frame, which slows the render.

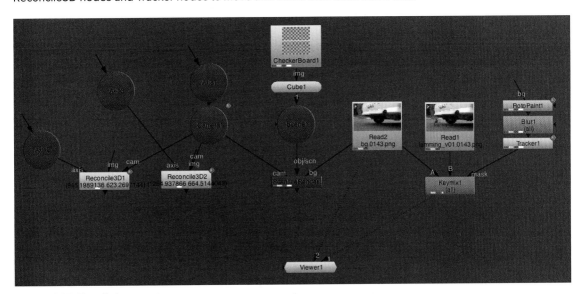

FIGURE 9.35 The whole messy tree.

FINAL DISCLOSURE

Now that you have finished this composite, I can tell you a little secret. The bit where you placed your Axis2 on what appeared to be the latch and Axis3 on what appeared to be the tail pipe? That was a lie. You couldn't possibly have placed the axes correctly by looking at just the 2D image. You have no way of knowing where those two elements are in 3D space.

So how did it work after all? And why did you have to go through this process if it's all a lie?

Well, it worked because this shot has what's called a *nodal camera*—a camera that's not moving. It's panning and tilting, and the zoom changes, but the location of the camera itself in space isn't changing. Therefore, there is no perspective change in the shot. All points in the shot move just as they would in a 2D move you would do using a Transform node in Nuke. Therefore, there is no meaning to the depth of the image, and placing the axes the way you did on the 2D image worked.

And why did you have to go through this? Well, first of all, because I wanted you to learn how to use Reconcile3D. Second, because it worked and it will always work on nodal cameras. And third, because in the next lesson you learn how to find locations in 3D space using Nuke's own built-in 3D CameraTracker node.

CAMERA TRACKING

Nuke 6.0v1 introduced the much-anticipated Camera Tracker to Nuke. The Camera Tracker enables Nuke to extract the camera location and movement from a moving shot. It uses a lot of *tracking points*, also called *features*, which are generated automatically. Then, through calculations of the parallax movement of different planes, it can extract the camera information, which includes its location and rotation on every frame as well as its field of view (parallax is explained in the following note). The tracking points used to create the camera information form a *point cloud*, a representation in 3D space of the location of each of these points.

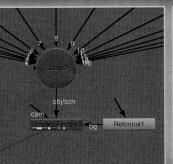
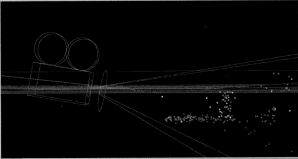

NOTE Parallax is the apparent change in the position of objects at different distances that results from changing the camera's position. If you move your head left and right, you will see that objects close to you are moving faster than things far away from you. This phenomenon is used to figure out distance in camera tracking technology.

FIGURE 10.1 The Camera Tracker is a NukeX only feature.

NOTE Many employers have NukeX—and they may expect you to have a full understanding of the CameraTracker node—so you will want to read and learn the information in the "3D Tracking in Nuke" section even if you only have standard Nuke.

The CameraTracker node is only available in NukeX—a more expensive license for Nuke which enables some advanced features. The good thing is that only the processing part of the Camera Tracker is disabled in standard Nuke, so you can run your track on a machine with the NukeX license, but then use it in standard copies of Nuke (**FIGURE 10.1**).

If you don't have a NukeX license, please read on anyway as only a small part of this chapter covers steps you won't be able to perform.

CALCULATING REFLECTION MOVEMENT USING CAMERA TRACKING

In Chapter 5's four-point tracking exercise, you composited a new picture into a frame and left it with no reflection on the glass. As promised, you will now add the reflection. To calculate the correct way the reflection will move on the glass, you need to use a reflective surface at the location of the frame and have it reflect something—preferably the other wall of that room. You also need to shoot that surface in the same way the original shot was shot. For that you need to extract the camera information for the shot.

Since you'll be tracking with the CameraTracker node you need to launch NukeX rather than standard Nuke. If you don't have a NukeX license, finish this section with your standard version of Nuke and then continue on with the steps from the "Loading a pre-generated CameraTracker node" section, and only do the steps in the "3D Tracking in Nuke" section you can do, which doesn't include the actual tracking process.

1. Launch NukeX. If you don't own NukeX, launch standard Nuke.

2. Open a Nuke script by pressing Ctrl/Cmd-O. Go to your student_files folder and double-click frame_v01.nk (**FIGURE 10.2**).

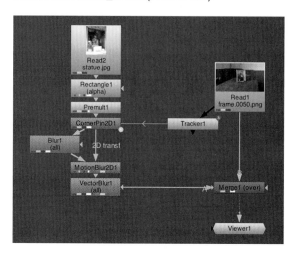

FIGURE 10.2 This is the script as you left it.

3. Save the script in your student_files directory as frame_v02.nk.

Next, you will use Nuke's Camera Tracker to extract the camera information from the scene. Another useful thing that will come out of this process is the point cloud, representing locations of several elements in the shot.

NOTE If you don't save your script as directed some steps later in the chapter won't work.

3D TRACKING IN NUKE

Nuke's Camera Tracker works in three stages:

■ Track Features is the actual tracking process. Nuke looks at the image and finds tracking points according to high contrast and precisely defined locations (such as dots and crosses), much as you would choose tracking points manually.

■ Solve Camera solves the 3D motion. Nuke looks at the various tracked points it has, throws away redundant points that didn't track well, and by looking at the movement, figures out where the camera is and where each tracking point is located in space.

■ Create Scene transfers all the gathered information into a basic Nuke 3D setup including a Camera node, a Scene node, and a Point Cloud node.

Let's track the shot.

1. Select Read1. This should be the clip containing the frame on the table.

2. Branch out a CameraTracker node from the 3D toolbox by holding Shift as you create it.

3. Make sure you are viewing the output of the newly created CameraTracker1 (**FIGURE 10.3**).

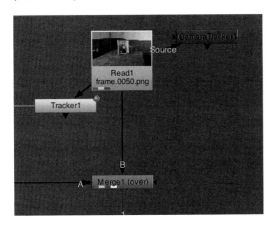

FIGURE 10.3 A newly branched Camera-Tracker node.

Tracking features

Your CameraTracker node is ready, but you can make several adjustments to make for a better track.

1. Switch to the Tracking tab in CameraTracker1's Properties panel (**FIGURE 10.4**).

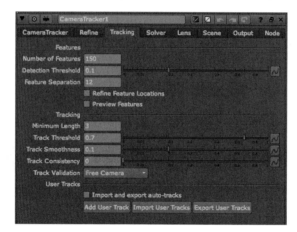

FIGURE 10.4 The Tracking tab.

Several properties in this tab can help you achieve a better track. Here are some important ones:

- Number of Features: The amount of automatic tracking points created by the tracker. If you increase this, reduce Feature Separation.

- Detection Threshold: The higher the number, the more precise the tracker has to be in finding trackable points.

- Feature Separation: The higher the number, the farther apart the tracking features have to be. If you increase Number of Features, reduce this value.

- Track Validation: This setting tells Nuke whether the camera is *handheld* or Free Camera, meaning a free-moving camera, or if it's *nodal* or Rotating Camera, meaning a camera on a tripod. Track Validation validates that the tracks are correct.

The camera in the shot is a free camera, so you'll leave the setting as is. It's not always apparent whether the camera was free—in fact, the best way to know is by being on set and writing it down. However, in this case it is apparent the camera is moving as there is parallax in the shot. These controls are good enough for this shot. It is good practice to try tracking using the default values; if that's not enough, start over with different values, depending on the shot.

2. Switch back to the CameraTracker tab (**FIGURE 10.5**).

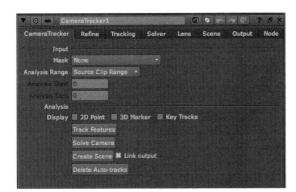

FIGURE 10.5 The CameraTracker tab.

The CameraTracker tab provides some properties to help out the tracker as well. The first one is called Mask. It controls Camera Tracker's second input, the Mask input (**FIGURE 10.6**).

FIGURE 10.6 Camera-Tracker's Mask input is the little arrow on the left of the node.

3D tracking only works on stationary objects. Objects that are moving will distract the solving process, as their movement is not generated from the camera's movement alone. If there's a moving element in the scene, you should create a roto for it, feed it into the CameraTracker's Mask input, and then use this property to tell the Camera-Tracker node which channel to use as a mask. If you're not sure where Camera-Tracker's Mask input is, drag the little arrow on the side of the node (**FIGURE 10.7**).

For now, you will simply run the tracking process and hope for the best.

FIGURE 10.7 Camera-Tracker's Mask input revealed.

3. Click the Track Features button at the bottom of the Properties panel (**FIGURE 10.8**).

FIGURE 10.8 Click the Track Features button to start the tracking process.

The CameraTracker node automatically tracks the length of the Input clip. It's doing it right now, as you can see from the Progress Bar that displays. If you want to change the tracking length, change the property called Analysis Range in the CameraTracker tab (**FIGURE 10.9**).

FIGURE 10.9 The Progress Bar showing the forward tracking stage.

The CameraTracker will track forward from the start; when it reaches the end, it will track backwards and then stop. You can see all the tracking points, or features, the CameraTracker tracked (**FIGURE 10.10**).

FIGURE 10.10 Tracked features display as orange crosses.

FIGURE 10.10 Tracked features display as orange crosses.

Solving the camera

The next stage is to "solve" the camera—to turn all these tracked features into camera information. There are properties you can adjust for this stage as well.

1. Switch to the Solver tab in CameraTracker1's Properties panel (**FIGURE 10.11**).

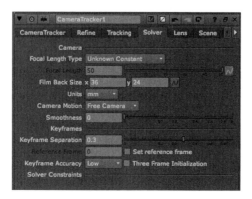

FIGURE 10.11 The Solver tab.

This tab offers several controls that can help reach a better solve.

- **Focal Length Type:** If you know anything about the focal length that was used when shooting, you can enter it here.

- **Film Back Size:** This is the size of the sensor used for capturing the image. The sensor can be the size of the camera's back in a film camera, or the size of the CCD in a digital camera. If exact scale doesn't matter in the end result of your track—that is, if you don't need to match to a specific real-world scale—then a ratio such as 4:3 or 2:1 will be enough, depending on your format.

- **Camera Motion:** This property is similar to the Track Validation property in the Tracking tab. If you know that the camera is a free (moving) one rather than a nodal (stationary tripod) one, choose it here so that the solve knows what it's looking for.

I know this shot was taken with a Panasonic HVX-200 camera. I know the zoom didn't change, but I don't know what the focal length was. Aside from what you see with your own eyes, this kind of information is not always available. This is one of the reasons VFX supervisors go on set—to jot down all this kind of information.

You will leave the Focal Length Type at Unknown Constant. If the zoom was working, you would have chosen Unknown Varying.

Because I know the camera make, I can easily find out what the Film Back Size is. Doing a quick Wikipedia search shows that this camera has a ⅓-inch sensor, which is 4.8mm x 3.6mm. Use this information for the Film Back Size.

2. Set the Film Back Size property to X = 4.8, Y = 3.6 (**FIGURE 10.12**).

   This camera is handheld, so you will leave the Camera Motion property's drop-down menu at the default of Free Camera.

FIGURE 10.12 Changing the Film Back Size property.

3. Now go back to the CameraTracker tab and click the Solve Camera button.

   Nuke is now processing the information and trying to re-create the real-world situation out of the features it tracked. The Progress Bar indicates how long this is taking.

It's done. Good for you (**FIGURE 10.13**).

FIGURE 10.13 Solved tracks are green and red.

As you can see, the tracks (features) changed colors to represent the tracks' status. Amber, as before, represents unsolved tracks. You can see that the majority of the tracks are green, representing tracks that were used for the solve. The red tracks were rejected by the solve as they didn't make sense with the majority of the other tracks.

Creating the scene

The last stage of using the CameraTracker node is creating the scene. This converts the tracked information and the solved camera into a useful Nuke 3D scene including a Camera node, a Scene node, and a CameraTrackerPointCloud node.

Properties for this stage are in the Scene tab. I usually change these properties after creating the scene (**FIGURE 10.14**).

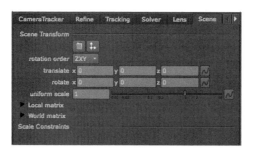

FIGURE 10.14 The Scene tab.

1. Make sure you are viewing the CameraTracker tab.

2. Click the Create Scene button (**FIGURE 10.15**).

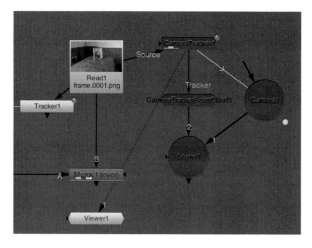

FIGURE 10.15 Three new nodes are created.

You now have three new nodes in the DAG. You have a Camera node, which is the main thing you were looking for. You have a Scene node, which simply connects everything, but is really redundant and will not be used. And you have a node called

CameraTrackerPointCloud1. This last node serves as a placeholder for the point cloud data. If you want to export the point cloud so it can be used in another application as a 3D object, you can connect a WriteGeo node from the 3D toolbox to it and render that out as an obj file.

LOADING A PRE-GENERATED CAMERATRACKER NODE

If you don't have a NukeX license, try the following steps. In fact, even if you do have a NukeX license, you should read this section because it explains the difference between using the CameraTracker with and without a NukeX license. If you did the steps in the previous section don't do the following steps, just read through them.

Not having a NukeX license means you can't click the three buttons in the Camera-Tracker tab: Track Features, Solve Camera, and Create Scene. But you can still use a pre-generated CameraTracker node as you do in the remainder of this chapter. Here's how to load the pre-generated CameraTracker node.

1. Delete CameraTracker1, which you created earlier.

2. Choose File > Import Script and import a script called CameraTrackerScene.nk from the chapter10 directory.

3. Connect Read1 to the input of the imported new CameraTracker1 node and arrange the imported nodes as in Figure 10.15 in the preceding section.

You are now ready to continue reading the rest of the chapter.

ALIGNING THE SCENE

When CameraTracker solves the camera and point cloud, it does it in a void. It can only figure out the relationship between the camera and the point cloud, but not the relationship to the world. In other words, it doesn't know which way is up. Because of this, the next step is usually to define the ground plane. You do this by finding several features you know are flat to the ground and then telling Nuke to align the scene to that.

In this case, the table is flat to the ground so you will use the table as the ground plane. Let's look at the point cloud in the 3D Viewer.

1. If you are not already viewing the 3D scene, hover your mouse pointer over the Viewer and press the Tab key to switch to the 3D Viewer.

2. Make sure CameraTracker1 is loaded in the Properties Bin by double-clicking it.

    You should now see points in 3D space. This is the point cloud. If you don't see this immediately you might need to zoom out a little.

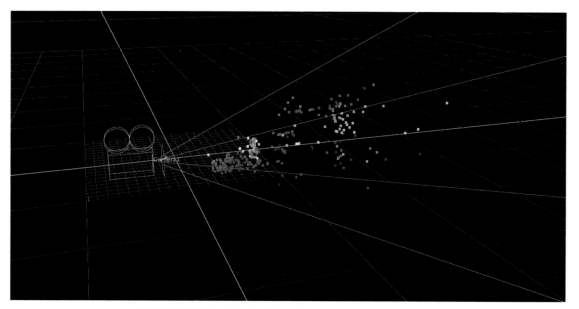

FIGURE 10.16 The point cloud from the side in the 3D Viewer.

3. Zoom out a bit and rotate so you can see the scene from the right (**FIGURE 10.16**).

    You can see that the points are spread out in a way that shows something flat at the bottom and something upright on the right. The bottom thing is the points representing the table while the upright points represent the picture frame. You want to make the table flat, not diagonal like it is at the moment.

You can only pick points in the 2D view, but it's better to see your selection in the 3D view—so you need two Viewers. Let's create a second Viewer.

4. Choose Split Horizontal from Viewer1's Content menu (**FIGURE 10.17**).

FIGURE 10.17 Splitting a pane horizontally.

5. In the new pane, choose New Viewer from the Content menu (**FIGURE 10.18**).

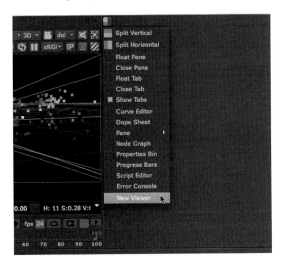

FIGURE 10.18 Creating a new Viewer in a new pane.

You now have a new Viewer and a new Viewer node in the Node Graph. You need to connect what you want to see to that new Viewer.

6. Drag Viewer2's input to CameraTracker1's output (**FIGURE 10.19**).

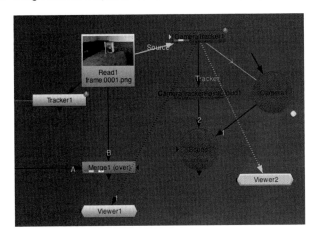

FIGURE 10.19
Connecting a new Viewer.

You now have two Viewers, one showing the scene in 2D and the other in 3D (**FIGURE 10.20**).

FIGURE 10.20 Two Viewers side by side.

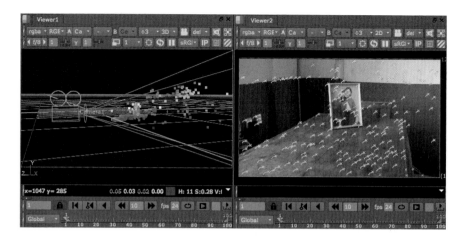

Let's select features, or points, on the table. You will define the ground plane on two axes. One for the axis going from the camera forward—the Z axis. The other going across, perpendicular to the camera—the X axis. Start with the Z axis.

7. In Viewer2, which is showing in the 2D view, select two points along the right side of the table. They should be far apart. Just click the first one and then Shift-click the second one.

    Notice that when you're selecting points in the 2D view they are highlighted in the 3D view. Make sure the points you select are part of the main point cloud area representing the table in the 3D view.

    You can see the two points I selected in **FIGURE 10.21**, both in 2D and 3D view.

FIGURE 10.21 Selecting points from the point cloud.

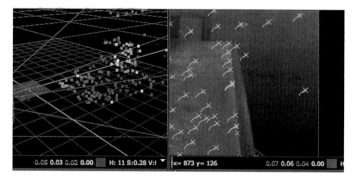

To define what the points represent, use the contextual menu.

8. Right-click (Ctrl-click) anywhere in the 2D Viewer. From the contextual menu choose Ground Plane, then Set Z (**FIGURE 10.22**).

    You can see how the point cloud in the 3D Viewer jumped so it's flat against the bottom of the window and aligned with the grid scene in the 3D Viewer.

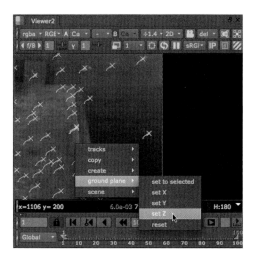

FIGURE 10.22 Setting the ground plane's Z axis.

You just told Nuke this represents the ground plane's Z axis. Now do the same for the X axis.

9. Again in the 2D Viewer, select two points, this time going across the screen from left to right. Make them as far apart from each other as you can to eliminate small rotation error and make sure they're a part of the main point cloud area representing the table (**FIGURE 10.23**).

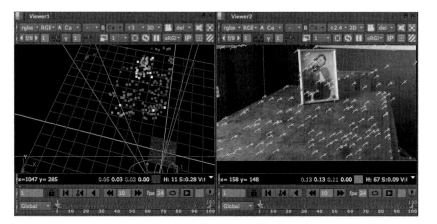

FIGURE 10.23 Selecting points for the X axis.

10. Right-click (Ctrl-click) in the 2D Viewer. From the contextual menu choose Ground Plane, then Set X.

   This sets the table so it's roughly on the X and Z axes of the world space, which will help you later in placing things in the world. The important thing is that the table is now flat and horizontal (**FIGURE 10.24**).

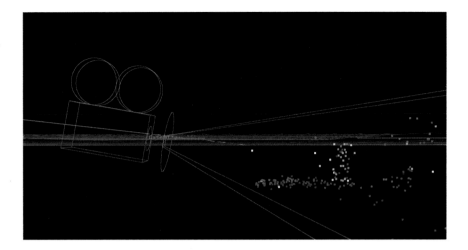

The realignment is complete. Let's tidy up the screen.

11. Choose Restore Layout 1 from the Layout menu in the menu bar.

12. Clear the Properties Bin.

    This removes the extra Viewer and brings the interface back to its default setting.

This ends the Camera Tracker part of the lesson, but what now? You need something to use as a reflection.

CREATING THE REFLECTION

To create the reflection, you need something for the frame to reflect. Unfortunately, I don't have a shot of the back of this room to give you—in real-world terms, let's say the production didn't have time to shoot this for you. What I do have, though, is a panorama of a swimming pool on a beach. True, it's of an outside scene with bright light and palm trees, not exactly interior, but it will have to do.

This is a complete Nuke script of its own. If you want to learn how I made it, visit the book's web site at www.peachpit.com/nuke101. You will now load this script in and use its output as a reflection map.

1. Save your script.

2. Make sure you navigate the DAG so there is a lot of empty space in the middle of the DAG window.

    This will be invaluable when you bring in the panorama script. Otherwise the newly imported script will overlay the current nodes in the DAG, and you'll have one big mess.

3. Choose File > Import Script.

4. Navigate to the chapter10 directory and bring in Pan_Tile_v01.nk. Don't click anything else!

   When you import another script, all the nodes that came with it are automatically selected, which makes it easy to move them.

5. Drag the newly imported nodes to the right of the rest of the nodes (**FIGURE 10.25**).

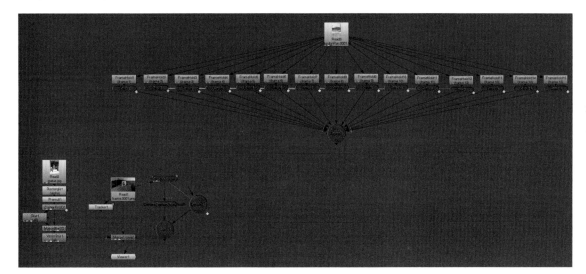

FIGURE 10.25 Place the imported nodes to the right of the existing nodes.

ScanlineRender nodes

Reflection maps tend to be full panoramic images, usually 360 degrees. That's exactly what you have in this imported panorama. It consists of 15 still frames shot on location with a 24-degree rotation from frame to frame. All these frames are sitting in 3D and forming a rough circle, producing a 360-degree panorama.

However, this is only a panorama in the 3D world, not the 2D one. You need to convert this into a 2D panorama for a reason explained later.

Nuke's ScanlineRender node usually outputs whatever the camera that's connected to it sees, but its Projection Mode property's drop-down menu (which sets the type of output mode) has other options. One of those is called Spherical, which is what you are after. Let's connect a ScanlineRender node to the panorama. But first let's look at the panorama in the 3D Viewer.

1. Double-click Scene2 (the Scene node at the end of the panorama script you just brought in).

2. Hover your mouse pointer over the Viewer and press the Tab key to switch to the 3D Viewer. If you are already in the 3D Viewer, there's no need to do this.

3. Navigate back and up in the 3D Viewer by using the + and – keys and by holding Alt/Option-drag. (**FIGURE 10.26**).

    This panorama is made out of the 15 frames textured on 15 cards spread around in a circle.

FIGURE 10.26 The panorama is spread out in the 3D Viewer.

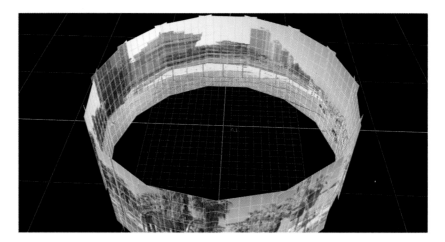

4. Switch back to the 2D Viewer.

Now for the ScanlineRender node.

5. Select Scene2 (the Scene node connecting our 15 Card nodes) and insert a new ScanlineRender node from the 3D toolbox.

6. In ScanlineRender2's Properties panel, change the Projection Mode drop-down menu from Render Camera to Spherical (**FIGURE 10.27**).

FIGURE 10.27 The Projection Mode setting controls what kind of render the Scanline-Render node outputs.

7. View ScanlineRender2. Make sure you're viewing in 2D (**FIGURE 10.28**).

FIGURE 10.28 The panorama in all its glory.

You can now see the whole panorama as a 2D image. There's no need to connect a camera to the ScanlineRender this time, as the camera has absolutely no meaning. You don't want to look at the scene from a specific angle—you just want to look at it as a panorama. However, you do need to input a background to the ScanlineRender, as spherical maps are usually a ratio of 2:1.

8. With no node selected, create a Reformat node from the Transform toolbox. You can also press the Tab key and start typing its name.

Usually, you use the Reformat node to change the resolution of an image. If you have an image that's full HD (1920x1080), for example, and you want it to be a 720p format (1280x720), this is the node to use. It can also change the format of an image beyond just resolution, change its pixel aspect ratio, and depending on the properties, crop an image (though that's rarely used).

In this case, using a Reformat node is an easy way to specify resolution. You don't really need a background image for the ScanlineRender node, you just need to enter a resolution, and so a Reformat node is perfect.

9. Choose To Box from the Type drop-down menu on Reformat1's Properties panel. This option lets you enter width and height values without having to create a new format.

10. Check the Force This Shape check box to enable both the Width and Height fields. Otherwise, you will only be able to specify Width, and Height will be calculated with aspect ratio maintained.

11. Enter **2000** in the Width field and **1000** in the Height field.

12. Connect ScanlineRender1's bg input to Reformat1 (**FIGURE 10.29**).

FIGURE 10.29 The
Reformat node deter-
mines the resolution
of ScanlineRender1's
output.

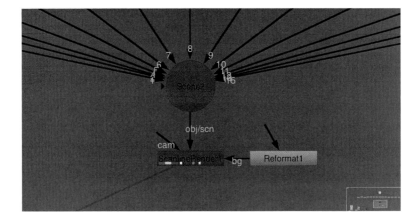

FIGURE 10.29 The
Reformat node deter-
mines the resolution
of ScanlineRender1's
output.

The resolution of the reflection map is now correct. Using a different aspect ratio would have eventually resulted in a squashed or stretched looking reflection (**FIGURE 10.30**).

FIGURE 10.30 The
correctly proportioned
panorama is now ready.

Creating the reflective surface

You need a flat surface to reflect on. A flat surface is sufficient to mimic the front glass on the picture frame. You will use a *Card* node for that. A Card node is a flat surface 3D piece of geometry. One way to create such a surface is to create a Card and then manually position it where the frame is located according to the point cloud. However, there is a simpler way:

1. Clear the Properties Bin.

2. Double-click CameraTracker1 to open its Properties panel in the Properties Bin.

3. Press the 1 key to view CameraTracker1 in the Viewer.

4. Select all the points inside the picture frame—except for the orange points or points on the frame itself or outside of it. You can do this by marqueeing them or Shift-clicking them (**FIGURE 10.31**).

FIGURE 10.31 Selecting all the points in the picture frame turns the points yellow.

5. From the Viewer's contextual menu choose Create, and then Card (**FIGURE 10.32**). (Right-click/Ctrl-click to display the contextual menu.)

FIGURE 10.32 Creating a Card at a point cloud location.

The Viewer now switches to the 3D view (if it doesn't you can press Tab to do so) and you can see that a Card was created at the location of this feature in the point cloud. It is placed well and at the correct angle. This saves you a lot of work (**FIGURE 10.33**).

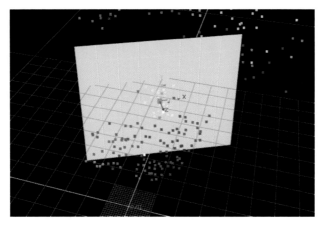

In the DAG, you now have a new Card node that should be called Card16. This is the card the CameraTracker node dutifully created for us (**FIGURE 10.34**).

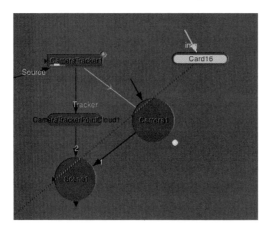

FIGURE 10.34 The new Card node is created at the center of the DAG.

You now have practically all the elements you need: A camera, a reflective surface, and something for it to reflect. Time to connect it all up. There are only two missing pieces to the jigsaw puzzle, discussed in the next section.

Environment light and specular material

Nuke's ScanlineRender node isn't a raytracing renderer and so it can't generate reflections. *Raytracing* means that light can bounce not only from its source onto a surface and to the camera, but also from its source onto a surface, then onto another surface, and onto the camera. So even though you have a surface and a reflection map, you can't tell the surface to mirror the reflection map. What Nuke does have is a light source called Environment, which shines light, colored by an input image instead of a single color, onto surfaces. These surfaces need strong specular material characteristics. *Specular* means objects (or parts of objects) that reflect a light source directly to the camera. A specular material, also called *shader*, can also be generated inside Nuke.

Let's connect the whole thing up. First you'll need to create the Environment light and connect the panorama to it, then connect everything up with a Scene node and finally another ScanlineRender node.

1. Select ScanlineRender1 and from the 3D/Lights toolbox insert an Environment node.

   The Environment node will now project the panorama on every piece of geometry that has a strong specular material. You need to add a specular shader to your Card16 node.

2. With nothing selected, create a Specular node from the 3D/Shader toolbox.

3. Connect Card16's input to the output of Specular1.

4. Set the white property in Specular1's Properties panel to 1.

   By connecting Shader1's output to Card16's input, you are telling Card16 to have that texture or shader. Changing the white value of our Specular1 shader to 1 will ensure full specularity, hence full reflectivity. This will let you control the strength of the reflection later on.

5. Select Card16 and Environment1 by marqueeing or Shift-clicking them; then, create a Scene node from the 3D toolbox.

   The newly created Scene3 node will connect the card and the Environment light so that they work together (**FIGURE 10.35**).

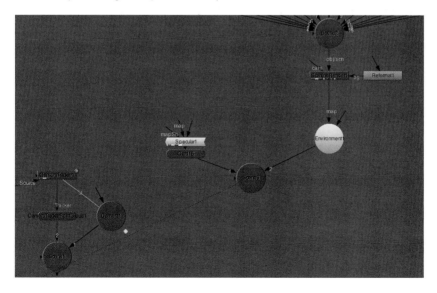

FIGURE 10.35 Another Scene node to connect the Environment light and the shaded Card16.

Now to add a ScanlineRender node to render this thing through a camera. Yes, this is when you connect the camera generated in the beginning of the lesson to the tree and use it.

6. Select Camera1 and Scene3, then press the Tab key and type Scan. Use the Arrow Down key until you reach ScanlineRender then press Enter/Return to insert another ScanlineRender node (**FIGURE 10.36**).

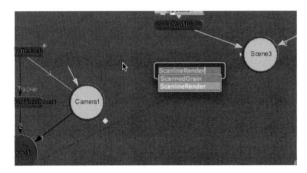

FIGURE 10.36 Connecting up all the elements and rendering the 3D elements.

7. View the newly created ScanlineRender2 by selecting it and pressing the 1 key. Make sure you're viewing in 2D mode.

8. Press Play on the timeline.

   What you are now seeing is the reflected surface showing the part of the panorama that is in front of it. You can choose another part of the panorama if you want, but first you'll make the render a little quicker.

9. Stop the playback and go back to frame 1.

10. View the output of ScanlineRender1. That's the one showing the panorama (**FIGURE 10.37**).

FIGURE 10.37 The panorama image.

As you can see in front of you, the bounding box, representing the part of the image that is usable, is all the way around the image—even though a good 66% of the image is black and unusable. You will make the reflection render faster by telling Nuke that the black areas are not needed.

11. With ScanlineRender1 selected, insert a Crop node from the Transform toolbox.

12. Move the top and bottom crop marks in the Viewer so they are sitting on the top and bottom edges of the actual panorama (**FIGURE 10.38**). This will make for a more optimized (faster) tree.

FIGURE 10.38 Changing the bounding box for a more optimized tree.

13. View ScanlineRender2 in the Viewer.

To choose a different part of the panorama, you need some kind of Transform node. For geometry—the panorama before the ScanlineRender node is just geometry, a collection of Cards, not an image—you need to use the TransformGeo node. Because you want to rotate all the Card nodes together, you can add the TransformGeo node after the Scene node that connects all the Card nodes together—Scene2.

14. Select Scene2 and insert a TransformGeo node from the 3D/Modify toolbox.

15. While still viewing ScanlineRender2, change TransformGeo1's Rotate.y property and see what happens (**FIGURE 10.39**).

FIGURE 10.39 The reflection image projected on the Card node.

As you bring the rotate value up, or clockwise, the image rotates counterclockwise and vice-versa. This is because what you are watching is a reflection, not the actual image. When you rotate the real image, the reflection, naturally, rotates in the other direction.

Cutting the reflection to size

You need to add this reflection to the frame image. At the moment, the reflection image is not the right size—it's a lot bigger than the frame. You need to create a matte that will cut the image to the right size. You already have all the stuff you need in the 2D Tracking part of your tree. You just need to manipulate it in a different way.

1. Navigate the DAG to the left, where you have the statue image connected to the Rectangle node.

2. Click VectorBlur1 to select it and press the 1 key to view it.

3. View the Alpha channel by hovering your mouse pointer in the Viewer and pressing the A key.

    That's the matte you need. No doubt about it. You just need to get it to the other side of the DAG.

I'm not sure where you placed all the bits and pieces of the somewhat disjointed tree I asked you to build. They might be far away. You are now going to drag a pipe from this part of the tree to that one, and I don't want you to lose it on the way. Let's make this a little easier for you:

4. With nothing selected, press the period (.) key.

5. Connect this new Dot's input to the output of VectorBlur1.

6. Drag this new Dot to the right, or wherever you placed your ScanlineRender2 node.

You will hold the ScanlineRender2 node inside this matte, which is connected to the Dot.

7. Select the Dot and press the M key to insert a Merge node.

8. Connect Merge2's B input to ScanlineRender2.

9. Change Merge2's Operation property from Over to Mask (**FIGURE 10.40**).

Now place the reflection on top of the rest of the composite.

10. Select Merge2 and insert another Merge node after it.

11. Connect Merge3's B input to Merge1 (**FIGURE 10.41**).

12. View Merge3 in the Viewer and make sure to view the RGB channels (**FIGURE 10.42**).

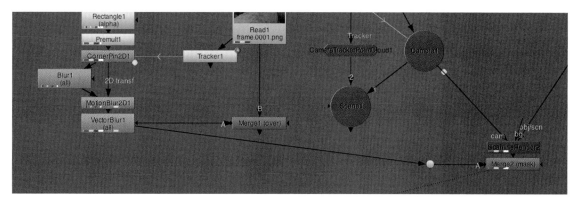

FIGURE 10.40 Using the frame's matte to mask the reflection.

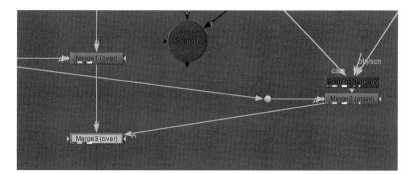

FIGURE 10.41 Another merge to place the reflection over the rest of the composite.

FIGURE 10.42 The reflection is placed perfectly inside the frame.

It's in there—now you just need to take it down a tad.

13. Reduce Merge3's Mix property to 0.05.

The comp is done. You added a very accurate, very sophisticated reflection to the composite.

To really understand how well this reflection works, render it and view it in Framecycler. You should know how to do this by now, so I won't bore you with instructions. (If you need a refresher, see Chapter 1.)

Remember that, if you want, you can still pick a different part of the panorama image to be reflected. You can do that with TransformGeo1. Just change Rotate.y as before. I left mine at 20. I also tidied up my tree a little so I can read it better. You can see it in **FIGURE 10.43.**

There are many other uses for camera tracking. Once you have the camera information for a shot, a lot of things that you would consider difficult suddenly become very easy. For example, I toyed with placing the doll from Chapter 2 on the table. Try it.

More advanced stuff coming up in Chapter 11.

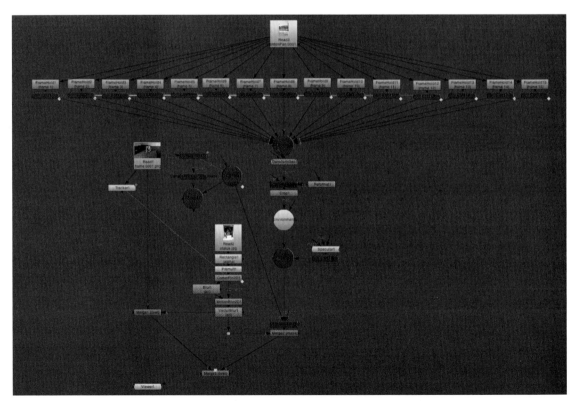

FIGURE 10.43 The final tree.

CAMERA PROJECTION

In this chapter you create a slightly bigger composite and combine a lot of the different tools you learned in other chapters to create the final image. You learn about *camera projection*, use 3D scenes, texture an imported model, and import a camera as well as do some traditional compositing using mattes, color correction, and paint.

Camera projection, a technique used primarily in 3D applications, was brought into Nuke and is proving to be a strong and useful tool. Camera projection is a 3D texturing tool that uses a camera as if it were a projector to project an image onto geometry. It becomes a useful tool when an image is being projected on geometry that was built to look exactly like it. Imagine, for example, an image of a building tilted at an angle. If you build the geometry of the building and place it in front of

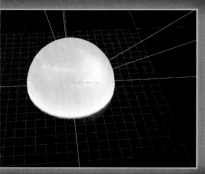

a camera so the alignment of the camera to the geometry produces the same general perspective as your image, you can use that camera to project the image onto the geometry. You can then make that image do things only a 3D scene can do, like move around it, for example.

Speaking of examples, let's dive into one.

BUILDING A CAMERA PROJECTION SCENE

To have a point of reference, let's start by importing an image.

1. From the chapter11 folder, import Ginza.jpg using a Read node (**FIGURE 11.1**).

FIGURE 11.1 The image you will use for the camera projection.

This is a photo I took of the Ginza Hermes building in Tokyo. You will make this still photograph move with true perspective and parallax as well as add some more elements to it. Its resolution is 1840x1232. Not exactly standard, but that doesn't matter. You will make the final composite a 720p composite. Let's set up the project.

2. While hovering the mouse pointer over the DAG, press the S key to display the Project Settings panel.

3. Set up the project as follows: Check Lock Range and choose New from the Full Size Format drop-down menu. Then, enter the following:

    *   Name = **720p**
    *   W = **1280**
    *   H = **720**

    Click OK (**FIGURE 11.2**).

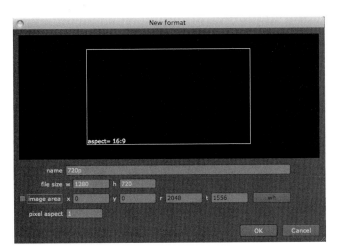

FIGURE 11.2 Creating a 720p format.

For camera projection to work, you need a 3D scene that is set up in the same way as the shot was taken. This means you need geometry for the buildings as well as a camera located where the camera that took the photo was (I asked somebody who uses 3D software to produce this). You just need to import the elements.

You'll start by reading in the geometry:

4. Click anywhere in the DAG to deselect Read1, and while hovering over the DAG, press Tab to create a ReadGeo node.

5. Click the folder icon next to the File property and navigate to chapter11/geo. Import Ginza_building01.obj.

6. Switch to the 3D view by pressing Tab while hovering the mouse pointer over the Viewer, and zoom out by scrolling out or hitting the − key repeatedly until you see a cube. Alternatively you can press the F key to frame the selected object to the Viewer (**FIGURE 11.3**).

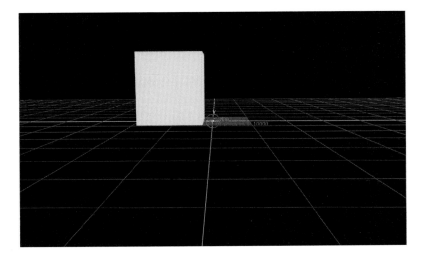

FIGURE 11.3 The imported geometry representing one of the buildings.

This cube represents one of the buildings—the one at the front left. Let's bring in the other two buildings.

7. Create another ReadGeo node by copying and pasting ReadGeo1. (Use Ctrl/Cmd-C to copy and Ctrl/Cmd-V to paste.) Double-click ReadGeo2 to display its Properties panel.

8. Simply change the 1 to **2** in the text for the File property's field. It should now say: Ginza_building02.obj (**FIGURE 11.4**).

FIGURE 11.4 Changing the text is quicker than a lot of clicking.

9. Repeat for the third building, replacing the number with **3**. Make sure that Read-Geo1 is building01, ReadGeo2 is building02, and ReadGeo3 is building03. I refer to the node's names rather than the buildings, to prevent confusion.

You now have all the geometry you need to replicate this scene in 3D. Notice that the geometry is a very basic representation, not a perfect copy. This is enough, because the texture is detailed enough all on its own (**FIGURE 11.5**).

FIGURE 11.5 All the geometry in the 3D Viewer.

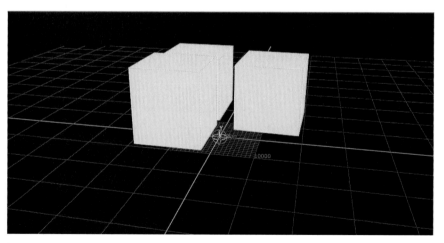

You now need a camera.

10. Create a Camera node from the 3D toolbox.

11. Check the Read From File box in Camera1's Properties panel.

12. Switch to the File tab and click the folder icon at the end of the File property.

13. Import chapter11/geo/Ginza_camera.fbx. Click Yes when asked if you want to change all properties to the imported ones.

You need to choose which camera from the imported data to use.

14. Make sure the Node Name property is set to Camera01.

    You now have a camera in your scene pointing up, which resembles the angle of the camera in the photo. If you move around the scene by Ctrl/Cmd-dragging, you'll see that the camera is way out in another location from the buildings (**FIGURE 11.6**).

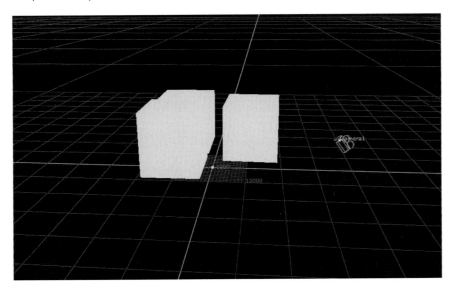

FIGURE 11.6 The camera has a good angle, but its location is off.

The geometry and camera were both generated in Autodesk's 3D Studio Max. This 3D application uses a different scale than Nuke. Because of that, some elements get transferred with the wrong location or size. The ratio in this case is 1:1000. Dividing each translation property by one thousand, therefore, brings the camera into its correct location.

15. Switch to Camera1's Camera tab.

Because Read From File is checked, the properties will keep updating from the file. To change some of the properties, you need to uncheck the box now.

16. Uncheck the Read From File box, click in the Translate.x field, and move the cursor to the end.

17. Enter **/1000** and press Enter/Return (**FIGURE 11.7**).

FIGURE 11.7 Manipulating the Translate.x field directly to change scale.

18. Do the same for Translate.y and Translate.z.

19. When you are finished, check that your values are approximately:

- Translate.x: **26.764**
- Translate.y: **24.250**
- Translate.z: **48.711**

The camera is now located in the correct place (**FIGURE 11.8**).

FIGURE 11.8 The correct location for the camera.

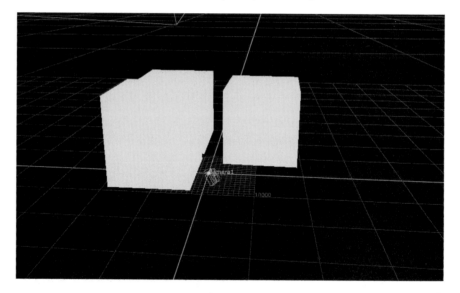

Camera projection means you are using a camera to project a texture onto geometry, remember. To use a 3D term, you will use a texture and a camera to *shade* geometry. You will find the camera projection node in the 3D/Shader toolbox. It's called Project3D.

20. Select Camera1 and from 3D/Shader choose Project3D (**FIGURE 11.9**).

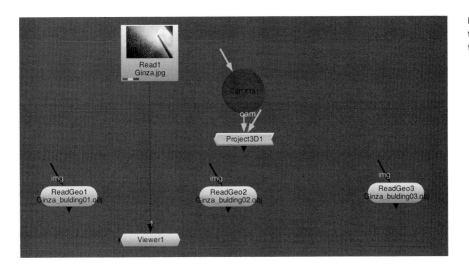

FIGURE 11.9 Inserting the Project3D node into the tree.

Project3D1's Cam input is already connected to Camera1. You need to connect the second input to the texture, which is, in this case, Read1.

21. Connect Project3D's second input to Read1.

You now need to use this texture setup on the geometry. One way to do that is to use ReadGeo1's input and connect it to Project3D1's output. However, there is another node that enables you to connect a texture to a piece of geometry anywhere in the tree. That ability can be useful at times.

22. Select ReadGeo1 and insert an ApplyMaterial node from the 3D/Shader toolbox after it.

23. Connect ApplyMaterial1's Mat input to Project3D1 (**FIGURE 11.10**).

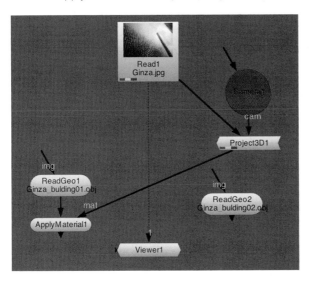

FIGURE 11.10 Connecting the camera projection setup up to the first piece of geometry.

24. Make sure you're viewing 3D in your Viewer (**FIGURE 11.11**).

The first building is now textured in the areas where you have texture for it. If you look at this textured geometry through the camera, it will look right. This technique allows some movement around this object—but only limited movement, as this texture is only really designed to be viewed from the angle it was shot in. If you look at it straight on, you will see noticeable *stretching* (deforming and scaling the texture unevenly over the geometry).

FIGURE 11.11 The texture is starting to appear on the building.

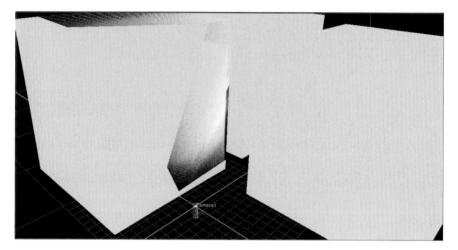

Let's repeat this for the other two buildings:

25. Select Project3D1 and ApplyMaterial1. Copy both selected nodes and, with nothing selected, paste.

26. Connect Camera1 to the Cam input of Project3D2, Read1 to Project3D2's other input, and finally ApplyMaterial2's other input to ReadGeo2's output.

27. Repeat again for the third building, or ReadGeo3.

28. For sanity's sake, arrange the node in a way that makes sense to you. I use a lot of Dots to help with that. Create a Dot by pressing the . (period) key (**FIGURE 11.12**).

Let's build the rest of the scene to connect this whole thing up. You need a Scene node, another Camera node, and a ScanlineRender node.

29. Create Scene and ScanlineRender nodes. Make sure that Scene1's output is connected to ScanlineRender1's Obj input.

30. Connect the three ApplyMaterial nodes to Scene1.

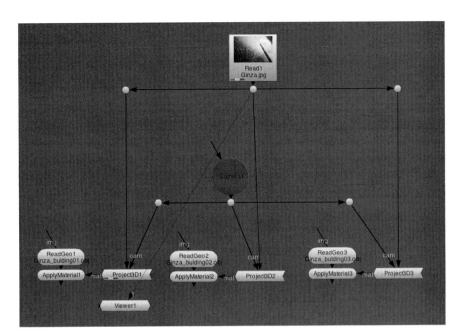

FIGURE 11.12 Using Dots to tidy up a script.

Now, why do you need a camera? You already imported a camera into the scene. Well, the camera you have, Camera1, is being used as a projector if you recall. So you need another camera to be able to shoot through. You also want to be able to move the camera to get the 3D movement you set out to achieve. If you move the projection camera, the texture will move, so that's not allowed. It's easier if the camera you shoot the scene with is based on the projection camera as a starting point, so that's what you will now do.

31. Copy and paste Camera1 to create another camera.

You now have two cameras. This can be confusing, so rename them to easily figure out which is which.

32. Double-click the original Camera1 and enter a new name, ProjectionCamera, in the field at the top of the Properties panel.

33. Double-click Camera2 and change its name to ShotCamera.

34. Connect ShotCamera to ScanlineRender1's Cam input (**FIGURE 11.13**).

You don't need a BG input because you don't need an actual background, and the resolution is set by the Project Settings panel.

FIGURE 11.13 The three
pieces of geometry
are now connected to
a Scene and rendered
through a new camera.

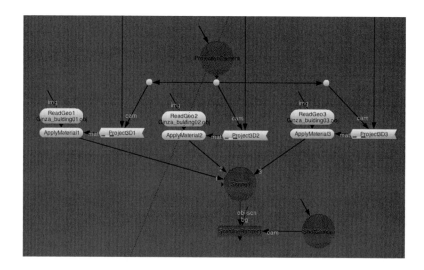

35. View the 2D scene through ScanlineRender1.

There's no point in including a figure here because what you are seeing is easily describable. Black. You should be seeing a lot of black, because the ShotCamera is too big (as it was when you brought it in from file) and its *near clipping plain*, which determines what's the nearest distance from the camera that the camera will include in its render, is farther away from the farthest building. There is no reason for this, it's just the way the camera came in from 3D Studio Max.

36. Double-click ShotCamera and switch to the Projection tab.

You can see the Near property is set to 1000, which is rather big for Nuke so you'll change this.

37. Change the Near property from 1000 to 1.

You can now see the projection setup working (**FIGURE 11.14**).

FIGURE 11.14 The basic
projection setup is now
working.

TWEAKING THE GEOMETRY

There are still some little tweaks to do. The geometry created in 3D Studio Max isn't precise enough. It is clear there is some excess texture on building02, for example. You're going to fix these kinds of problems before moving on.

1. While viewing ScanlineRender1, select ReadGeo2 and disable it by pressing the D key.

   You can now see the misalignment between the texture and the geometry in building01 (**FIGURE 11.15**).

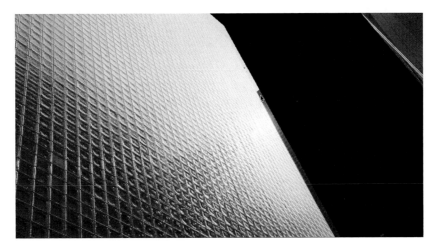

FIGURE 11.15 Some of the background building is showing through on the foreground one.

By translating building01's geometry a little, the texture will fall on it in a better way. For that you will use a TransformGeo node.

2. Select ReadGeo1 and insert a TransformGeo after it from the 3D/Modify toolbox.

3. While looking at the Viewer, decrease TransformGeo1's Translate.x property until you no longer see the other building projected on it. I ended up with –140.

4. To fix the second building, first select ReadGeo1 and press the D key to disable it. Then select ReadGeo2 and press D again to enable it.

This time the geometry is too high and includes a good part of the sky in it. Repeat what you did above for building01.

5. Select ReadGeo2 and insert a TransformGeo node after it by pressing Tab and typing.

6. For this building to match, you need to tweak both the Translate.x and Translate.y properties. I ended up with Translate.x = –180 and Translate.y = –1110.

7. Enable ReadGeo1 by pressing the D key while it's selected (**FIGURE 11.16**).

Grand. You now have your geometry set.

ANIMATING THE CAMERA

Now that the projection setup is good, you need to move a camera and get the perspective movement for the shot.

Keep the default position for the ShotCamera so you always know where you started.
Use an Axis node to move the camera instead.

1. Create an unattached Axis node from the 3D Toolbar.

2. Connect ShotCamera's input to Axis1's output (**FIGURE 11.17**).

   Now you have an Axis with which you can move the camera.

3. While on frame 1, choose Set Key from the Animation drop-down menu for Axis1's
   Translate properties. Do the same for Axis1's Rotate properties.

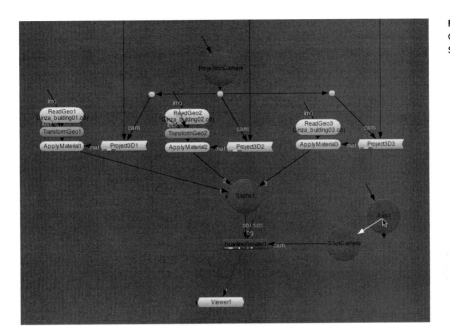

FIGURE 11.17
Connecting Axis1 to
ShotCamera.

The kind of movement you will create for the shot starts at the current location (which is why you added a keyframe on frame 1) and then moves up along the building and forward towards the building while turning the camera to the left.

4. Go to frame 100.

5. Play with Axis1's Translate and Rotate properties until you reach something you are happy with. The values I ended up with were Translate: 100, 1450, –2200 and Rotate: –3, 7, 0.

Now watch the animation you did in the Viewer. To get a good rendering speed, it's a good idea to switch to proxy mode.

6. Switch to proxy mode by either pressing Ctrl/Cmd-P or clicking the Toggle Proxy Mode button in the Viewer.

7. While viewing ScanlineRender1, click the Play button in the Viewer to see your animation playing.

Now that's a wonderful tracking shot, don't you think? Notice that on the left of building02 (the back building) something odd is happening. As more of building02 is exposed, you get more of the texture of building01. This is because there is no more building02 texture—only what was shot. You will have to create more texture for that part of the building.

TWEAKING THE TEXTURE

Right now, there isn't any "extra" back building hiding behind the front building. What you have is what you have. You need to extend the texture for the back building so there will be something else to expose as the camera moves.

1. Create an unattached RotoPaint node from the Draw toolbox and insert it between Read1 and Project3D2 (**FIGURE 11.18**).

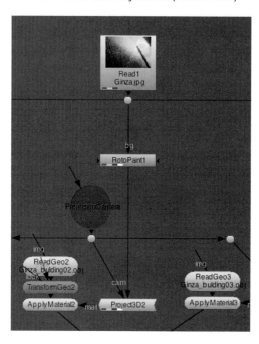

FIGURE 11.18 Inserting a Roto-Paint node between the texture and the projection node.

The good thing about your tree is that each geometry has its own pipe coming from the texture. This gives you the option to tweak the texture of each geometry separately.

2. View RotoPaint1.

Use the RotoPaint node to clone some texture where you're missing it.

3. In RotoPaint1, select the Clone tool.

4. Using the Tool Settings bar, make sure you're painting on all the frames.

5. At the top of RotoPaint1's Properties panel, uncheck the Rgba.alpha so you don't paint in it (**FIGURE 11.19**).

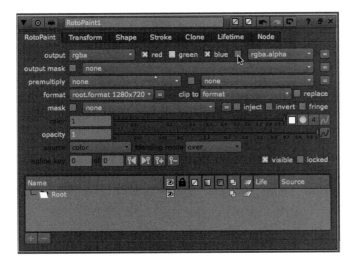

FIGURE 11.19 Turning off the Rgba.alpha channel in the Properties panel.

6. Align your brush using the lines on the building. Because there's perspective change throughout the height of the building, you'll have to change the alignment as you go up and down the building. Start painting (**FIGURE 11.20**).

FIGURE 11.20 Using the window edges to align the clone brush.

Here are a couple of tips while painting:

▨ As you go, view the output of ScanlineRender1 once in a while to make sure you have everything you need covered.

▨ You might want to switch back from proxy mode to full mode to make sure your paint strokes look right.

Painting should take some time because of the perspective change on the buildings as you go down towards the ground level. Follow the above tips and you should be fine. You should have something like **FIGURE 11.21** in the end.

FIGURE 11.21 Using RotoPaint to add more texture.

7. When you're done, go back to viewing the output of ScanlineRender1, make sure proxy mode is on, and click Play in the Viewer.

The texture should now be fixed, and the shot comes to life as "more" of building02 is being exposed. This kind of move could not be achieved using normal 2D transformations.

USING A SPHERICALTRANSFORM TO REPLACE SKY

The current composite has no sky. It was lost through the way this composite was done. You can create another piece of geometry for the sky and continue projecting there, too. However, the original sky in this image is very flat and is not worth the work needed to get it to fit throughout the shot. Better to replace it with a slightly more interesting sky. You can do that by using another sky texture and a sphere geometry.

1. Read in the SkyDome.png image from the chapter11 directory (**FIGURE 11.22**).

2. Make sure proxy mode is off.

Look at the bottom-right corner in the Viewer. It says square_2k. This is a format defined in Nuke by default, which is why the name is displayed here instead of as a set of two numbers. The format means this is a 2048x2048 image. It's a mirror ball map, which is one way of transforming a spherical image into a flat image—taking a photo of the reflection of half a chrome-painted ball. To place the image on a sphere geometry, you need to turn it into a *lat long* map—a flat representation of the sphere as it is being unraveled. The SphericalTransform node is used to transform between several different ways of displaying spherical shapes in a flat image.

FIGURE 11.22 The sky texture you will use.

3. Select Read2 and insert a SphericalTransform node after it from the Transform Toolbar.

SphericalTransform's default is exactly this—changing from a Mirror Ball input to a Lat Long Map output. You just need to change the resolution. You can look at a sphere as an object that is twice as round as it is tall (360 degrees around, 180 degrees in height). And so the resolution of the texture should be twice as wide as it is tall. You'll need to change the Output Format property.

4. Change the Output Format resolution by selecting New from the drop-down menu and then creating a format called 2:1 with a resolution of 2048x1024 (**FIGURE 11.23**).

FIGURE 11.23
A transformed sphere.

5. Create a Sphere geometry from the 3D/Geometry toolbox and attach its input to SphericalTransform1's output.

6. View Sphere1, making sure you're viewing the 3D Viewer.

You're probably not seeing much. This is because spheres are, by default, created with a size of 1. The buildings, on the other hand, are very big. Because your perspective camera (the one you're viewing the 3D scene through) is probably set to view the buildings, the sphere is too small to be seen. You'll have to scale the sphere up. It's supposed to be as big as the sky, after all.

7. Change the Uniform Scale property of Sphere1 to 500,000. If you still can't see the sky, move back by using the − key or the scroll wheel until you do.

You should now see the sky dome (**FIGURE 11.24**).

FIGURE 11.24 The sky dome, half a textured sphere.

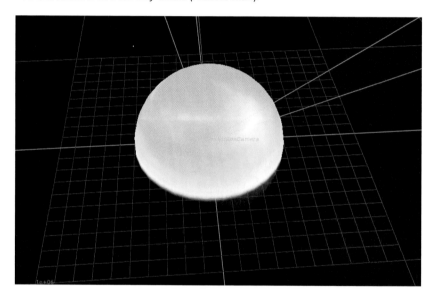

8. Connect Sphere1's output to another input of Scene1.

9. Select ScanlineRender1 and press the 1 key to view it. Make sure you are viewing 2D.

You just did a sky replacement. A pretty sophisticated one as well. There's still work to do on it, though—as in, compositing.

COMPOSITING OUTSIDE THE SCANLINERENDER NODE

At this point, you need better control over the kind of composite you are producing between the buildings and the sky. At the moment, the ScanlineRender and Scene nodes are doing the composite, but because Nuke is a compositing package it would be better to do the composite using normal compositing tools.

Cloning nodes

To have two layers available for compositing outside the 3D scene, you need to split the geometry into two sets and render each separately. You will need two Scanline-Render nodes. However, with two ScanlineRender nodes, changing properties in one means you have to change properties in the other. This is because you want both of them to render the same kind of image.

Instead of having to keep changing two nodes constantly, you can create a clone of the existing ScanlineRender node. A *clone* means that there are two instances of the same node. One is an exact copy of the other. Both have the same name, and if you change a property in one, it is reflected in the other.

1. Select ScanlineRender1 and press Alt/Option-K to create a clone.

    Notice that cloned nodes have an orange line connecting them to show the relationship. They also have an orange C icon at the top left of the node to indicate they are clones.

2. Connect ShotCamera to the Cam input of the newly cloned ScanlineRender1.

3. Drag from the newly cloned ScanlineRender1 node's Obj/scn input to Sphere1's output.

4. Drag and let go on the pipe leading from Sphere1 to Scene1 to disconnect it.

5. Select the original ScanlineRender1 and press the M key to create a Merge node.

6. Connect Merge1's B input to the new cloned ScanlineRender1 (**FIGURE 11.25**).

    You have now made a composite between two separate 3D scenes. The ScanlineRender nodes are cloned, so if you change something in one it changes in the other.

FIGURE 11.25 The
cloned ScanlineRender
nodes.

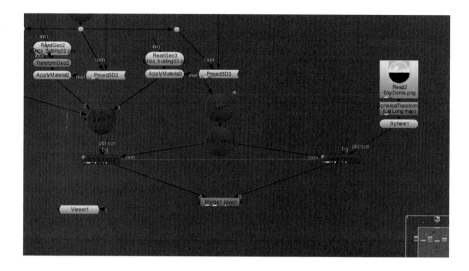

If you look carefully, you'll see that the edges of the buildings are very jagged. This is because you haven't turned on any anti-aliasing for the 3D render (**FIGURE 11.26**).

FIGURE 11.26 Jagged
edges on the building
because of no anti-
aliasing in the Scanline-
Render node.

7. Double-click one of the ScanlineRender1 nodes (it doesn't matter which since they are clones).

8. In the ScanlineRender tab, change the Antialiasing property to Low, which should be enough for now.

Final adjustments

The sky is a little blue for this image. You will color correct it to match the foreground better.

1. Select SphericalTransform1 and insert a Grade node after it by pressing the G key.

2. Tweak Grade1's properties to create a better match of the sky to the buildings. I ended up changing only the Gain property as follows: 1.3, 1.1, 1.0.

There must be another part of the sky dome that will fit the buildings better— something with a highlight that will match the highlight on the buildings. You can use the Sphere geometry's Rotate properties to pick a different part.

3. Using Sphere1's Properties panel, change the Rotate.y property until you find something more fitting for the buildings. I stopped at 70 (**FIGURE 11.27**).

FIGURE 11.27 Rotating the sky to find a better spot.

The composite is looking better, but the edges of the buildings still need a little work. You want to slightly erode the matte. Because this will change the relationship between the RGB and alpha channels, you will need to break up the premultiplied buildings image first.

4. Select ScanlineRender1 (the original one creating the buildings image) and insert an Unpremult node from the Merge toolbox.

5. Insert an Erode (filter) after Unpremult1 and a Premult node after that (**FIGURE 11.28**).

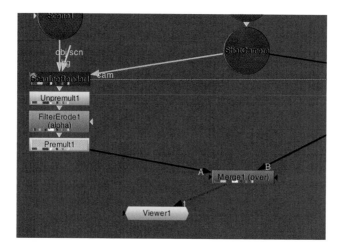

FIGURE 11.28 Inserting an Erode node in between Unpremult and Premult nodes.

The FilterErode1 node has a default value of 1, which is enough in this case. However, you want to have sub-pixel eroding, and that needs to be turned on.

6. Choose Gaussian from FilterErode1's Filter drop-down menu. Leaving it on Box won't allow for sub-pixel eroding.

This concludes this part of the exercise. However, let's make this shot a little more interesting by adding TV screens.

2D COMPOSITING INSIDE 3D SCENES

This is Tokyo after all, and as far as you can see at the moment, there is not a single TV screen in sight! This needs to be rectified posthaste!

You will create a TV screen using a Photoshop file a designer has prepared for an airline called Fly Ginza. You will start by working at a different area of your DAG and then connect your new tree to the main tree later.

Importing Photoshop layers

Nuke can bring in Photoshop files—that's basic stuff. Nuke can also split those files into the layers that make them up, however Nuke only produces the layers themselves. It doesn't include any of the other settings that are part of the file, such as how opaque a layer is or what layer style it has. It will just contain the pixels that make it up, which in this case is enough.

1. Navigate the DAG so the tree is far on the right.

2. Read in chapter11/FlyGinza.psd with a Read node and view it in the Viewer (**FIGURE 11.29**).

FIGURE 11.29 The Fly
Ginza poster.

What you see now is the Fly Ginza logo on a background. You would like to add some
LCD screen effect to this image, but you don't want it to affect the type, just the background. For this reason, you'll need to split up this Photoshop file into layers.

3. Using the left-most Viewer channel button, see the different channel sets you
    have available (**FIGURE 11.30**).

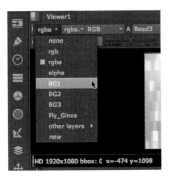

FIGURE 11.30 Some new
channel sets are available.

You can see four additional channel sets: BG1, BG2, BG3, and Fly Ginza. Let's look at
one of them.

4. From the left-most Viewer channel buttons, click BG3 (**FIGURE 11.31**).

FIGURE 11.31 The channel set BG3 is exposed.

I don't remember seeing this image in the final composite. Let's figure this out as you go.

5. Go back to viewing the RGBA channel set in the Viewer.

To split this into separate layers, you will use a few Shuffle nodes.

6. Click Read3 and insert a Shuffle node after it.

7. Choose BG1 from the In 1 drop-down menu.

   You should now see the first part of the background—an orange image (**FIGURE 11.32**).

FIGURE 11.32 The orange part of the background.

8. Click Read3 to select it and Shift-click to branch another Shuffle node. This time choose BG2 from the In 1 drop-down menu.

9. View the output of Shuffle2 in the Viewer.

   You should be seeing some green lines (**FIGURE 11.33**).

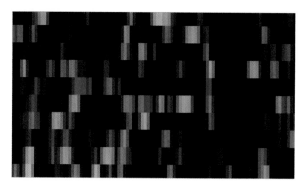

FIGURE 11.33 Some green lines as the second part of the background.

10. View the alpha channel.

You can see the alpha channel is white. You need to find a way to connect this layer up with the first layer, which doesn't need an alpha channel.

11. Repeat the process a third time, this time with BG3 for the In 1 property. You already saw this part of the background earlier.

12. Repeat this process one last time for the Fly Ginza layer and view it in the Viewer (**FIGURE 11.34**).

FIGURE 11.34 The Fly Ginza logo.

If you'll look at the alpha channel, you notice that this image has an alpha channel that outlines the Fly Ginza text.

The best way to know how to layer this is to open it in Photoshop and see what the layering operations are and what opacity is used. If you can't do that, then it's just guesswork. I did it, so follow my instructions.

13. Click Shuffle2 and press M on the keyboard to insert a Merge node.

14. Connect Merge2's B input to Shuffle1 and view Merge2 in the Viewer.

This looks nothing like what the RGBA channels look like. You need to change the Operation property for Merge2 to Plus to mimic Photoshop's operation.

15. Change Merge2's Operation property to Plus.

That's better—now for the next layer.

16. Click Shuffle3 and insert another Merge node after it.

17. Connect Merge3's B input to Merge2, and view Merge3.

Again, this needs some tweaking, as this texture is hardly there in the final composite.

18. Change Merge3's Operation property to Color-dodge and reduce the Mix property to 0.2.

Now the last layer:

19. Click Shuffle4 and insert another Merge node after it.

20. Connect Merge4's B input to Merge3 and view Merge4 (**FIGURE 11.35**).

You have successfully rebuilt the Photoshop setup and have controls over each and every layer separately.

FIGURE 11.35 The tree mimicking the Photo-shop setup.

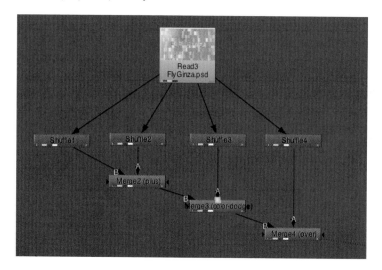

Now you want to create some kind of "dot LED" look, so you need some kind of grid-looking element. You can make that inside Nuke. The main thing you need is a grid of spaced dots. You'll use a Grid node from the Draw toolbox for that.

21. Click Read3 to select it, then Shift-click to branch a Grid node from the Draw toolbox, and view it in the Viewer.

You don't need it to be composited over this image. You just did this in order to get the right resolution. You can replace the whole image with the grid image.

22. Select the Replace checkbox in Grid1's Properties panel.

You need to create exactly even squares, as wide as they are tall, but the way the amount of lines are chosen in this node is through the Number property. This property relates to the resolution of the image, meaning: How many lines per resolution (X, Y). To have an even number of horizontal and vertical lines, take resolution into account and make a quick calculation. The nice thing is that Nuke can make that calculation for you as you type.

In input fields, you can use the words "width" and "height" to ask Nuke for the current resolution as a number. This is very useful for a lot of things. If you need to know the middle of something, for example, you can just enter **width/2** for the horizontal middle point.

23. At the far right of Grid2's Properties panel, click the 2 next to the Number field to enable both fields (**FIGURE 11.36**).

FIGURE 11.36 Enabling the X and Y Number fields.

24. In the Number.x field enter **width/16**.

25. In the Number.y field enter **height/16**.

You now have perfect squares that are 16 pixels wide and 16 pixels tall.

26. Change the Size property from 1 to 6.

You now have an LED screen (**FIGURE 11.37**).

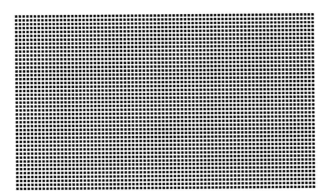

FIGURE 11.37
The grid is ready.

Now to have it affect the background layers of the sign.

27. Insert a Grade node after Merge3.

28. Connect Grade2's Mask input to the output of Grid1.

29. Decrease Grade2's Gain property to something like 0.4 (**FIGURE 11.38**).

FIGURE 11.38 The
grid is added to the
composite.

Creating the frame

Now to create the frame for this lovely screen to sit in. The frame is going to be a
simple affair for now. Just a color with an alpha. Later on you will add a little something to it to make it look more believable. You'll make it in context—while looking at
the final composite—which will make your work even better.

1. Create a Constant node from the Image toolbox.

2. Change the Channels drop-down menu to RGBA, and change the Format drop-
    down menu to HD.

You want the frame to not be darker than a dark color in the original image. Otherwise it will feel fake.

3. View Read1 (the buildings image).

4. Click the Sample color from the Viewer button to the right of Constant1's Color
    property and Ctrl/Cmd-click to choose a dark color from the Ginza image. I
    selected 0.003, 0.003, and 0.001.

5. Change the Alpha value to 1 (**FIGURE 11.39**).

FIGURE 11.39 Setting
a basic color for the
frame.

To make this into a frame, you'll start with a copy of this frame, make it smaller, and
use it to cut a hole in the frame.

6. While Constant1 is selected, insert a Transform node after it.

7. Change the Scale property to 0.95.

8. Insert another Merge node after Transform2.

9. Connect its B input to Constant1.

10. Change Merge5's Operation to Stencil to cut a hole in the frame.

This is the frame. Nothing much to see before placing it over the image itself.

11. Insert another Merge node after Merge5 and connect its B input to Merge4.

12. View Merge6 (**FIGURE 11.40**).

You now have a screen with a frame. Hoorah. You used a separate tree for this. You'll need to connect it up now (**FIGURE 11.41**).

FIGURE 11.40 The image with its frame.

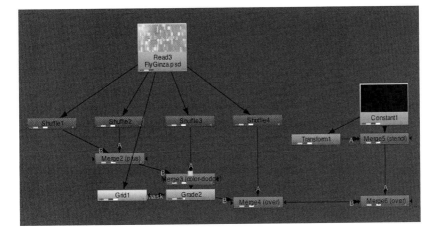

FIGURE 11.41 The screen tree.

Compositing the screen into the 3D scene

You can connect this screen to the 3D camera projection scene in many ways, but in my opinion, for this purpose, compositing it on the original image is probably going to be the best thing. Use a CornerPin and a Merge to do that.

1. Insert a CornerPin node after Merge6.

2. Select CornerPin1 and insert another Merge node after it.

3. Insert Merge7 in between Read1 and Project3D1.

4. View Merge7.

Use the CornerPin node to place the screen in perspective.

5. Move the four pins to place the screen on the front building in a convincing way. Use the lines created by the windows for correct perspective (**FIGURE 11.42**).

FIGURE 11.42 The screen in perspective.

Notice that the building has a very strong highlight top right. The frame doesn't.

6. Select Constant1 and insert a Ramp node after it from the Draw toolbox.

The Ramp node is a simple two-point gradient producing one color that fades along the ramp. Use this to create a highlight on the frame.

7. Move Ramp1's p1 on-screen control to top right of the frame and p0 to roughly the center of the frame (**FIGURE 11.43**).

FIGURE 11.43 Adding a highlight to the frame.

You have now added a matte to the buildings—a matte that wasn't there before. This causes problems with the camera projection setup because it has assumed so far that the matte is white. Now that you Merged a matte into the original image using Merge7, this changes things. Reset that using a Shuffle node.

8. Insert a Shuffle node after Merge7.

9. Change Shuffle5's Alpha to 1 as shown in **FIGURE 11.44**.

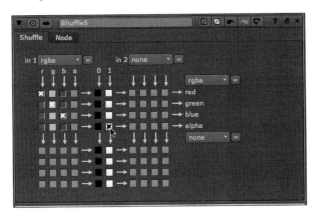

FIGURE 11.44 Setting the Alpha value to a perfect white.

Rendering the Scene

The projection shot is now ready. It has everything you set out to put in it. You should now render the tree, and to do so you need a Write node.

1. Insert a Write node (remember, just press the W key) at the end of this comp, right after Merge1.

2. Click the little folder icon to tell Write1 where to render to and what to call your render. Navigate to your student_files directory and name your render ginza_moving.####.png.

3. Make sure you are not in proxy mode and click the Render button.

4. When the render is finished—and it can take a while—look at your handiwork in the player or Framecycler and be proud (**FIGURE 11.45**)!

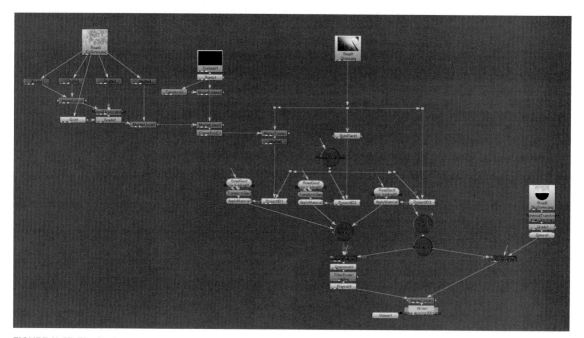

FIGURE 11.45 The final tree.

CUSTOMIZING NUKE WITH GIZMOS

One of the wonderful things about Nuke is that it's completely and utterly open.

By *open* I mean that it's customizable in a way that I haven't encountered before in a compositing application. You can change the interface, add functionality, and change the behavior of so many parts of the application that you can really make it do anything! If your coffee machine were connected to your network, it would make coffee for you, too.

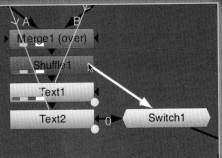

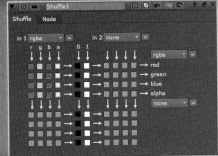

Nuke offers several levels of customization. I showed you very basic customization in Chapter 1—customizing the interface by changing the size of the panes and what they contain. Other levels include Python scripting and Gizmos.

Python scripting, which I touch on in the appendix, lets you do intensive customization by writing code that can control Nuke, your operating system, and any other application or device that allows for such manipulation.

Gizmos are what this chapter is about. They are nodes that you create by adding together other nodes and wrapping them into a custom tool with a user interface, knobs, sliders, and even on-screen controls. Doing so lets you automate mundane tasks—which you would otherwise do over and over again—or create completely new functionality.

ABOUT SAFETY AREAS

As you may have noticed, Nuke doesn't come with any kind of on-screen guides—not for aligning things together, not for the center of the screen, and, indeed, not for safety areas.

In case you don't know what *safety areas* are, here's an explanation. In TV and in some film formats, not all parts of an image end up on-screen. Some get cropped by the TV or projector. It's just the nature of these mediums. Because of this, many programs show guides, usually as boxes on-screen, to approximate where the image will get cropped and where it's safe to place text. Safety areas may be displayed as two boxes, one within the other. The outer one is called *Action Safe*, and the inside one, *Title Safe*. They are usually defined as a percentage of the image's resolution, such as Action Safe at 10% and Title Safe at 20%. Safety areas vary from one TV format to another (4:3, 16:9, and so on) and from country to country (**FIGURE 12.1**).

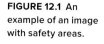

FIGURE 12.1 An example of an image with safety areas.

Nuke's lack of these guides is sometimes problematic. You have to create safety areas yourself and add them to your trees manually every time. Instead of having to do that every time, this chapter shows you how to build a tool that generates this functionality for you automatically. Neat, huh?

BUILDING THE GIZMO'S TREE

The first stage of making a Gizmo is to create a tree in the DAG with the functionality you want. Because you want the tool to be easily controllable, you use a few expressions along the way to link properties together and change them according to various situations. It is important to have the tree work with any image as its source—the whole point of this tool is to be able to add guides to any project you are doing. The main difference to consider from image to image is the resolution.

Let's begin:

1. In a new, empty script, create a Rectangle node from the Draw toolbox and view it in the Viewer.

   You'll use this node to draw the Action Safe box. Right now it is just a white box, and you only need its outline edge. For that you can insert an EdgeDetect node after Rectangle1. Notice that after you create an EdgeDetect node it will be called EdgeDetectWrapper in the DAG.

2. Add an EdgeDetect node from the Filter toolbox.

   Not much different—or is it?

3. In the Viewer, look at the alpha (**FIGURE 12.2**).

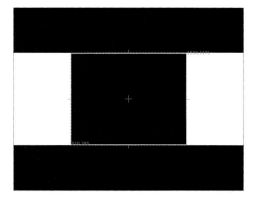

FIGURE 12.2 What happened to the alpha here?

You can see that at the top and bottom you have lines, but the sides are all funny. This is an odd thing that happens due to the bounding box. With the bounding box on the edge of the rectangular shape, the EdgeDetect operation does not work properly. You need to make the bounding box larger so it's not exactly at the edge of the rectangle. You can use a Crop node for that as it will, by default, make the bounding box the same size as the resolution of the image:

4. Insert a Crop node by clicking Rectangle1 and inserting the Crop from the Transform toolbox.

    The lines are there, but you can't see them very well because of Rectangle1's on-screen controls.

5. Clear the Properties Bin and look at the Viewer (**FIGURE 12.3**).

FIGURE 12.3 The outline you will use for the Action Safe guide.

Start changing the size of Rectangle1. As mentioned, the size of the rectangle is expressed as a percentage of the source image resolution. The percentage is determined by the user, and the image will be the input image (whatever it will be).

Let's add an expression to Rectangle1's Area property. This property has four Input fields for the location of each side of the rectangle (measured in pixels). You want to be able to control the location as a derivative of the resolution, so you use the expressions "width" and "height" again.

6. Double-click Rectangle1 to load its Properties panel into the Properties Bin.

7. Choose Edit Expression from the Area property's Animation menu (**FIGURE 12.4**).

FIGURE 12.4 The Area property Expression panel.

Here you can see four lines, one for each of the properties available. You used the Expression panel before when you linked the CornerPin to the Tracker in Chapter 5. This time, you're not going to link at this stage, just use basic math.

The X property is the distance from the left side of the frame. Let's say you want your Action Safe area to be 5% away from the left side of the frame.

8. In the X expression field, enter **width*5/100** (FIGURE 12.5).

FIGURE 12.5 Writing the first expression.

On the right you can see the result of the expression: 102.4.

Next, do the Y property, using the "height" expression.

9. In the Y expression field, enter **height*5/100**.

The result here is 77.8.

The next two properties are R and T, which stand for *right* and *top*. Here you would like the same distances, just from the right edge and the top edge. You simply need to subtract the results in X and Y from the width and height of the image, respectively.

10. In the R expression field enter **width-width*5/100**.

11. In the T expression field enter **height-height*5/100** (FIGURE 12.6).

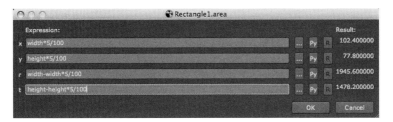

FIGURE 12.6 All the expressions and their results.

12. Click OK.

13. Hover your mouse pointer over the Viewer and press O on your keyboard to temporarily remove the on-screen controls (also called *overlays*, hence the O hot key) so you can see the change in the Rectangle (FIGURE 12.7).

FIGURE 12.7 The new Rectangle1 should look like this now.

Great. So you now have a line shaped like a box all around the edges of your frame, 5% from the edge. What if you want it to be 7% from the edge? You have to change each of the four expressions to have a 7 instead of a 5. This can be unintuitive and quite annoying. There is another, better, way: Create a User Knob.

CREATING USER KNOBS

NOTE The NoOp node is exactly what it says it is: It has no initial function-ality. You can use it for various things, but mainly you will use it for the kind of task shown here.

You need to create a property for the percentage value so that you and any other user of your Gizmo will have something easy to manipulate. Nuke lets you create user properties called *User Knobs*. Now you'll make another node to hold your User Knobs.

1. Create a NoOp node from the Other toolbox.

2. Right-click (Ctrl-click) somewhere in NoOp1's Properties panel. From the contex-tual menu click Manage User Knobs (**FIGURE 12.8**).

FIGURE 12.8 Accessing the User Knobs panel.

As mentioned, a knob is just another name for a property. Managing User Knobs means to manage the user-generated knobs. This loads the User Knobs panel for this node (**FIGURE 12.9**).

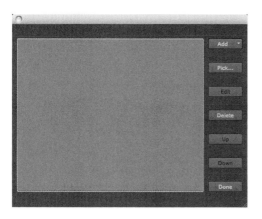

FIGURE 12.9 The User
Knobs panel.

On the right, the two top buttons are Add and Pick. Both are ways to create new knobs. The first lets you choose from a list of available knob types, such as a slider, a Size Knob, a Text Input Knob, and so forth. The second one lets you pick from existing properties (discussed later in the chapter).

You want to be able to change the percentage in both X and Y. You can use a Width/Height Knob that by default appears as one slider, but can be split into two separate fields.

3. Choose Width/Height Knob from the Add button/menu (**FIGURE 12.10**).

FIGURE 12.10 The Width/
Height Knob panel opens
so you can define the
knob's properties.

The Width/Height Knob panel opens so you can define the knob's properties. There are three properties:

- Name is the true name of the knob, used for calling the knob through expressions.

- Label is what appears in the white text to the left of the slider. The Name and Label don't need to be the same—although they usually are. Sometimes, however, when one knob name is already taken, you want the Name to be unique so you use something longer. But you need the Label to still be short and easily readable.

- Tooltip appears when you hover your mouse pointer over a property for a few seconds. It's a little bit of helper text that can remind you (and other users) of the functionality of the knob.

4. In the Name field, enter **actionSafe**. Spaces are not allowed in the Name property, but you can use an underscore in it if you like.

5. In the Label field, enter **actionSafe**. Spaces are allowed in the Label property, but I like to keep things consistent. Suit yourself.

6. In the Tooltip field, enter **Controls percentage of Safe Area** (**FIGURE 12.11**).

7. Click OK (**FIGURE 12.12**).

   You now have two lines in the User Knobs panel. The first one reads User and the second one reads ActionSafe. You only made the one called actionSafe. User was created automatically and is the name of the tab where the User Knob will appear. If you don't want this tab to be called User, you can click to select this line and then click the Edit button and rename it in the panel.

FIGURE 12.11 The filled Width/Height Knob panel.

FIGURE 12.12 The User Knobs panel now has two knobs in it.

8. Click the Done button in the User Knobs panel (**FIGURE 12.13**).

FIGURE 12.13 A new knob appears in the NoOp node's Properties panel.

You have just created a tab called User. Inside it you have a knob called Action-Safe. (I don't call it a property because it doesn't do anything yet. If you play with the slider, nothing happens, because this is just a knob.)

9. Experiment with the ActionSafe knob. When you're finished, leave it on 5.

Remember, if you tie it to something in some way, it then acquires functionality. I already explained what this knob is to be used for: as the Percentage property for Rectangle1. Let's connect this up.

First you expose the two separate parts of the ActionSafe knob.

10. Click the 2 icon—the individual channel's button, to the right of the slider you just created.

    You now have two Input fields instead of the slider (**FIGURE 12.14**). Note that the first Input field is called W and the second H.

FIGURE 12.14 Your Width/Height Knob's two Input fields exposed.

You will replace the percentage in Rectangle1's Area property's expression with a link to this knob. To call up this property from another node, you first call the name of this node, then the name of your property, and then the Input field you need.

11. In Rectangle1's Properties panel, choose Edit Expression from the Area property's Animation menu.

12. In the first line, for the X property, replace the digit 5 with **NoOp1.actionSafe.w**.

13. For the Y property, replace the digit 5 with **NoOp1.actionSafe.h**.

14. For the R property, replace the digit 5 with **NoOp1.actionSafe.w**.

15. Finally, for the T property, replace the digit 5 with **NoOp1.actionSafe.h** (**FIGURE 12.15**).

FIGURE 12.15 Changing the expressions to make use of the new User Knob.

16. Click OK.

    Your new User Knob is now part of an expression and it acquires functionality.

17. Go ahead and play with your ActionSafe fields. You can bring it back to being a slider or leave it as two Input fields. The expression will not break. You can see the box on-screen change size horizontally and vertically. When you're finished, go back to a value of 5 and a single slider.

Right. Now that you have this, you should make a safety area for titles. I will quickly guide you through repeating most of what you already did for the action safe area:

18. Select Rectangle1, Crop1, and EdgeDetectWrapper1. Copy them with Ctrl/Cmd-C.

19. With nothing selected, paste what you've copied using Ctrl/Cmd-V.

20. Click EdgeDetectWrapper2 and press M to create a Merge node. Connect Merge1's B input to EdgeDetectWrapper1 (**FIGURE 12.16**).

FIGURE 12.16 A new branch for the second safe area.

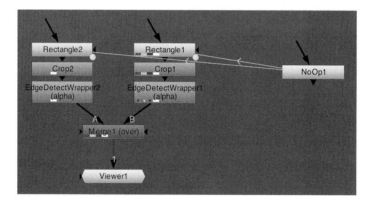

You now have a whole other set of nodes that will create the second safe area for you. You'll need another percentage knob.

21. In NoOp1's Properties panel, right-click (or Ctrl-click) and choose Manage User Knobs from the contextual menu.

22. Click ActionSafe to select it and then click Add > Width/Height Knob.

23. Write **titleSafe** in both the Name and the Label Input fields.

24. In the Tooltip field, enter **Controls percentage of Title Safe area.** (**FIGURE 12.17**).

FIGURE 12.17 These are the settings for the second User Knob.

25. Click OK. In the User Knobs panel, click Done (**FIGURE 12.18**).

You now have another User Knob called TitleSafe under your existing ActionSafe Knob.

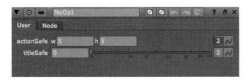

FIGURE 12.18 The new Knob appears under the previous Knob.

26. Set your new TitleSafe slider to a value of 10.

Now you need to change the expression in Rectangle2 to link to this new Knob—TitleSafe—instead of the old ActionSafe Knob.

27. Load Rectangle2's Properties panel into the Properties Bin.

28. Choose Edit Expression from the Area property's Animation button/menu.

29. Change every occurrence of ActionSafe to **titleSafe** (**FIGURE 12.19**).

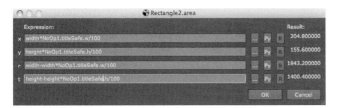

FIGURE 12.19 The expressions after replacing all ActionSafe occurrences with TitleSafe.

30. Click OK.

31. Make sure you are viewing Merge1 and still viewing the alpha channel (**FIGURE 12.20**).

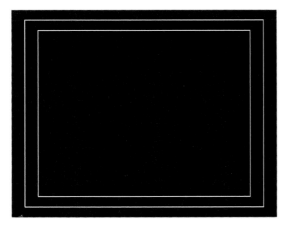

FIGURE 12.20 Two boxes for the two safe areas.

You hard work is paying off. You have two boxes—one for each safe area—and you can manipulate them using User Knobs.

32. Switch to viewing the RGB channels in the Viewer.

A big white rectangle—that's not what you want at all. You need to move the alpha channel into the RGB channels as well.

33. Click Merge1 and insert a Shuffle node after it.

34. Shuffle the alpha channel into all four channels (**FIGURE 12.21**).

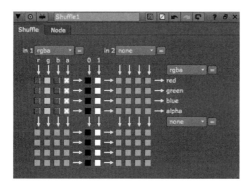

FIGURE 12.21 Shuffle1's Properties panel.

It's also a good idea to create something that gives feedback in the Viewer about the size of the safe areas. You can easily do that using Text nodes and some basic scripting for automation.

SCRIPTING WITH A LITTLE TCL

The TCL scripting language was the main language in Nuke until Version 5, when Python scripting replaced it. Nuke can still use TCL, but mostly everything has moved to Python. A few things have remained TCL by default, mainly Text Input fields. You can practice this here briefly:

1.   Click Shuffle1 and insert a Text node from the Draw toolbox after it.

Use this Text node to write the size of the Action Safe area. To begin, place the text so that it's placed at the bottom left corner of the Action Safe area and automatically moves with it. The Text node places the text inside a box, and you will need to place the left and bottom sides of this box where the left and bottom sides of the Action Safe area are.

2.   At the bottom of Text1's Properties panel, open the Transform group by clicking the triangular arrow to the left of that name (**FIGURE 12.22**).

FIGURE 12.22 Open the
Transform group using
this triangular arrow.

3. Click inside the box.x property's Input field and press = (equals key).

This is the hot key for loading the Edit Expression panel. It only loads the Edit
Expression panel for this specific part of the Box property, not all four parts.

4. Enter **Rectangle1.area.x** and click OK (**FIGURE 12.23**).

FIGURE 12.23 A simple
linking expression.

This places the left side of the box at the left side of the safe area.

5. Click inside the box.y property's Input field and press =.

This loads the Edit Expression panel for the second part of the Box property.

6. Type **Rectangle1.area.y** and click OK.

This places the bottom side of the box at the bottom side of the safe area.

At the moment, the actual text is set to be drawn at the left and middle of the box.
You want to change that to left and bottom.

7. For the Justify property, choose Bottom from the second menu.

The Text "frame 1" should now appear exactly on the edge of the Action Safe area
(**FIGURE 12.24**). You will change the actual text in a second, but first, it would be nicer if
there were a little room between the line and the text.

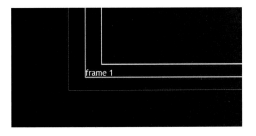

FIGURE 12.24 The text
is now attached to the
Action Safe area.

8. Click inside the box.x property's Input field and press =.

9. To the expression you already wrote, add +20 (**FIGURE 12.25**).

FIGURE 12.25 The adjusted expression.

10. Do the same for the Y property. You should end up with: **Rectangle1.area.y+20**.

    Now there's some breathing room for the text. To change the actual text, you will use TCL.

Look at the large Message Input field. At the moment it says: frame [frame]. The first word is an actual word. The second, in the square brackets, is a TCL script. On-screen the text says: frame 1. 1 is the frame number you should be on. [frame] is a script indicating to look at the current frame, hence it's returning a value of 1. Anything you put in square brackets is interpreted as a TCL script. You can use TCL scripts to call up the value of a property. Simply open square brackets and type.

11. Replace the current Message property with [**value NoOp1.actionSafe**].

Here you are asking for the value of the ActionSafe property in the node called NoOp1.

If you followed everything correctly, the text "frame 1" was replaced with a 5. This is great! Your ActionSafe value should indeed be 5 and this is reflecting it. But it might be prettier if this was a little more verbose.

12. Change the Message property to: **Action Safe** [**value NoOp1.actionSafe**]%.

    Look at the Viewer and you should see **FIGURE 12.26**.

FIGURE 12.26 The text in the Viewer is more easily understandable.

Now, to do the same for the Title Safe area:

13. Click Text1 in the DAG, copy it, and then paste it.

    Text2 should now be inserted after Text1. You only have to change a few simple things.

14. Double click Text2 to load its Properties panel.

15. Change your TCL expression to replace all occurrences of the word *action* with the word *title*. Note that scripts are case sensitive, so keep uppercase and lowercase consistent. It should read: **Title Safe [value NoOp1.titleSafe]%**.

    You have now changed the written text to Title Safe and changed the TCL expression to read the value from the TitleSafe Knob.

You now need to change the expression that places the text.

16. In Text2's Properties panel, click inside the box.x property's Input field and press = to load the Edit Expression panel.

17. In the expression that's already there, replace Rectangle1 with Rectangle2.

18. Do the same for the box.y expression (**FIGURE 12.27**).

FIGURE 12.27 Changing the expression to link to the other Rectangle node.

You should now have lovely text attached to both your Safe Areas.

19. Clear the Properties Bin and then double-click NoOp1 to load its Properties panel back into the Properties Bin.

20. Play with the two Knobs and see how everything changes in the Viewer. When you're finished, bring back the values to 5 and 10 (**FIGURE 12.28**).

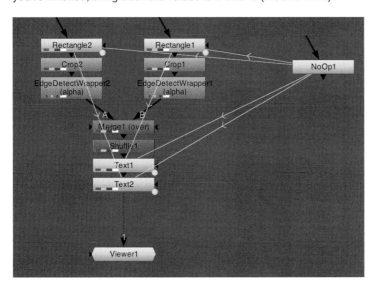

FIGURE 12.28 Your tree should look something like this at the moment.

TESTING THE GIZMO'S TREE

OK, so the functionality is there, but let's test what this looks like on an image and see if the current tree is missing anything. Let's call it beta testing the Safe Area tool.

1. From the Image toolbox, create a ColorBars node.

    The ColorBars node generates color bars used in video image adjustments. In this case, you will just use it as a background image for the Safe Area tool.

Now where should you connect the ColorBars node? Seems like there is already something missing. If you connect ColorBars1 to the input of either Rectangle node, you will pass them through the EdgeDetect and Shuffle nodes. That's not part of the functionality planned for; you need to add another Merge node.

2. Click Text2 to select it and press M to create another Merge node.

3. Connect Merge2's B input to ColorBars1 (**FIGURE 12.29**).

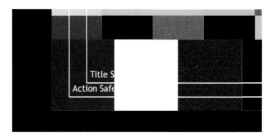

FIGURE 12.29 Not every part of the Safe Area is readable.

You should now see the Safe Area guides composited over the color bars. You can't read the text well in this case because there is a white box where the text is supposed to appear. Maybe another operation (instead of over) would be better in this case.

4. Change the Operation property in Merge2 properties from "over" to "difference."

    You can now see the text better.

Let's try a different resolution for the ColorBars1 node.

5. In the ColorBars1 Properties panel, choose HD from the menu.

Boo-hoo. It's all broken. There is no Action Safe guide on the right, and nothing at the top (**FIGURE 12.30**). This is because—although you made the box a derivative of the resolution—I didn't show you how to connect the Rectangle nodes to the source resolution.

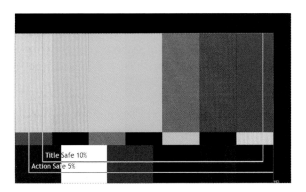

FIGURE 12.30 Changing the resolution broke the Safe Area.

6. Connect Rectangle1's and Rectangle2's inputs to the output of ColorBars1.

OK, so now the resolution will be correct since the Rectangle nodes will draw around the input resolution. But you don't want to actually use the color bars image as part of the Safe Area tree. If you select the Replace check box, only the resolution of the input image will be outputted but the actual image won't be (it will be replaced by the image generated in the node—in this case a rectangle).

7. In Rectangle1's and Rectangle2's respective Properties panels, select the check box called Replace.

    The problem is now fixed. Whatever resolution you bring into this tree will change the size of the Safe Area boxes.

Notice that your test image has three outputs. Since this image is something you'll need to replace constantly, it would be a good idea to have only one output.

8. Click ColorBars1 and press . (period) on the keyboard to create a dot.

And there you have it. The next stage will be to wrap this tree up in what's called a Group.

WRAPPING IN GROUPS

A *Group* in Nuke is a node that holds another tree inside of it. You can still access what's inside of it and manipulate it, but you can also treat it as one entity. It's useful to wrap little functionalities, or trees that you know are taking care of a certain element of your comp, in a Group. Some compositors use them more and some less. To create a Gizmo, you have to first create a Group.

Like every other node, a Group node can hold User Knobs.

Everything in the DAG except for ColorBars1 is in charge of making the Safe Area guides. So that's what you are going to place in the Group.

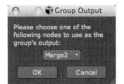

FIGURE 12.31 The Group Output panel.

1. Select all nodes in the DAG except for Viewer1 and ColorBars1 and press Ctrl/Cmd-G.

The Group Output panel that pops up wants to know which node that you selected will be the Group's output. Just as in any other node in Nuke, a Group node can have many inputs, but only one output. In this case, there are only two nodes for which the output is not in use: Merge2 and NoOp1. The output of the tree is the output of Merge2—not NoOp1, which is unconnected to anything and is only used as a holder of Knobs (**FIGURE 12.31**).

2. In the Group Output panel that pops up, make sure that Merge2 is selected and click OK (**FIGURE 12.32**).

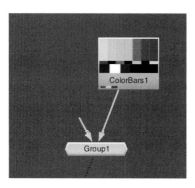

FIGURE 12.32 A Group is created instead of the tree.

Your tree was replaced with a Group node called Group1. Notice it has two inputs: One was the Dot's input, and the other NoOp1's input. Let's look inside.

You should now also have the Group1 Properties panel loaded. Notice it has a new button that other nodes lack—the S, or Show, button (**FIGURE 12.33**).

FIGURE 12.33 The Show button is unique to Group nodes.

Clicking this button opens another Node Graph panel and shows the tree that is held inside the Group node.

3. In Group1's Properties panel, click the S button (**FIGURE 12.34**).

In the DAG you can see that your Safe Area tree appears again. If you look closely at the tabs of the current pane, where the Node Graph is, you'll see that you are no longer in the Node Graph, but rather in the Group1 Node Graph. You can move back and forth between the Node Graph and the Group1 Node Graph.

In this DAG, you can also see three new nodes you didn't place here: Input1, Input2, and Output1. These nodes were created when you created the Group. The Input nodes appear as inputs in the main DAG; these are inputs 1 and 2 that you saw before. And the Output node indicates where to output the tree, normally at the bottom-most node. You only need one input: the one connected to the Dot. The Input node connected to NoOp1 was created because NoOp1 had a free input, and that's how the Group creation works.

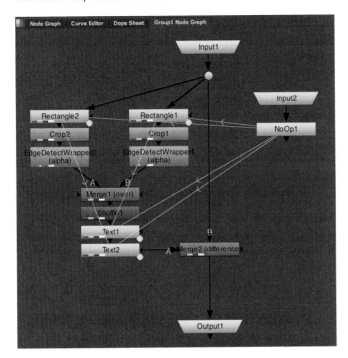

FIGURE 12.34 The Group1 Node Graph.

Since Nuke creates these nodes automatically, I don't know which node is Input1 and which is Input2 in your tree. Delete the one called Input2 because deleting Input1 will cause a bug to happen where the deleted input still appears in the main Node Graph though doesn't exist anymore as a node. If Input2 is the node connected to the Dot you will have to still delete it and then move the output of Input1 so it is connected to the input of the Dot.

4. Click Input2 and click Delete to delete it. If you need to, connect the Dot's input to the output of Input1.

5. Switch to viewing the main Node Graph by clicking its tab.

    You can see that the second input is now gone.

Now you would like to change the Action Safe area, but your Knobs are not available—they moved to within the Group with NoOp1. This is not convenient at all. Furthermore, this Group node can hold Knobs without needing a NoOp that does nothing. The Group node can both group trees together and hold User Knobs. Time to put that NoOp1 node to rest and move all its functionality into Group1. First to generate some Knobs, including a new type of Knob to begin with.

6. In Group1's Properties panel, right-click (Ctrl-click) an empty spot and choose Manage User Knobs from the contextual menu.

Now you're going to add another Knob you didn't have before. Remember that you changed the Operation property for Merge2 to Difference. There are other useable operations, and it's nice to have this property ready to be changed right here in the Group's Properties panel. Instead of adding this Knob from the Add menu, you can pick this Knob from your existing Knobs in the tree held within the Group, using the Pick button.

7. Click the Pick button (**FIGURE 12.35**).

FIGURE 12.35 The Pick Knobs to Add panel.

From the Pick Knobs to Add panel, you can expose any Knob from the tree held in the Group. You just need to find it. You're looking for a node called Merge2 and a property called Operation.

8. Navigate and open submenus until you find the Operation property, as shown in **FIGURE 12.36**. Then select it and click OK.

FIGURE 12.36 Finding the right property requires a little digging.

In the User Knob panel you now have two entries: *User* and *operation* with some curly brackets and some code in them. You can click this entry and then click Edit to change things in there. But there's no need. I will have you change the name of the tab, though (**FIGURE 12.37**).

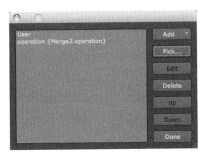

FIGURE 12.37 Two entries in the User Knob panel.

9. Click the User entry and then click Edit.

10. Change the Name and Label to **SafeAreas**. Click OK.

11. Click Done.

You now have a new type of Knob that you created (well, sort of—you actually copied it): a pull-down menu called operation. Changing it changes how the Safe Areas are composited over the image (**FIGURE 12.38**).

FIGURE 12.38 Your new Knob is a pull-down menu.

Now to create the two Knobs to replace the Knobs in NoOp1. Let's run through this:

12. Right-click (Ctrl-click) an empty spot in Group1's Properties panel and choose Manage User Knobs from the contextual menu.

13. Click the Add button and from the pull-down menu click Width/Height Knob.

14. Name this **actionSafe** and label it **actionSafe**. In the Tooltip field, enter **Controls percentage of Safe Area** (**FIGURE 12.39**). Click OK.

FIGURE 12.39 Recreating the Action Safe area Knob.

Now for the Title Safe area Knob:

15. Choose Width/Height Knob from the Add button/menu.

16. Name this **titleSafe** and label it **titleSafe**. In the Tooltip field, enter **Controls percentage of Title Safe Area**. Click OK.

Have a look at the User Knob panel. You now have four items in it. Move the User Knob panel a little if necessary to see the actual Properties panel (**FIGURE 12.40**).

FIGURE 12.40 The order of Knobs in the User Knobs panel is repeated in the Properties panel.

Notice that in the User Knobs panel the Operation Knob is now last, and it's the same in the Properties panel. The order of the Knobs in the User Knobs panel determines the order of the Knobs in the Properties panel.

You would like to have the Operation Knob at the top, so:

17. Click Operation in the User Knobs panel and click the Up button twice to move it in between SafeAreas and ActionSafe.

18. Click Done.

This Knob is now at the top.

19. Set the values again for ActionSafe and TitleSafe: 5 and 10 respectively.

You now want to change all the expressions that point to NoOp1 to point to the Group's User Knobs. Let's do one.

20. Click the Group1 Node Graph tab.

21. Double-click Rectangle1.

22. Click in the "area.x" Input field and press = to load its Edit Expression panel.

You now need to replace the NoOp1 part of the expression with something—but what? At the moment, Rectangle1 is sitting inside Group1. There's a hierarchy there—the Group1 node is Rectangle1's parent. Instead of calling up Group1 by name, simply ask Rectangle1 to look for an ActionSafe Knob in the parent node:

23. Replace the word "NoOp1" with "parent" (**FIGURE 12.41**).

FIGURE 12.41 Calling for one level up in the hierarchy using the parent expression.

You need to change this for every other instance of an expression referencing the NoOp1 node. In the next section, instead of doing it again manually, you use a different method.

MANIPULATING THE NUKE SCRIPT IN A TEXT EDITOR

Here's a surprise: Save your script in your student_files directory, name it SafeAreas_v01, and quit Nuke!

That's right. Something to note about Nuke scripts, which I have mentioned before, is that they are actual scripts. This means they are made out of normal human-readable text. That means you can change the script using a text editor. The search and replace functions in text editors are uniquely suited for this type of work.

1. Navigate to your student_files directory, where you will find your last saved Nuke script, which should be called SafeAreas_v01.nk.

   There may be another file next to it called SafeAreas_v01.nk~. Disregard that—Nuke uses that for temporary caching.

2. Open this file in your favorite text editor. By default, it's Notepad on Windows and TextEdit on Mac.

You need to find every occurrence of the text "NoOp1." (the dot is important) and replace it with "parent." (also with the dot). The reason the dot is there is so you won't replace the actual node name of NoOp1.

3. Find the Replace function in your text editor. Normally it's in the Edit menu. It might be called Find instead, and may include a replace function within Find. In Windows Notepad press Ctrl-H. On Mac TextEdit press Cmd-F.

4. Use the search function to find the words "NoOp1." and replace them with "parent." (**FIGURE 12.42**).

FIGURE 12.42 Setting up the Find dialog box in the Mac's TextEdit.

NOTE Use only text editors (rather than word processors) for working with Nuke scripts. Word processors such as Microsoft Word and OpenOffice Writer tend to add all sorts of extra formatting characters (many of them invisible) that can break the Nuke script. You should always work with text editors that show you everything they put in the file and don't hide anything—for example, Notepad in Windows, and TextEdit on the Mac.

5. Use the Replace All function (you should have one).

   TextEdit, which I'm using, told me it replaced the text nine times—which is good, that's what I was expecting. This single click just saved a lot of time and labor.

6. Save the changes and then double-click the file again to open it in Nuke again.

7. Double-click Group1 to load its Properties panel.

8. Click the S button to open the Group1 Node Graph (**FIGURE 12.43**).

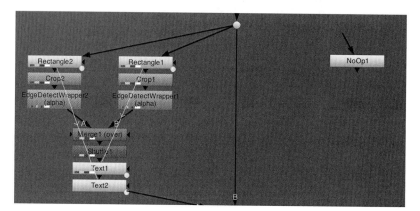

FIGURE 12.43 The green expression line connecting NoOp1 is gone.

You can now see that NoOp1 is no longer being used. There are no green expression lines pointing to it. All the expressions pointing to it have been changed to point to the new Knob in the Group.

9. Change the ActionSafe and TitleSafe properties in Group1 and see your safe areas change in the Viewer.

10. Reset the properties to 5 and 10 when you're finished.

11. The Knobs you created in the Group now control everything you need. You no longer need the NoOp1 node so simply delete NoOp1.

Now let's add one more function to the Group and tree. The text showing Action Safe and Title Safe isn't always necessary, so I would like to add a switch to turn them off. Start by adding another node to the tree in the Group1 Node Graph.

12. Click Text2; from the Merge toolbox, insert a Switch node.

13. In the DAG connect Switch1's input called 1 to Shuffle1 (**FIGURE 12.44**).

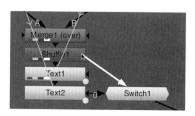

FIGURE 12.44 Connecting the Switch node.

The Switch node does exactly what it says. It has a single property called Which and it switches between its inputs using a slider (**FIGURE 12.45**). This way input 0 is a "which" value of 0, and input 1 is a "which" value of 1. This is a useful tool to pick different branches or, in this case, bypass parts of the tree. Choosing a value of 1 makes the text disappear.

FIGURE 12.45 The Switch Properties panel.

You'll need to create a Knob to change the Which property. An easy solution is to create a slider just like this. But it's a lot more intuitive to add a check box. The check box has two possible values, a value of 0 when unchecked, and 1 when checked. First, you will create the Knob.

14. In Group1's Properties panel, right-click (Ctrl-click) an empty spot and choose Manage User Knobs from the contextual menu.

15. Choose Check Box from the Add button/menu.

16. In the Check Box panel that opens, give this new Knob the name "text." But for the label, enter something that's a little clearer: **Text On?** (**FIGURE 12.46**).

FIGURE 12.46 Setting up the new Check Box Knob.

17. Click OK.

You want this Knob to be the bottom one in the interface.

18. With your new Knob selected in the list, press the Down button three times, then click Done to close the User Knob panel (**FIGURE 12.47**).

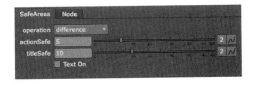

FIGURE 12.47 A new check box appears.

For now, this new Check Box Knob does nothing. You'll link it to an expression.

19. You should already have the Properties panel loaded for Switch1 and Group1. If you don't, please load it now.

20. Ctrl/Cmd-click and drag from the actual check box you created to Switch1's Which property's Input field (**FIGURE 12.48**).

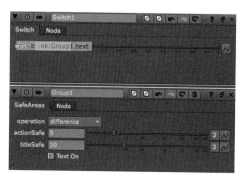

FIGURE 12.48 Dragging to create an expression link.

21. Click your newly created and linked check box, then look at the Viewer.

The functionality is reversed. When the check box is checked, the text disappears from the screen. With a small change to the expression you can reverse this and make 1 into 0 and 0 into 1.

22. Click in Switch1's Which property's Input field and press = to load its Edit Expression panel.

23. Place your cursor at the very left and enter 1-.

The expression should now read: 1-parent.text.

24. Click OK. The functionality is now reversed.

TURNING A GROUP INTO A GIZMO

You have finished building the SafeAreas Group. For now this is still just a Group. You can save it and bring it in later as a script. But the real smart way of using this is by turning this into a Gizmo that you can always access through a button in the interface.

It's a good idea to name your group something that makes sense for the Gizmo.

1. Change the name of Group1 to SafeAreas.

2. In the SafeAreas Properties panel, switch to the Node tab (**FIGURE 12.49**).

3. At the bottom of this window you can find the Export as Gizmo button. Click it. (Note that only Group nodes have this button.)

FIGURE 12.49 The Export as Gizmo button in the Node tab.

4. Name the Gizmo SafeAreas and save it on your Desktop.

5. Save your script and quit Nuke.

Installing the Gizmo

To install the Gizmo, first you need to know where Nuke saves its customization files. According to the manual, these are the default locations:

- For Linux: /users/login name/.nuke

- For Mac: /Users/login name/.nuke

- For Windows XP: drive letter:\Documents and Settings\login name\.nuke

- For Windows Vista onwards: drive letter:\Users\login name\.nuke

On Linux and Mac, folders that start with a dot are hidden by default. You need to find a way to find the folder then. On the Mac, press Cmd-Shift-G to open the Go to Folder dialog box, enter ~/.nuke/ ("~" means your home folder), and press Enter.

In this folder you can drop all kinds of files defining your user preferences and added functionality. These can include favorite directories, new formats, Python scripts, and Gizmos amongst other things.

1. Locate your .nuke directory.

2. Drag the SafeAreas.gizmo from the Desktop into your .nuke directory. This is all you need in order to install the Gizmo.

3. Launch Nuke.

4. Click File > Recent Files and choose safeareas_v01.

Where did the Gizmo go? You haven't told Nuke where you want it to appear yet.

Testing the Gizmo

Gizmos that are just dropped into the .nuke folder appear in the All Plugins submenu under the Other toolbox.

1. Click the Other toolbox, click All Plugins at the bottom, then click Update (**FIGURE 12.50**).

FIGURE 12.50 Updating the All Plugins submenu.

2. Again access the All Plugins submenu.

This time you will see that where you only had the option to update, you now have a submenu of the alphabet. Under each menu you have all the tools whose name starts with that letter. This includes all tools, the ones that come in with Nuke and the Gizmos and scripts you create or bring from elsewhere.

3. Go to the S submenu to find SafeAreas. Click it to create it (**FIGURE 12.51**).

SafeAreas1 is created. In its Properties panel you can see all the Knobs you made, play with them, and make Safe Areas that fit your needs.

4. Bring in an image from chapter04/IcyRoad.png.

5. Clear the Properties Bin.

6. Connect SafeAreas1 to Read1.

7. View SafeAreas1.

FIGURE 12.51 This is how you create a copy of the Gizmo you made.

Great! You have Safe Areas for this image as well. Working in this way, though, isn't that convenient. Safe Areas should be part of the Viewer, not part of the tree.

USING THE VIEWER INPUT PROCESS

The Nuke Viewer can accept trees held in Groups and Gizmos into the Viewer Input Process. These trees are then applied to the image before it is viewed in the Viewer (and only in the Viewer). The Viewer Input Process will not be rendered on final output. This is designed exactly for things like the Safe Area guides and other on-screen tools.

To load something into the Viewer Input Process, use the contextual menu.

1. Disconnect the pipe connecting Read1 and SafeAreas1.

2. View Read1 in the Viewer.

3. Click SafeAreas1 to select it, then right-click (Ctrl-click) to display the contextual menu. Choose Node then Use as Input Process from the menu (**FIGURE 12.52**).

FIGURE 12.52 It's a long way to go, but the Use as Input Process option is there in the end.

Even though SafeAreas1 is not connected to anything, you can now see it in the Viewer. Whatever you add to your tree now, the Input Process will be composited on top of it. You can still double-click SafeAreas1 to change properties and that will still reflect in the Viewer.

If you want to turn this off, you can do so:

4. Right-click (Ctrl-click) in the Viewer and choose Enable Input Process from the contextual menu. You can also use the hot key Alt/Opt-P.

MORE ABOUT GIZMOS

There's one final thing to know about Gizmos—and it can help you a lot later on. Follow these few steps first:

1. Double-click SafeAreas1 to load its Properties panel.

2. Switch to the Node tab.

3. At the bottom of this tab find the Copy to Group button. Click it (**FIGURE 12.53**).

   This takes the Gizmo and reverses the operation, turning it back into a Group.

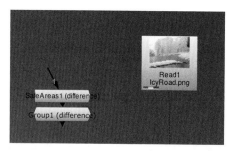

FIGURE 12.53 Click the Copy to Group button to make the Gizmo back into a Group.

4. Double-click the newly created Group, and click the S button at the top right of its Properties panel (**FIGURE 12.54**).

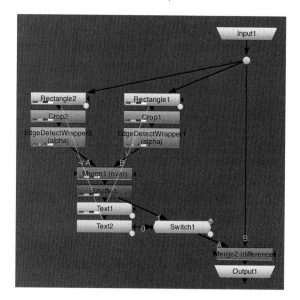

FIGURE 12.54 The original tree has been embedded in the Gizmo the whole time.

You can now see the original tree that made up this Gizmo.

Gizmos can be found all around the web. There's a big depository at nukepedia.com. Downloading Gizmos, installing them, and then looking at how they're built is a great way to learn advanced features in Nuke.

There is also a way to create real buttons inside real toolboxes for your Gizmos instead of using the Update button. This requires a little Python scripting. If you are interested in that, look at the appendix at the end of the book.

CUSTOMIZING NUKE WITH PYTHON

A lot of features might seem to be missing from Nuke—things you may be used to from other applications, or that seem like they would be nice to have. Maybe you keep doing a series of procedures for which you wish there were a single button. Well, some of these missing features can be solved with Gizmos, as discussed in Chapter 12. But other features, such as automation and user interface customization (amongst other things), need a more open and robust framework. This is where Python scripting comes in.

Python is a scripting language that was introduced into Nuke to replace the aging TCL scripting language. Python is now the main scripting language in Nuke. It is a widely used scripting language, and learning it for use in Nuke may prove useful when working with your operating system and other software applications. In fact, you can control your operating system and other applications that support Python from within Nuke, making Python a powerful tool in your arsenal.

NOTE This appendix assumes you have completed Chapter 12. If you haven't, you won't understand some of the terms used here and you won't have the correct files in place to complete the steps as written.

In this appendix, I only cover how to use Python to do very basic things that I believe are absolutely necessary if you use Nuke anywhere—except for in a big organization that has people who take care of all customization for you. But I encourage you to learn Python, as it can really become a very powerful tool at your disposal.

PYTHON SCRIPTING BASICS

In Chapter 12 you learned how to build a Gizmo. To access it, you used the toolbox called Other and the Update button to load all plug-ins from all paths into an alphabetical list. Sure, you can keep doing that—but it's nicer to be able to simply get to the Gizmos you use with an easy-to-access button in an easy-to-access toolbox.

An easy request, but for that to happen you need to learn a little about how Nuke's Python customization setup works. Remember, Nuke is a production tool that relies on hardcore knowledge of advanced systems. You need to know a little Python scripting to be able to do that. Let's start.

FIGURE I.1 Loading the Script Editor.

1. Open Nuke.

2. Choose Script Editor from the Content menu on the right pane (**FIGURE I.1**).

The Script Editor is split into two panes. The bottom half is where you write your commands (the Input pane). The top half provides feedback about what's happening when you execute your commands (the Output pane).

There is a row of buttons at the top. **TABLE I.1** explains what each button is called and what it does, from left to right.

Creating a button in the Nodes Toolbar requires a Python script that starts by calling up the Nodes Toolbar, populates it with a new toolbox, and populates that with a new button, which then calls up a node.

Python uses different terminology for certain user interface elements and functions. I point out these distinctions as they're encountered.

Under Python, Nuke calls the various panels, panes, and toolboxes "menus." The Nodes Toolbar you use all the time to grab nodes from is a menu simply called Nodes under Python. Here, you will add a new toolbox menu to the Nodes menu and call it User. You are then going to tell Nuke to place a link to your Gizmo in the new User menu.

TABLE I.1 The Script Editor's Buttons

Icon	Name	Description
	Previous Script	Loads previous command.
	Next Script	Loads next command.
	Clear History	Clears command history.
	Source Script	Loads and runs a script from disk.
	Load Script	Loads a script from disk.
	Save Script	Saves a script to disk.
	Run Current Script (Run for short)	Executes the current script.
	Show Input Only	Shows only the Input pane.
	Show Output Only	Shows only the Output pane.
	Show Both Input and Output	Shows both the Input and Output panes.
	Clear Output	Clears the Output pane

CREATING A BUTTON WITH PYTHON

Your first line of code will be to call up the Nodes menu and call it by a name (toolbar), so that you can easily refer to it in the next lines of code. Calling a command by name is called *assigning a variable* in scripting. The Nodes menu will have the variable toolbar assigned to it.

1. As the first line in your Script Editor's Input pane, enter the following:

    ```
    toolbar = nuke.menu('Nodes')
    ```

2. Click the Run button at the top of the Script Editor to execute this command.

The command you wrote disappears and the following appears in your Output pane:

```
toolbar = nuke.menu('Nodes')
# Result:
```

This means the command executed with no error. Let's make sure the new variable toolbar is now defined.

3. In the Input pane enter toolbar and press the Run button.

The result of this should be something like this:

```
# Result: <Menu object at 0x15cc80f0>
```

Keep adding to the script, line after line, so you end up with one long script containing all the commands you wrote, one after another. You use the Previous Script button to bring back the previous command to the Input pane.

4. Click the Previous Script button twice to bring back the full toolbar = nuke.menu('Nodes') command.

Now to create the new menu inside of the newly defined variable toolbar.

5. Press Enter/Return to start a new line and type the next command:

```
userMenu = toolbar.addMenu('User')
```

NOTE As mentioned in the beginning of this appendix, Nuke uses different names for things than the interface itself. In this case, the Python name "menu" refers to a lot of things, but can refer to a toolbox as well. I switch between the names depending on whether I want to describe what you're doing when writing the code or what you're doing in the interface.

You just created a new menu called "User" with the addMenu command. (In interface terms you made an empty toolbox called User in the Nodes Toolbar.) All this is performed inside the toolbar variable. This new menu is also assigned a variable called userMenu.

You can now run these two commands to create an unpopulated menu.

6. Click the Run Current Script button again.

If you look carefully at your Nodes Toolbar, you will notice you now have a new toolbox at the bottom with a default icon (**FIGURE I.2**).

7. Hover your mouse pointer over this new menu and you will see from the pop-up tooltip that it is called User.

If you click the menu, nothing happens because it's still empty.

Now call up the Gizmo:

8. Click the Previous Script button to bring back the two previous commands.

9. Press Enter/Return to start a new line and enter the next line:

FIGURE I.2 A new toolbox is born.

```
userMenu.addCommand('Safe Areas', "nuke.createNode('SafeAreas')")
```

10. Click the Run button at the top of the Script Editor to execute this list of commands.

    This new command tells Nuke to look for a Gizmo called SafeAreas (in the second part of the command) and give it the name Safe Areas (note the space).

11. Click to display the User menu you just created.

    The menu now contains a Safe Areas option (**FIGURE I.3**).

12. Clicking Safe Areas creates a SafeAreas Gizmo (provided you have it in your .nuke directory from Chapter 12).

FIGURE I.3 The User menu is now populated with a Safe Areas node.

Essentially, this is it. You have created a menu called User under the Nodes Toolbar and placed a link to your SafeAreas Gizmo in it. You can, however, make it more interesting (keep reading).

ADDING A HOT KEY

You will use this Gizmo to add safe areas to images all the time, so wouldn't it be convenient to have a hot key that calls this Gizmo? It's easy to do in Python.

1. Click the Previous Script button to bring the three lines of code back to the Input pane.

2. Change the third line so it looks like this (with the little bit at the end added):

```
userMenu.addCommand('Safe Areas', "nuke.createNode('SafeAreas')",
'^+z')
```

The last bit of code tells Nuke to use Ctrl-Shift-Z as the hot key for the SafeAreas Gizmo (**FIGURE I.4**). (You can also type that out as Ctrl+Shift+Z or Cmd+Shift+Z—but you have to type Alt not Option.) The symbols for the hot keys work as follows:

^   Ctrl/Cmd
+   Shift
#   Alt/Option

FIGURE I.4 The new menu populated by a link to the Gizmo and a hot key to boot.

3. Click the Run button at the top of the Script Editor to execute this command.

You should be very proud of yourself here. Pat yourself on the back. But one problem is that if you quit Nuke and restart it, all this disappears, which is a shame. But there is a remedy.

MAKING CUSTOMIZATION STICK WITH THE MENU.PY FILE

When Nuke loads, it looks for a file called menu.py in the .nuke directory. This is a text file with a .py (for Python) extension instead of the default .txt extension. This file will hold all the customization you want to add to Nuke.

NOTE If you're not sure where the .nuke directory is on your system, see Chapter 12 to refresh your memory.

You can use Nuke's Script Editor to create this file—but it's best for quickly testing things as you write them, not for long coding sessions. You can use any text editor you prefer instead. I recommend using very simple text editors (like Notepad on Windows and TextEdit on the Mac) or code-oriented text editors (such as ConTEXT on Windows and TextMate or TextWrangler on the Mac). Whatever you do, don't use big word processing software because it adds all sorts of styling and formatting code to your text file, which Nuke can't read. The text that displays in your file is what should be in your file when Nuke reads it. This is not the case with Microsoft Word's .doc files, for example.

In this case, you already created all the code inside Nuke's Script Editor. You just need to save it in your .nuke directory and call it menu.py.

1. Click the Previous Script button to bring back the three previous lines of commands (including the hot key part of the code as well).

2. Click the Save Script button. This is the Save Script button in the Script Editor, not the Save Script menu item.

3. In the browser window navigate to your .nuke directory (if you can't see the .nuke directory in your home directory, start typing .n and it will come up).

4. Name the file menu.py and click Save.

    Your menu.py file is now saved with the commands for creating the User menu in the Nodes Toolbar and adding a link to the SafeAreas Gizmo in it.

5. Quit Nuke, then open it again.

    The User menu is now there.

Creating and adding an icon

"Daddy, why do all the other toolboxes and commands have nice icons and ours doesn't?"

"Why, we can make icons as well, son."

Really? Can we, please? After all, nothing says "we care" like an icon. *Icons* in Nuke are 24x24 pixels in size and are saved as either .png or .xpm files in the .nuke directory. Let's make a couple.

The first one will be an icon for the User toolbox itself: simple white text on a black background. The second will be an icon for the SafeAreas Gizmo: a single safe area box on a black background.

If you want to design your own icons instead, that's up to you. Just remember to make them with the requirements mentioned in mind. Otherwise, follow these steps:

1. Create a Constant node from the Image toolbox.

2. Choose New from the Format drop-down menu.

3. Name the new format **icon** and set the File Size to 24 and 24. Click OK.

4. With Constant1 selected, insert a Text node after it from the Draw toolbox.

5. View Text1 in the Viewer.

6. In Text1's Message property field, type **User**.

7. At the bottom of the Properties panel, click the black arrow to display the Transform submenu.

8. Change the Box property to: 0, 0, 24, 24.

9. Change the Size property at the top (under Fonts) to **10** (FIGURE I.5).

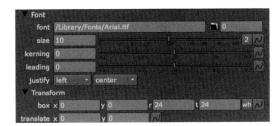

FIGURE I.5 Text1's properties.

The icon for the User menu is ready! Now you will render it (**FIGURE I.6**).

10. Select Text1 and insert a Write node after it.

11. Click the File Browser icon and navigate to your .nuke directory.

12. Name the file **user_icon.png**.

13. Click the Render button; in the Render panel that opens, click OK (**FIGURE I.7**).

FIGURE I.6 The final icon in all its glory.

FIGURE I.7 The first icon's tree.

Now to make the second icon, this time for the Gizmo itself.

14. Copy and paste the three existing nodes to get another, unattached tree.

15. View Write2 in the Viewer.

16. Double-click Text2 and change the Message property to **Safe Areas**.

17. Also change the Size property to **8** and the Justify property's first drop-down menu from Left to Center.

18. With Text2 selected, press Shift-Ctrl/Cmd-Z to insert a SafeAreas node.

19. Change SafeAreas1's ActionSafe and TitleSafe properties to a value of 1 to create a single white outline around the edge of the frame (the small resolution of the icon doesn't allow for two thin safe area boxes—**FIGURE I.8**).

FIGURE I.8 The second icon should look like this.

20. Double-click Write2 and change the name of the file to **safeAreas_icon.png**.

21. Click the Render button; in the Render panel that opens, click OK.

22. You can save your icon project in your student_files directory if you'd like.

    Both icons are ready and are saved in the .nuke directory, making them available to be called via Python.

You now need to tell Nuke (in the menu.py file) to attach these icons to the menu and Gizmo commands.

23. Open a Script Editor in the right-hand pane in the same way you did at the beginning of the chapter.

24. Click the Load Script button, navigate to the .nuke directory, and double-click menu.py.

25. You should have the following in your Input pane now:

```
toolbar = nuke.menu('Nodes')
userMenu = toolbar.addMenu('User')
userMenu.addCommand('Safe Areas', "nuke.createNode('SafeAreas')",
'^+z')
```

26. Change the second and third lines so they look like this:

```
toolbar = nuke.menu('Nodes')
userMenu = toolbar.addMenu('User', icon='user_icon.png')
userMenu.addCommand('Safe Areas', "nuke.createNode('SafeAreas')",
'^+z', icon='safeAreas_icon.png')
```

Adding the last bit of code tells Nuke to use an icon that contains the name between the apostrophes. You don't need to include a full directory path to the icon file name since Nuke will simply look for the icon in the .nuke directory.

27. Click the Save Script button in the Script Editor.

28. In the File Browser, navigate to your .nuke directory and click the menu.py file.

29. Click Save. When asked, approve overwriting the existing file by clicking OK.

30. Close Nuke and open it again to load menu.py.

You should now have icons associated with your toolbox and Gizmo (**FIGURE I.09**). Hurrah!

FIGURE I.9 Successfully adding icons to the user interface.

Other uses for menu.py

You can do many other things with menu.py. Things placed in menu.py are loaded on Nuke startup, so it's a convenient place to add Python commands that will create things you need all the time. There's a lot more about this in the Nuke documentation, and I encourage you to have a look.

First, you can add many more Gizmos to your already created User menu. You do that by simply duplicating the third line and changing the name of the Gizmo, the hot key (if you want any), and the name of the icon file.

But that's just skimming the surface. There are a lot more things you can add to the menu.py file. One example is adding a format to the default format list. Adding a line like the following one adds a format called 720p to the format list with all the right sizes. Just add this line at the bottom of your menu.py (you can add a couple of spaces to separate the Gizmo code and the format code) and then choose File > Save.

```
nuke.knobDefault("Root.format", "1280 720 0 0 1280 720 1 720p")
```

INDEX

WATCH READ CREATE

Unlimited online access to all Peachpit, Adobe Press, Apple Training and New Riders videos and books, as well as content from other leading publishers including: O'Reilly Media, Focal Press, Sams, Que, Total Training, John Wiley & Sons, Course Technology PTR, Class on Demand, VTC and more.

No time commitment or contract required! Sign up for one month or a year. All for $19.99 a month

SIGN UP TODAY

peachpit.com/creativeedge

creative edge